TURNING ME TO WE

THE ART OF PARTNERING WITH MINDFULNESS

*Shifting competition and narcissism (ME)
to collaboration and connection (WE)*

BY DR BETH GINERIS, MA, MBA, MSOM

Copyright © 2013 Dr. Beth Gineris, MA, MS
All rights reserved.

ISBN-10: 1478351683
EAN-13: 9781478351689

Library of Congress Control Number: 2012920458
CreateSpace Independent Publishing Platform
North Charleston, South Carolina
Library of Congress cataloging-in-Publication Data
Gineris, Beth
Turning Me to We: The Art of Partnering with Mindfulness/ Beth Gineris. - 1st ed.
p.cm
[1. Family & Relationships.] 2012920458

PRAISE FOR DR. BETH GINERIS'S WRITING AND WORK:

"Beth's work inspires listening to the quiet whispers of your heart and trusting your intuition to guide the soul. Her work is so easily accessible. Through shifting the perspective, she works toward healing the soul, returning to balance, and building a joy filled life."
—Rachel Boston, Actress/Producer

"If my experience is any measure, this book will be useful to many. I have been using Beth's victim scenarios and mindfulness guiding principles in my practice for years with excellent success."
—Ron Romanik, MD, Psychiatrist, Integrative Medicine Practitioner

"Beautifully and deeply helpful..." Dr Claudia Welch, DOM, Ayurvedic Educator and
—Author of Balance your Hormones, Balance your Life

"Powerful, insightful and transcendent energy to clarify right relationship among partners, love it! Beth's presence in my life as an intuitive-life-coach, friend, and author, has been transformational."
—Jeremiah Samuels, Executive Producer

"Beth's energy is like magic in how she can assist others to shift their perspective, come together without losing themselves, and transform their lives. She has been a powerful change-maker for my patients."
—Dr. Bill Wolfe, DDS, NMD, Creator of Dr Wolfe's energetic healthcare products

"Beth's perspective and tools shift the energy in a multidimensional way to advance healing and release toxins in the sprit/mind/body fields."

—Pamela Costello, MD, PhD,
Holistic Neurosurgeon, Integrative Neurological Medicine

"Beth's work is transformative."
—Ava Keenen Kurnow, MA, Educator, Director of Life-long Learning

"Beth's work is perfect for creating the space to facilitate transcendence in the leadership process. Her conflating eastern and western concepts combined with her own integral spiritual ideas are truly a gift to the planet."   Lisa Aldon, MA, author of
—Transcendent Leadership and the Evolution of Consciousness

"I have been waiting for this book for a long time. Finally, all of Beth's pithy deconstuction of psychology, language, relationship and how to be your best self, bound together for easy access."
—J. M. Romanik, JD, MBA, Founding Partner Secourier, LLC

"Useful information for teambuilding, with easy to utilize tools and techniques."
—Jeff Sullivan, Director of Student Affairs, ITT-Tech, Alb., NM

DEDICATION AND ACKNOWLEDGEMENTS

Dedicated with love to:

My brothers *Marc Gineris* and *Peter Gineris,* whose different styles of loving and relating helped me define the importance of temperament and through whom I developed my first knowings of the value in creating and maintaining enduring relationships. *Ken and Pat Roth*, dear friends who exemplify the interdependent We-style relationship. And, my magnanimous, supportive husband *Ron Romanik*, who reminds me to play and is a dynamic partner in the triple play of career, family, and personal development.

I want to acknowledge my dear friends:

Doug Arent, with whom I first experienced the joy and safety in being seen,

Sue Alschuler, who showed me the internal strength found in a trusting female friendship, and *Lisa Aldon*, with whom I clarified the power of faith, perseverance, and care; and, my beloved partners of my youth whose lessons paved my philosophical beliefs and defined the importance of cultural connections to paradigms and relationships.

This book is also in honor of my many clients and patients who have entrusted me with their stories and relationship struggles. I want to offer my gratitude and joy in their courage to trust in me, face their challenges, and create happiness in life.

CONTENTS

Preface xiii
Introduction to the Me, I, We styles of Relationship 1
Quick Review of Sociology and Relationship 7
   10 What Matters

Paradigm Recognition, *Paradigm Shifting*,
& Paradigm Integration 15
   19 Application of Mindfulness Toward Your and Your Partner's Paradigms
   24 The Importance of Being a Translator in Relationship
   29 Understanding Increases Through Communication
   34 The Function of Hearing and Listening in Relationships
   39 My Personal Adventure: a Mini Cultural Revolution
   47 Give &Take: We-style in Relationship Creates Mutual Care & Sustenance
   50 Inside-Out Change: The Equation that Paradigmatic Beliefs Drive Behavior
   56 Using Humor to Shift Your Perspective to Neutral
   60 Defining Boundaries Increases Your Sense of Space and Connection

Survivor Scenarios: Choose Thriver over Survivor 67
   73 Survivor Scenarios: Savior, Survivor, Protector
   76 The Power of the Thriver Attitude
   80 The Effect of Trauma in Self-Identity Creation
   84 Release Childhood Ghosts: Reveal Your True Self
   91 Mindfulness and Time Travel
   96 The 3 Ds in the Art of Verbal Aikido Create Harmony

Temperament and Relationship Style 101
   103 Understanding Styles of Temperament
   111 Discernment and Judgment; Holding On and Letting Go

- 113 Styles of Temperament in Relationship: Collaborator or Individualist?

MAAPS, Five Guiding Security Principles of Relationship: Money, Achievement, Attachment (Connection), Power (Freedom), & Structure 117

- 120 Self-Confidence Leads to a We-style Relationship
- 123 Security Drivers Defined and Clarified, a Negative Need Base
- 136 Reclaiming your Inner Security, Moving from Need to Preference
- 140 Balance the Power Differential in Relationship Through Detachment
- 143 Negotiating with Empowerment: The We-Style of Relationship
- 146 Mindful Speech, Mindful Action
- 149 Trust Creates Security
- 152 Heart-Led Action Transforms the Effects of Loss in Relationship Style
- 155 Graciousness Leads to Inner Strength and Outer Durability

Belief Systems Affect Your Relationship Style and Your Sense of Security 161

- 165 Turning Over a New Leaf—Inverting a Belief
- 170 Apply the Metaphor of Spring Cleaning to Get Rid of Misbeliefs
- 175 Daytime Sleepwalking Through Your Life, Wake Up!
- 178 You in the Driver's Seat of Your Life

Inner Guidance: Integrating Spirit & Mind 183

- 184 Truth Within: Right Relationship
- 186 Rebalancing: Empathy, Ego, and Spirit
- 191 Multidimensional Sight: Right Mindfulness
- 194 Inner Guidance IV: Inner Truth Infusion

Toward a Union of We: Shifting Your Consciousness 199
- 202 Consciousness Evolving I
- 206 Consciousness Evolving II
- 209 Leadership and Inner Strength of Will: Creating Space for We
- 212 Less Attitude, More Gratitude: Increase Altruism and Empathy
- 216 Love Heals, Love Binds, Love Frees
- 219 We-ness: Win–Win or No Deal, and a Word about Psychopaths

Mindful Living in the We-style of Relationship: How to Integrate Your Personal Sensory Guidance System Into Your Daily Life 225
- 227 Model Critical Thinking, Eschew Propaganda
- 232 Finding Your Way: Culling Through the Propaganda,
- 235 Piercing Through Seductive Logic to Truth
- 240 Shifting the Substrate: Creating Change Without Drama
- 242 Lead Through Joy: Focus on Connection and Empowerment
- 246 Forgiveness and Curiosity Rather Than Defensiveness
- 251 Seeing from Four Dimensions at Once: The 4D We-style Relationship
- 254 Shifting the Energy of Disappointment to the Power of Courage: Me to We
- 257 Focus Your Energy and Breathe: Respond From an Inner Balanced State
- 260 Your Heart Center Links Meditation and Mediation
- 263 Embracing Your Flaws, Shifting Your Attitude Creates A We-style Outcome

Reference 269

Suggested Readings 285

INDEX OF IMAGES

Figure 1,..17
Figure A 32
Figure B..32
Figure 2, Photography Credit: Charlotte Elconin.........................38
Figure 3..51
Figure 4, Photography Credit: Denise Bryce 64
Figure 5, Photography Credit: Lisa Aldon 73
Figure 6, Photography Credit: Laura Wolf.................................80
Figure 7, Photography Credit: Ron Romanik 90
Figure 8..106
Figure 9..149
Figure 10..158
Figure 11..166
Figure 12..190
Figure 13..215
Figure 14, Photography Credit: Ron Romanik 235
Figure 15..250
Figure 16, Photography Credit: Lisa Aldon 263
Figure 17, Photography Credit: Laura Wolfe............................267

PREFACE

Turning ME to WE: The Art of Partnering with Mindfulness; Shifting competition and narcissism (Me) to collaboration and connection (We). This book delineates quick and easy tools for developing profoundly successful relationships in work, home, and love. Intertwined within these strategies are ways of resetting, refocusing and realigning your internal compass to create a new space for collaboration and connection while allowing space for your personal self to grow along with your relationship/partnership. It focuses on an integrated spirit-mind-body approach dealing with communication, context, paradigmatic beliefs, and form. Information about how you develop your personal style of relating and partnering clarifies what is working for you. And, this book offers ways to shift out of various paradigmatic forms of thinking/seeing/communicating styles and contexts that are problematic, do a disservice to you in relationship, or interfere with connecting and collaboration.

There are different forms of how we can relate in groups that are forms of relating Me and I perspective. As you read you will learn about how these are part of certain psychosocial stages. Some styles of relating are contorted aspects of relationship that serve to keep you in a less than equal relationship. *Co-dependence* is a skewed perspective of Me, it is not a true We experience. This is a situation where the core Me has not efficiently developed into a whole self-sufficient being. In a co-dependent relationship each Me is acting to create dependence, each person is an incomplete Me with a tenuous cording between them. This cording gives the experience of connection for the Me-style, however it is fragile and offers little security or inner strength to the whole. Each Me in the relationship is focused on maintaining the connection but this is accomplished through a sense of fear of abandonment rather than resilience or dependability. When looking at this kind of relationship each Me is acting as half of the whole so that the coming together is a smaller sphere. Each Me gives up something to make the co-dependent relationship work. It is co-dependent rather than interdependent.

In an I-style relationship, each person is a more self-contained and self-dependent, however, the relationship is without interdependence. The style of connection is through exchange patterns and a tally-sheet. This style of relationship is competitive. Here each individual feels right or correct and fights to prove their rightness. As with the Me-style of relating, the I-style of relating is an important psychosocial development stage.

The We-style of relating is *interdependent;* it incorporates each perspective and then threads the two perspectives to create an infusion of innovation and paradigmatic shifting to rise above the limitations of each single entity to create a fluid, collaborative, relationship between the two individuals. It is here that creation happens. It is here that 2+2 equals more than 4 or as the Buddhist principle holds true, 2+2 equals the interconnectedness of all.

The We style of relating is the natural outcome of a successful resolution to the psycho-social development stages of childhood through adolescence into adulthood. Various insecurity issues can develop throughout this process of development, that interfere with a successful resolution to these stages or with a fixed style of relating. Individuals who have experienced injury, loss, abandonment, or a skew through cultural or limiting belief systems, can develop habit reaction patterns and get stuck at either Me or I-style of relating.

This book offers a way to release yourself from that patterning and create internal healing and understanding so that you can interact in relationship and partnership through a We-style of interdependence.

Shifting ME to WE is a paradigm shift, an inversion that allows an evolution of your consciousness in your psychosocial development. The innovative information herein offers a new vision of relationship. How you partner and act in relationship is a weaving of

- 1/ your paradigms, how you view partnering
- 2/ your temperament style
- 3/ your belief systems
- 4/ your core security driver, MAAPS: **M**oney, **A**chievement, **A**ttachment (connection), **P**ower (freedom), **S**tructure – MAAPS - to feel secure.

Your partnering paradigm and your core security driver evolve through your developmental resolutions to Erikson's psychosocial stages.

This book delineates each partnering style and provides tools for you to shift out of an ineffective partnering style to create powerful, sustaining, and mutually successful partnerships. Your style is personal to you and falls on a developmental continuum of relating. The developmental aspect is moving from Me-dependence, through I-independence, to We-interdependence.

This book is divided into ten sections: Introduction to the Me, I, and We-styles in Relationship; Sociological Underpinnings; Paradigm shifting; Survivor scenarios; Temperament and relationship styles; MAAPS, the five styles of security; Belief systems; Inner Guidance;

Toward a Union of We; and Mindful Living in the We-style of Relationship. Each section has a general presentation of the information followed by subsections that provide a deeper perspective of the section topic; together these subsections impart an integrated understanding of the section topic and within each subsection there will be suggested exercises, mantras, or practices that you can try to enhance your understanding and incorporation of the chapter information. The sections are meant to work together to provide the different elements of how to transform your relationship into a prosperous, mutually satisfying relationship or to clarify for yourself what drives your style of relating.

These sections are best read in order for the highest clarity. This is especially true for the first six sections as these provide the core of the information, however you can read those sections to which you are drawn in the order you choose. The final section offers material that you can use to support your process of change. The reference section has several articles and meditations from my previous book *Turning No to ON: The Art of Parenting with Mindfulness* and definitive information on works cited throughout this book about relationship theories and studies.

This material is dense. It is offered in a non-judgmental, objective, loving manner to assist you in attaining your highest good. It is meant to be uplifting and supportive. If you find, as you are reading, you begin to get upset or angry about the information, take your time to review what you read and the meaning of the words that have charge for you. To work-through this feeling, you may want to look-up the meaning of the words in a dictionary to help clarify if you are experiencing a personal reaction to the words. Read all the meanings for the word to ascertain how it is meant in context, and apply the knowledge that my intent is to be non-judgmental and loving. These mindful actions can help you to neutralize the charged-reaction to the word, phrase, or concept.

Journaling or writing about your feelings may be helpful to determine what may be driving your strong, negative reaction. Get a break from the material by reviewing a different chapter or subsection; return to the area that was upsetting once you feel less reactive.

Each section will have tools, questions, exercises, or techniques for you to practice to increase your understanding and facility with this information.

A note about gender pronoun use in this book. To avoid the distance from the material created by using *they, their,* and *them* for the sake of gender neutrality, I have chosen to alternate the use of male and female pronouns when discussing specific experiences. Although the editing desire for gender neutrality is laudable, writing from a *they* perspective distances you from directly connecting to the material and relating it to yourself and your experiences. This is a common automatic psychological defense.

In order to assist you in getting the most out of the book, I endeavor whenever possible, to use the pronouns *you* and *your* so that you can experience me sharing with you directly. This increases connection to the material and integration of the concepts into your world-view so that you can mindfully evaluate how and if they apply to you. When using *you/your* is inappropriate I have opted to use singular pronouns alternately, *with the understanding identified here that while these specific pronouns are used, the information in the sentence applies to either gender.*

INTRODUCTION TO THE ME, I, AND WE-STYLES OF RELATIONSHIP

Your personal style of relationship incorporates threads from your sociological paradigmatic world-views, values, and temperament. Whether you utilize a Me, I, or We-style of relating, your personal style is based in this weaving of:

1) How you view partnering (your partnering paradigm)
2) Your temperament
3) Your belief systems
4) Your core security driver, MAAPS - **M**oney, **A**chievement, **A**ttachment (connection), **P**ower (freedom), or **S**tructure. Your partnering paradigm and your core security driver evolve through your developmental resolutions to Erikson's psycho-social stages.

Turning Me to We: The Art of Partnering with Mindfulness delineates each partnering style and provides tools for you to shift out of an ineffective partnering style to create powerful, sustaining, and mutually successful partnerships. Your style is personal to you and falls on a developmental continuum of relating. The developmental aspect is moving from Me-dependence, through I-independence, to We-interdependence.

THE ME-STYLE IN RELATIONSHIP:

The Me-style of relating is a dependent state. It is the natural beginning state of relationship. The Me-style of relating appears narcissistic and feels needy and clinging in relationship. This style of relating lacks true empathy. This is because the Me aspect overrides seeing the other's needs or point of view; even actions that appear generous on closer view are conditional. Me-style relates only from personal perspective and experience; even a personally experienced event is not translatable to another's experience, especially when there is a competing need in the relationship.

Generosity is simply a way to meet an inner self-need, which is to keep the other entwined to him. The Me-style lacks a capacity for true self-knowledge of boundaries, strengths, or weaknesses. This makes it difficult for an individual in a Me-style to negotiate. When trying to resole conflict an individual in the Me-style can be very concrete and have difficulty abstracting information, or trusting his partner. Fear of abandonment drives an intense need to create dependence.

The Me-style is dependent and co-dependent and can indicate an injury in the first stage of *Erikson's psychosocial stages, birth to eighteen months old*, where the primary development milestone is that of *trust* that the primary caregiver or the society at large is dependable. In general, this Eriksonian stage centers around feeding, nutrition, and sustenance necessary for survival, which can include spiritual and emotional sustenance. The loss of a significant caregiver or an injury or disruption in the smooth flow of care during this time, can derail the individual's ability to develop a successful resolution to this first psychosocial stage. (For more information about these stages and ways to heal various kinds of injuries experienced in childhood, you can review *Every Twelve Years*, in the *reference* section of this book.) Just as children develop into adolescents, psychosocial development moves from dependent to independent, and the Me-style gives rise to the I-style of relating.

THE I-STYLE IN RELATIONSHIP:

The I-style of interacting is independent and solitary in nature. Independence is a paradigm wherein individual credit and competition are paramount. The I-style incorporates an ongoing tally-sheet of each other's actions to delineate connection. With the focus of connection being competition and exchange, the I-style of relating lacks empathy and negotiation. Unlike the Me-style that lacks capacity for empathy and negotiation due to a lack of boundaries, the I-style has an understanding of and capacity for empathy and negotiation but enforces boundaries that preclude the utilization of these due to a foundational insecurity of autonomy and competence.

The latent MAAPS core insecurity driver of the I-style relates to an injury during one of these *Erikson's psychosocial stages: 2- autonomy shame/doubt* (two to three years); *3- initiative versus guilt* (three to five years); *4- industry versus inferiority* (six to eleven years); and to some degree *5- identity versus role confusion* (twelve to eighteen years), which focuses on a strong self-knowing or weak sense of self.

The I-style paradigm focuses on exchange patterns, competition, and independence. Freedom, winning, and being right are highly valued in this style of relating. As with the Me-style of relating there is an underdeveloped sense of trust. This lack of trust presents differently; the I-style fears compromising self, instead using exchange patterns. The I-style paradigm picture is that of insulated parallel *Is* walking side-by-side. The I-style feels isolated and lonely; both parties feel unseen and unheard by each other. There is an underlying tone of defensiveness, competition, and arbitration. With the constant defense of position, rights, achievements, and accomplishments, this relationship style lacks dependability. There is a fear of engulfment into the other or destruction, without the constant redefinition via the tally-sheet of exchanges. In the I-style each party keeps his or her own money, material acquisitions and sense of survival squarely in his or her own court to maintain that sense of freedom from destruction or engulfment. Hurts and repayment for hurts are part of the tally-sheet.

The Me and I-styles have significant latent conflict. A superficial presentation covers a deeper convoluted tapestry and interplay of needs, agreements, and conditional contracts. With these styles of relating there is a lack of security in self and other, which results in withholding, aloofness, neediness, and an unstable foundation. What passes for cooperation and interaction is a thin veneer based on a set of conditional agreements. These agreements are often covert and unequally interpreted.

THE WE-STYLE IN RELATIONSHIP:

The interdependent We-style of partnering evolves out of a successful set of resolutions to the first five stages of Erikson's psychosocial development. Psychosocial development moves from Me to I to We or dependent to independent to interdependent.

The developmental stages of Me and I are required to then create a solid sense of self for interdependence. Dependence on others→Independence of self → Interdependence, wherein you can trust yourself and other to be mutually caring and supportive. The natural outcome to the developmental stages is the capacity for interdependence.

The interdependent We-style of relating is secure; negotiates with open communication, resilience, and synergy. It is overt; information is shared honestly; agreements are entered into with genuineness. Conflict is resolved to meet the needs of both partners; there is a lack of covert agenda in the relationship. Empathy is paramount. Interdependence in the Me-style is depending on the other without losing a sense of internal power, autonomy, or self-reliance. The two parties are able to work together toward shared goals; focusing support toward individual and collective goals, highlighting one without diminishing the other in the process. Communication and collaboration are highly valued. There is dependability with a natural ebb and flow of inter-dependence and utilization of resources within the partnership.

The tone, tenor, trustworthiness, and dependability of the We-style makes it highly desirable. Using mindfulness in partnering assists you to release old habits of seeing and acting, so that you can create a more satisfying style of relating.

So, the Me, I, and We-styles of relating are based in this *weaving of*
1/ how you view and look at partnering (your paradigms);
2/your temperament style;
3/your cultural/sociological/religious belief systems; and
*4/your core security driver: how you may use MAAPS - **M**oney, **A**chievement, **A**ttachment (connection) **P**ower (freedom) **S**tructure —to feel secure.*

Now, let's look at how your sociological groups, paradigmatic views, and temperament components play into the each style of relating and partnering.

QUICK REVIEW OF SOCIOLOGY AND RELATIONSHIP

The sociological perspective offers distinct information about how to view partnering and relationship in society. Social development evolves through stages but what informs each individual through that process is his or her primary agents of socialization: family of origin, cultural beliefs and norms, ethnic/racial status, social class status, spiritual/religious group and beliefs, and gender status. Identification within each of these groups and your biography and location in time inform you as to how to develop socially: what to believe, how to think about your environment, how to behave and act in the world, how to work through problems and how to partner. Your experiences profoundly affect who you are and how you act.

Temperament has a role in defining your style of partnering and relating. The groups to which you belong are outside influences that have significant affect on how you develop. Knowing your temperament will assist you in the relationship aspect of choosing a partner and developing a style of inter-relating that suits both of your needs. Understanding your agents of socialization helps you to shift partnering habit-styles that are inefficient, ineffective and not inherent in your basic nature.

Think of it this way, you have to manage your temperament style; it is an integral aspect to your personality. It can be fine-tuned and modified but it is in a sense hardwired. However, the aspects of how you see the world, and what you perceive as the rules of social engagement that come from your socialization are habits; these are not hardwired but coding downloaded or modeled from your group connections. These are completely malleable and changeable. Once you understand the personal historical significance and foundation behind these various beliefs you can choose to let go of the un-useful habits, paradigm shift, uplevel, and socially develop into an interdependent style of relating that is a higher level of consciousness.

This book offers a new vision about relationship, incorporating information on how different sociological groups view partnering in relation to security, belief systems, support, connection, exchange patterns, and paradigmatic belief structures (like romantic love) which are all aspects of relating that are borne out of cultural beliefs that are simply fed to you via your primary *agents of socialization* (the information you incorporated from your family of origin, cultural beliefs and norms, ethnic/racial status, social class status, spiritual/religious group and beliefs, and gender status), your *biography* (what happened to you in your life, and how you interpreted it) and your *location in time* (what was socially popular or thought to be deviant when you were being raised).

This is the idea that *you don't see the world as it is you see the world as you are*; your perspective is personal and it is a dynamic interpretation of the above three things sociological agents (group connections), biography (your personal experiences), and location in time (this is the effect of generally accepted belief systems about behavior that are inculcated through society; ie: in the 1950's in America there were various ideas about behavior regarding race/ethnicity, marriage/divorce, and gender roles that is dramatically different in the 2010 time period).

A good start to investigate the etiology of your beliefs is to write down what you believe *love, relationship, partnership, strength,* and *success* look like and entail. Then see if you can connect these core beliefs to people, or specific agents of socialization in your environment. Define the following words:

Partner _____

Lover _____

Spouse _____

Breadwinner _____

Homemaker _____

Strength _____

Powerful woman _____

Powerful man _____

Empowerment _____

Security _____

Happiness _____

Success _____

Good person _____

Reasonable _____

Use the chapters that follow to discover how you may be stuck in your social development. Take the time to develop a personal understanding of yourself, your beliefs, your code of honor, your style of relating and partnering. This review will assist you in identifying what habits you want to keep and which you want to discard.

Another useful task is to look at how you seek security. Endeavor to understand what actions you take to create an internal sense of security for yourself. From there, you can review your style of Me, I, or We in partnership and relationship. Pay attention to what makes you feel fearful, insecure, powerful, weak, confident, connected, and isolated. These feelings are cues to what matters to you in developing social relationships and partnerships.

WHAT MATTERS

What matters is connected to a person's belief system. If family matters you makes choices to care for family above other things. If money matters then making and keeping money has a higher priority than caring for family or relationship.

From an existential perspective, it is a general rule of behavior that people act in accordance with their primary core values: so actions are the true template of your core beliefs. People do what they want to do, so when you say you are doing something you don't want to do then you are either being deceptive or acting and speaking from an inner conflict.

What matters to a person is seen in her actions. Actions align your best interests according to your core belief systems. So, when a person says *I don't want to do this* endeavor to discover *why are you doing it*; what matters to her is revealed in her answer, as to what is the motivation for the behavior.

Knowing yourself is a function of knowing what matters; when you know yourself then living is easy, it follows a simple set of rules of acting in ways to support and keep close what matters to you. This is an important tenet in relationship: *Trust actions over words when the actions and words are in conflict.* When actions conflict with, or are incongruent with, what another says matters then you want to trust the *actions as the actual thing that matters*, rather than trusting the words. People mistakenly do the opposite of this, often being drawn to trust the words rather than the actions. When the truth is discovered they are confused, hurt or feel betrayed. In reality they betrayed themselves by trusting the words rather than the actions.

For example, if your partner says I love you, I am loyal to you, and will not betray that loyalty, however his actions exhibit disloyalty and betrayal, if you continue to ask *do you love me, are you loyal* and trust his verbal answer with actions that are in conflict with his words then you are ignoring the actions and trusting the words.

This is how individuals stay in relationships that do not serve them by trusting words over actions. Their relationships are serving what matters in their belief systems but are not be truly supporting their authentic, whole, congruent self.

Developing an understanding of yourself requires an ability to look at figure and ground, stay present in the moment, pay attention to your sensory cues (what bothers you and causes feelings, that something is off, or feelings of anger, hurt, and fear), and be willing to let go of habit reaction patterns and survivor scenarios as well as be flexible about how you incorporate your belief systems into your behavior.

It requires a vigilant eye to maintaining an internal consistency in actions, words, and beliefs. This takes a deep understanding of yourself and a willingness to apply mindfulness to your relationships.

You can use simple cues to discover how you are out of sync:

- Pay attention to inner dissonances, when something feels off, or sounds off or seems incongruent in your own sense of beliefs, actions, and words or in those of your partner.

- When you find yourself saying that you are doing something that you don't want to do, delve deeper to understand what drives your actions and how these are incongruent with your words.
- Stop the actions that are incongruent with your beliefs or words. Feel if there is a tension or conflict that presents itself for you to resolve. Strive to speak and act in a congruent manner.

Knowing what matters to you and acting from that space allows for self-confidence and increases your capacity for success in relationship and toward your goals. Knowing what matters to your partner offers a path to either create success toward your established goals or clarifies that the relationship is not worth pursuing. Getting out of a stuck situation takes a lot of energy. Release of an unhealthy relationship frees up more available energy to live and partner in a congruent fashion. When you focus on this issue of congruence you increase opportunities for mutuality in relationship.

PARADIGM RECOGNITION, *PARADIGM SHIFTING*, & PARADIGM INTEGRATION

Powerful paradigm shifting results from a fluid movement of sense perceptions between figure and ground: if you are watching TV and there are men working outside on the street, your hearing differentiates between the sound attributed to the work outside (back*ground* noise) and the TV audio or the storyline of the television program you are watching (*figure*). And just as you can recognize the information in the program while hearing the background noise from the men working you can shift your perception and attention to hear what the men are saying if you identify something of importance in their conversation. When this shift happens the conversation becomes the figure upon which you are focusing and the TV program becomes the background noise.

Visually your eyes determine figure and background to make sense of portraits or any visual field. For wine tasting, you distinguish between the taste of the background of the wine, dry or sweet, while identifying specific flavors attached to various herbs and fruits, clove, blueberries, or citrus, the figure.

All of your senses can distinguish ground and figure and shift between the two as part of your sensory guidance system. This capacity and inclination to discern figure and ground is built into your personal sensory system to assist you in negotiating life. It is essential in determining what stimulus is important and what is unessential at any given moment, in each situation.

Paradigm recognition, shifting, and integration are fundamental tools used in creating successful social interactions, negotiation, learning, leadership, and innovation. From a psychological perceptual perspective, figure-ground perception applies to paradigm recognition and shifting from the perspective of beliefs, values, behavior patterns, and communication.

The figure or foreground of something to which you attend or are bothered by, and the ground or background of your own values paradigm or belief system can be one way in which you identify whether you are safe, in love, or in danger.

An example of this is how you might interpret butterflies in your stomach:

- If you are looking at an attractive person whom you recently met and it is apparent this person desires a relationship, which you also desire, - then the feeling in your stomach, the butterflies, might be interpreted positively as a sense of excitement. And your action might be to encourage contact.
- If you feel the individual is threatening then the butterflies in your stomach might be interpreted by you as a negative gut response, an anxiety, and the approach of the person feel dangerous. This might result in you avoiding and discouraging contact with the person.

In this example the butterfly feeling in the stomach is the same and it is your interpretation within the context, the ground of the event that defines how to attend to the figure. Fluid shifting between figure and ground is required for negotiation, relationship, and communication processing, and working-through in the therapeutic environment. This concept of figure/ground perception was first applied in psychotherapy and health promotion by Fritz Perls in his book *Gestalt Therapy Verbatim(1969, 1992)*. It has since been applied to business communication development in negotiation and communication in leadership training programs. The common visual example of this is the vase (figure) and the two profiles surrounding the vase (background). There are many optical illusion pictures that show the transition from figure to ground. The exercise of moving from focus on the figure image and then focus on the background image allows for two completely different truths to be presented simultaneously. This is a shifting of focus to see through a different paradigmatic perspective.

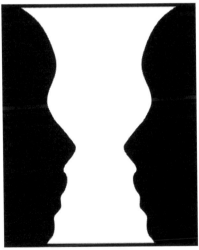

FIGURE 1
FIGURE/GROUND OPTICAL,
WINE GLASS AND FACES

This visual exercise of seeing one image and then the other can create the kinesthetic *aha* experience that allows you to have an integrated see/knowing experience of each perspective inclusive of a deeper understanding of the meaning connected to each. The value in this is profound when used in leadership, communication, relationship, parenting, and negotiation because it moves each person from a position of adversary to mediator. It transforms the sense of right/wrong to a space where healing, solutions, and resolutions can take place.

Being willing to see and understand the 'rightness' of another's perspective while simultaneously knowing the underpinnings of the 'rightness' of your own perspective gives you space to see where the two 'rights' connect, dovetail, share a common space. This shift frees you to work together with the other person to define a way for both truths to be accepted and seen. This is negotiation that embraces differences without denigrating the other while developing a shared perspective that encompasses both. This kind of interaction can only be created within the We-style of relationship or partnership. The I and Me-styles of relationship are based in rigid attachments that interfere with the flexibility of shifting between perspectives.

Practicing the visual exercise of paradigm shifting, mindful meditation, breathwork, seeing through compassionate eyes, and the practice of yoga can increase your capacity to paradigm shift in your everyday interactions in the world. This allows you to shift from a Me or I-style of relating to a We-style of relating. This is a way that you can choose to change your style of relating. While it doesn't require that the other person shift with you, your change will affect the relationship and may open the space for you both to uplevel in your awareness to each other. So you can shift into a We-style of relating through these practices even if your partner is stuck in a Me or I-style of relating. Over time your shift may be the catalyst that encourages your partner to shift his style of relating.

APPLICATION OF MINDFULNESS TOWARD YOUR AND YOUR PARTNER'S PARADIGMS

Partnering is an important and tricky venture. The way in which partners come together is not as straightforward as you may think. What holds people together has to do with a matrix of underlying paradigms of *how partnership should go*. Each person has an inner map or structure of how things 'should' look that is based in that matrix of belief systems, personal history, and sociological programming.

Agreements are set down in relationship, *I'll do this for you - you do this for me*. This is the model of how partnerships develop. These agreements can be explicit or implicit but they are there. All three styles of relating, Me, I, and We contain these types of agreements. The difficulty with the Me, and I-styles is that there is less space in the relationship to renegotiate or communicate about what aspect of the agreement isn't working or needs to be adjusted as the relationship develops. The Me-style of relationship has many more agreements or expectations that are underground, covert or unspoken. The I-style of relationship contains contractual agreements that are rigid and lack flexibility.

The dramatic interchange between partners breaking up or during divorce is a function of these issues. As you develop your relationship pay attention to what you agree to implicitly.

One way you can get a sense of an implicit agreement is by paying attention to the division of labor in a relationship. Look for the inferred exchange that is not clarified verbally. This will be discussed in more detail later in the book. To elucidate whether you may be participating in an implicit agreement pay attention to your personal sensory guidance system.

CHECK IN WITH YOUR PERSONAL SENSORY GUIDANCE SYSTEM

Your personal sensory guidance system is an integrated system of your five senses and your intuition. Paying attention to how you feel is a way of communicating with yourself. Your senses and intuition inform you like a compass as to the best path through life. Most people have learned to ignore these senses as they have incorporated the social constructs of their environment, but in actuality this refusal to pay attention to your inner knowing is a way in which you can get off course in relationship and life. To re-acquaint yourself with your personal sensory guidance system (think of this like your personal internal gps) use a check-in style of communicating. To do this, use a listening/feeling method of attending to your inner self. Your senses communicate through feelings that something is good or bad, safe or dangerous, right or wrong. To check in with these you do an interior body scan of your senses. This means to *check in with your feelings*. Ask yourself "does it feel right? Is something off? This is usually subtle. Strong feelings like intense fear that is incongruent with the situation are triggers back to an historical, past bad situation. This will be delineated in detail in the chapter on *Survivor Scenarios*. An indications that something is awry could be that something doesn't *smell right*, or he left you with a *bad taste in your mouth*, or something about her story *doesn't sound right or ring true*. You may feel dizzy, or even feel a knot in your stomach.

These are cues from your personal sensory guidance system that something is out of place. Part of this system is intuition, which is an integration of your five senses responses. You have intuition even if you do not use it. Often intuition is ignored or explained away. Not listening to intuition is similar to trusting words over actions; it leads to self-betrayal. Intuition is generally a gut feeling or a quiet voice that either encourages you toward or discourages you from a task or action. It is easy to ignore these cues; they are quiet, light, and can be brushed away by your mind's reinterpretation of the situation. Also, if you have had trauma or injury in childhood, sometimes the way in which you have survived is to ignore your own needs in order to take care of the other person for your perceived safety at the time. In this instance, you may have developed a mindset to expel these cues without attending to them.

In order to create a mutually satisfying We-style relationship, it is important to develop this freeway of information from your personal sensory guidance system.

When relationships break apart the more the agreements were implicit the more there is disagreement about those implicit agreements. The less spelled-out, clarified, or identified the equation of exchange, the more each party puts his or her own spin on the particular exchange components and expectations. This is especially true in Me or I-style of partnerships where one party gets a lot of recognition for what both parties are creating.

This is usually a power exchange. *I will do this to promote you* and *you do this to promote me*. The one who doesn't get the recognition feels betrayed but it is difficult to really get to what the true exchange was. These agreements may be spiritual, emotional, or physical. Problems develop on both sides. When the individual who gets more recognition, does so through a covert, unacknowledged dependence on the less recognized partner, then there is an implicit agreement. This can result in problems within the relationship due to the dissonance and also when the partnership breaks apart due to the incongruity. The person receiving the recognition without identifying the work of the behind the scenes person may take all the goodies with him. Or the person who was actually doing the work may leave and create a void that results in the partner who was receiving the recognition looking like a fraud.

From the less recognized perspective if the person getting the recognition is able to use that to move into another position and doesn't take the less recognized partner with him, then, the person who has actually been doing the work may be left with nothing. This is something that is seen in work partnerships. The undersecretary may actually be the person who has the skills and the person in the limelight may use this to move ahead, without bringing into the light the credit to the undersecretary. This can result in a traumatic ending to the relationship and a lack of credibility toward the person who was actually more responsible for the success. This kind of implicit agreement is seen in the Me-style of relating; it is co-dependent in nature. The less recognized person acts from a one-down position as a result of a problem with self-esteem, or a paradigm of being les-than when looking to partner. As a result, the two give the aggregate energy to promote the one. When the promoted one leaves he takes with him the success and the person who stays is even less strong than before the relationship.

The Me-style of relationship where this implicit energy exchange is most painful is when someone is exchanging work to receive love. This has a spiritual component to the broken agreement and injures the person who sees the love leave with the partner.

KNOW YOURSELF, KNOW YOUR PARTNER, USE MINDFULNESS

Overtly and explicitly identify what you see, feel, hear in your interactions and what you want to give and get from the relationship. When creating partnerships, avoid making assumptions that you and your partner have the same understanding about your participation and outcome. Be prepared to have a full and complete conversation about what you desire from and want to give to the partnership. Use your senses, to guide you. Look underneath the surface of what your partner is offering so that you get a full understanding. This is to say pay attention to his words and actions and what you see has happened previously with that person, in relationship. In general, people have a pattern in relationship so the history of how your partner has acted and created in relationship gives you information about your future with him or her. One mistake that can be made in this evaluation process is to think that somehow you can change your partner's habits. This is a mistake because you only have power to change your own habits. Your partner may change from how he has acted in the past but this will be a result of a paradigm shift. The best way to assist in the creation of a paradigm shift is to communicate your needs, wants, and perspective and understand your partner's needs, wants and perspective to see if you have agreement. It is important that you personally evaluate your true intention and agenda in the partnership.

Be open to the fact that you and your partner are dynamic and therefore your, or your partner's needs, expectations, and capacities may change over time. So it is important to keep the conversation going, check in verbally any time you have a funny feeling, and make adjustments.

These actions increase your ability to keep the partnership going and increase the health, mutuality, and success of the partnership. These actions can also lead to dissolution of the relationship when such is in the best interests of both parties, and under circumstances that promote your and your partner's health rather than injury.

THE IMPORTANCE OF BEING A
TRANSLATOR IN RELATIONSHIP

It is my observation and assertion that each person has a unique language. Words carry meaning that is personal. This personal meaning is a product of history, experience, and your own biography. Words have what I call *charge* in the power they contain because of the personal and/or social meanings attached to them.

Sociology posits that what underlies our capacity to create society is our ability to speak and have shared meanings and symbols. It is through this shared symbolism human groups create goals, have knowledge of the past, can live under specific rules of law, and can create a share vision. Language is what allows humans to have a shared past, present, future, and to have core values that bind the group together. Words are the building blocks that contain the symbolism and meaning that connect humans to each other, and connect humans to their perceptions of the earth, other species, plants and their perceptions of spirit or god.

There is an agreed upon meaning to words and then there are personal meanings to words. Arguments between partners are based on the interpretations of the shared and personal meanings in a personal way. For example, the word *belie* means to misrepresent and carries a connotation of intentionality, but it also means to contradict or negate which could be interpreted as unintentionally diverging or deviating, rather than intentionally misrepresenting or representing falsely. These different definitions are like different perspectives or paradigms. If you are in a discussion with a person who only knows the first definition, then he will respond defensively as if you are calling him a liar. If the person with whom you are talking is prone to being in an I-style of relating, then he will react to the word negatively and aggressively. If the person is prone to a We-style of relating he may inquire what your understanding of the word is and then respond with an interest in negotiating more fully the situation when you offer the second definition. I-style of relating is prone to defensiveness, aggressiveness, and attack. This style of relating has difficulty being a translator in relationship, as the idea of paradigm shifting is blocked by the need for independence and 'rightness' required in the I-style of acting in relationship. The We-style of relationship embraces paradigm recognition, shifting, and integration to develop connections, and strengthen both parties, the partnership, or group. The We-style of relating is prone to investigating ways to translate word meanings and language, so that a deeper understanding can be attained.

Successfully negotiating relationship is the process of learning each other's language and then being a translator.

Some small groups have a particular shared language that is highly personal and not directly related to dictionary definitions of words. This shared language has charged, intense meaning and can be used like shorthand to communicate an entire paradigm via gesture, sigh, tone, or word. This is great for quick interactions on the fly and great for winning parlor games, because each can telegraph a large amount of information with a single word or gesture. However, it is very difficult when the couple or partnership has reached a standstill. In these instances, the shared language blocks real and full communication. Individuals in long-term relationships, children and caregivers, and close siblings (especially twins) have their own shared-language.

This increases the intimacy between the shared language pair or group and excludes those outside the group. This is a secondary problem with how language connects. It can also disconnect, create isolation, and create battles between groups. You can see this in high school where small groups develop new words with personal meanings that hold them together as a group and exclude those who don't know the language. This creation of in-group/out-group is one of the most disastrous elements in society. It would not have power and could be easily resolved if individuals lived in the We-style of relationship. The We-style of relationship disallows this kind of in-group/our-group behavior through the focus on understanding, inclusion, and resolution through paradigm recognition, shifting and integration.

What words mean to you, how you see the world and communicate within it, these paradigms are dramatically affected by your experiences and your interpretations of those experiences. That whole internal, multidimensional meaning is called a frame of reference. Since everyone has a unique personality and unique experiences then this process results in unique meanings in language and even interpretation of behavior and actions. This as a phenomenological process; phenomenology identifies how phenomenon and objects of experience inform or uplevel your consciousness.

Two wonderful books on the phenomenology of words and language in developing meaning and connecting humans to their groups are from Martin Heidegger *On the Way to Language*, (1971) and Russell Lockhart, *Words as Eggs, Psyche in Language and Clinic*, (1983). The image of words as eggs is indeed apt as it centers you directly on the complete universe held within each word.

Let's use a word to illustrate this point: *Grace*. The word *grace* has religious connotations. It signifies beauty of a delicate nature, and movement that is easy and looks effortless, graceful. It can be interpreted as beneficence, prayer, a state of being under divine influence, and good will. I have a personal meaning to grace that describes being in line with your spiritual life-path, being in-sync with your true nature. For me this word is a gestalt of personal meaning that encompasses gifts from the exterior universe and the universe within, simultaneously, in complement.

How do you define *Grace*? How you interpret *Grace* or translate that word for yourself has to do with your experiences and internal relationship to that word. If you belong to a religious group with a specific interpretation to Grace then it will be imbued with that specific meaning for you.

Knowing yourself means understanding what has meaning for you and how much of that is transferable to and/or agreed on in your relationships, work, groups, and situations. It's important to know yourself, and know the person with whom you are in relationship, at this fundamental level.

Interpretation is one of the ways that communication breaks down because each individual interprets from his own frame of reference rather than that of the speaker. When there is a stall in communication, use a We-style of relating. Focus on paradigm recognition, shifting, and integration to shift the break-down into a break-through.

This underscores the importance of being a translator, clarifying your meaning and language, your frame of reference, as well as to spend time learning about the other's meaning and language, her frame of reference. Doing this creates the opportunity for full communication, resulting in an exchange of meaning and understanding. This is an act of mindfulness and allows a synergistic relationship of the two languages to be achieved. In groups there are as many languages as there are people involved. So this is an awesome task.

USE THE STOP, LOOK, AND LISTEN STRATEGY IN INTERACTION WITH OTHERS

Begin to identify and translate meaning in your own language and that of those close to you by noticing when you have/hear emotional expression with specific words.

Stop, look, and listen. This phrase will help to focus you into the present moment and onto the interchange, your emotional/sensory/feeling response, and the reaction in the other. It seems like a lot to focus on but you can do it though a simple check-in process, viewing and taking note in an interested but not determinant way. You are gathering information from these sources to clarify where a mis-step, or misunderstanding, in communication may have happened. This gives you the information needed to translate and communicate more fully.

Stop acting, talking, reacting, *stop doing*; *Look* at yourself, the other person, your face, your energy, her face, her energy, take note of what you see; *Listen* to the word and your inner experience as well as the other person's tone and her reaction. Then respond in the moment with *what did you hear me say?* or *I heard you say this, is that what you meant?* This style of communication moves the interaction into a neutral space. This will increase your success in investigation and translation of what has happened in the verbal exchange, so that you can clarify the meaning of the words used, and translate the languages. When you respond to sensory awareness in present time, you can act in a neutral/unattached, compassionate, and mindful way. Follow the thread of emotional expression back to its etiology when you are noticing an emotional attachment to a word either in yourself or your partner. Use the *stop, look and listen*, it can be revealing.

UNDERSTANDING INCREASES THROUGH COMMUNICATION

Underlying most disagreement in partnerships and relationships is ineffective communication. Conflicts are healthy opportunities to resolve areas of disagreement but when the conflict is met with ineffective communication it breaks down the structure of the partnership or relationship resulting in a tearing away and dissolution from within.

Unresolved conflict is the largest barrier to maintaining a healthy relationship. Me and I-styles of relating use ineffective communication tools. The underlying glue to these relationship styles interferes with the utilization of effective, direct, compassionate, forgiving, loving, strength-promoting communication. The We-style of relationship encourages this kind of multilevel communication. For successful conflict resolution to occur the communication and interaction between people requires receptivity to paradigm shifting, an attitude of openness and belief alignment.

One book in particular transformed how this was understood to happen, it addressed the process of attitude and belief change, and coined the term *paradigm shifting*: Thomas Kuhn, *The Structure of Scientific Revolutions*, (1962). The basis of the book is that the structure of scientific revolution is quantum shifting, rather than a linear acquisition of knowledge. The way in which the paradigm shifts is through a holistic shift in seeing, knowing, and understanding of a paradigm where a new conceptual worldview encapsulates or replaces the previous one. This had far-reaching applications into many fields of study. It defines how attitude and belief structures change and shift in people and groups.

Paradigm shifting is the basis of effective communication and paradigm integration is the basis of mutuality in partnership. The focus is on how to view various paradigms from within the structure as well as in relation to other structures. This is the ability to view situations from both a figure and a ground perspective, and then to shift back and forth between the figure and ground until you can perceive both simultaneously. This is a skill. It requires a willingness to accept all perspectives as true within context.

All perspectives are truth from within the perspective. Once you perceive all perspectives as true and you are not trying to 'pick' or 'prove' which is the *most true* (thereby shifting out of an I-style of relating), you take a neutral attitude which gives you a bird's eye-view. This allows you to view the conflicts and miscommunications in relationships and interactions as just that, misunderstandings and disconnects. This is a We-style of relating. I and Me-styles of relating have a rigid incapacity to perceive the other person's point of view, either due to a lack of psychosocial development, the Me-style of relating, or an unwillingness due to independence, competition, and defensiveness, the I-style of relating.

In disagreements, each party may describe an injury or problem with the situation that is true from his or her own perspective. When neither is able to see the other person's point of view there is a standstill, an obstacle that is immovable. The issue is from what paradigm or perspective they are arguing. If they are each focusing on different things they feel very assured they are right while unable to understand the other person's point or communication. Both parties describe feeling the same thing, unheard, unlistened to, or injured by the other's lack of empathy. This is a cue that a shift in perspective is needed.

Hearing and listening are important in discerning what is the core issue so a resolution may be created. Hearing and listening are not the same thing. Hearing is a passive, interpretable experience, where the person hears but may not extract meaning. Listening is an active process where another focuses mindful attention to what underlies the words, the content, the tenor, the tone, and the abstract issues that are in play.

This is when it is useful to focus on *connection rather than being right*. Use the *stop, look and listen* method to move you away from being tethered to your perspective toward being receptive to both perspective and a resolution.

My first goal in communication skills training is *connecting*, not judging or assessing right/wrong. Since both are right from each personal perspective and wrong from the other perspective the latter focus doesn't really open up any new avenues or allow for resolution. Only through a focus on increasing connection or understanding will the two individuals or group find resolution and solutions to their conflicts.

This is the concept of figure and ground in paradigm shifting. Here you could assign figure as the focus on the specific issue, situation, and ground as the focus on the background information. So that the figure component encompasses the words and ground perspective encompasses the tone, tenor, and unspoken information.

For a deeper understanding on this issue of figure and ground perspective and paradigm look at these two figure ground illusion images: In Figure A, The ground perspective is in Black – two faces, and the figure perspective is in white – a wine glass.

FIGURE A,
FIGURE/GROUND ILLUSION IMAGE
WINEGLASS, TWO FACES

FIGURE B
LEFT/RIGHT PERSPECTIVE ILLUSION,
DUCK, BUNNY

In Figure B the perspective shift is a right/left paradigm shift; looking at the image with a right facing perspective, the image looks like a *bunny*, from a left pointing perspective the image looks like a *duck*.

If two individuals are both looking at this image, from opposite perspectives there is sure to be disagreement about which animal is represented. The person who sees the duck only knows he is right and the person who sees the bunny only knows she is right — it is only through the capacity to see the other image via paradigm shifting that a resolution can be discovered.

There is a tendency to see either one or the other consistently when you first see the picture then after you learn about the other image in most situations you can go back and forth between the figure and ground. This is true with any paradigm. Your world-view is a paradigm and it has this figure-ground quality. It is through this paradigm you relate to others in your environment. This paradigm includes your political beliefs, your religious beliefs, your sociological/cultural beliefs, your attitudes and your values.

This next example shows how your cultural beliefs affect your perception. Look at the following set of words.

>axe,   log,   shovel,   saw

Group them into the three words that go together and the one that doesn't.

If you chose log that doesn't belong then you are looking at grouping them into *tools* and non-tool. This connotes a categorization with utilization.

If you chose shovel as the one that doesn't belong then you are looking at the log, saw and axe as connected by their *function* to each other – the log can be cut by the axe and saw but what can you do to it with the shovel? This connotes a categorization with functionality.

When I have used this technique with literature students they identified that three words were verbs and one word, *log* was not. However, when I have given it to a group of techies, they identified that all four were indeed verbs because they used the word log, as a verb in their computer experience.

How you group the words is a function of your cultural background and your personal experience in the world. It is your cultural phenomenon that informs you which is the right answer. Indeed all are correct as each relates to each perspective. If you saw that there were two (or more) answers right away before the answers were revealed, you have an affinity for seeing many points of view and are probably great at mediating and conflict resolution. Seeing the relationships among these words is a paradigm affected by your environment, upbringing, and your basic temperament.

Paradigm shifting, and figure/ground as applied to communication, team building parenting, and partnering is a way of increasing understanding between and among individuals to increase creativity, connection, and conflict resolution. This is a We-style of interacting, relating, negotiating, and partnering.

You can increase understanding through sharing your perspective while clarifying that of the other person. Use this information to review what may be creating a block or disconnect in your relationship. You can apply these ideas to a recent disagreement and see if the fundamental issue is a communication problem of paradigm alignment void of recognizing differences in perception.

Remember to use the stop, look, and listen method to investigate the underlying makeup of the obstacle. And question what your partner heard, when you feel you are in a conflict that you didn't intend. These neutral techniques help to diffuse the defensiveness and reactivity that can erupt when paradigms bump up against each other.

THE FUNCTION OF HEARING AND LISTENING IN RELATIONSHIPS

When interacting in a We-style of relationship a foundational tenet is to maintain connection and alignment with self while simultaneously connecting with your partner. You have to have a sense of what matters to you, your goals, your talents, and your limitations so that you can negotiate the common ground of the relationship.

This is harder to accomplish than your may think because humans have a tendency to hide information from themselves, or distort authentic truth, in order to obtain approval from others, feel accepted, or fit into their chosen group. This tendency to hide internal needs in your youth may assist in avoiding difficult situations or surviving difficult environments, but the habit later becomes a powerful deterrent to a successful partnership.

Seeking internal guidance and developing an image of your self that coordinates all of the necessary components of your being into a congruent and coherent whole is the first step. Seek first to know thyself; this suggestion is centered in the understanding that through self-knowledge you can attain your highest goals easily and happily. Once you have an understanding of who you are you can then begin to connect with another in partnership. When you begin the connection process with another you need to have an integral knowledge of yourself, then you can focus your attention on understanding the other. Through this investigative process you develop the connecting points of your relationship. The better developed your hearing and listening skills, the more facile your capacity to develop relationships.

When beginning a self-discovery, first be willing to accept yourself precisely where you are. It is only through this acceptance that you will have the strength, understanding, and compassion to love yourself. From that space you can change that which you do not like. In order to change you have to accept yourself as a whole. And through this self-acceptance you can then determine if you have things you would like to change in yourself.

Self-knowing is a starting place for self-development, and relationship development. Self-knowing is the process that allows for you to shift out of a Me or I-style of relationship into a We-style of relationship. This is a powerful, empowering, exciting, and humbling process. Once you have developed a more integrated sense of knowing of yourself then you can engage your sensory guidance system to assist you in communicating about what you have discovered with your partner. Remember to utilize paradigm recognition, shifting, and integration as your guide and to maintain a calm, neutral, and caring state in communication.

This step can be difficult because sometimes others are not as interested in you changing. They may prefer the benefits they receive even when it is not beneficial to you. Know that ultimately it is a positive shift for the relationship as a whole for you to increase your personal empowerment, mutuality, and connection with your partner. Move through this process with lovingkindness and compassion toward yourself and your partner. Use clarification and openness to keep your focused on your personal needs as well as the needs of your partner.

One common problem that happens with hearing in relationship is that people get into a habit of hearing what has been said in the past or hearing with a historical negative energy; so that they aren't actually listening but rather already preparing a defense to what they think they heard. This is especially true in I and Me-styles of relating.

You can discern this is happening when you feel surprise at your partner's response. For example you say something innocuous and they respond by yelling or with a very negative attitude. Through your listening skills you hear the dissonance between what you meant and what was heard by your partner. Make a habit of clarification; avoid mounting your own defensive action. Ask this question, *what did you hear me say?* This will get you and your partner refocused into the present so you can communicate more clearly. And then you can each listen to each other more fully, respectfully, and lovingly. This hearing in history is true for love and work relationships.

You will find it in any relationship that has a history of interaction that has become habitual with historical unresolved conflict.

Listening and speaking in a thorough manner when developing the expectations in any relationship will assist both parties in getting what they truly want and connecting more deeply. This is an important aspect of living in a We-style of relationship. This is the basic description of mindfulness. Discovering another's paradigm, as well as your own, and then shifting these to see the connecting threads is the place of the We-style of relationship. This We-style of relating offers a deeper level of connection intimacy, love, and mutual care.

Attend to subtlety without judgment; focus on connection and clarity with acceptance, compassion, and dispassionate observation. It requires hearing and listening both. Hearing being that component of noticing when something is off, changes in another's tone, and tenor. Listening being that component of content, meaning, and feeling that we need to listen to from within us, and from the perspective of the other.

When I am hearing on a multidimensional level the information of another, I feel her meaning from within me and when I am listening, I am aware of not just what I perceive but her perspective as well. Hearing and Listening to another is the ultimate gift of care. It reveals important aspects of another and results in visibility. The insecurity that underlies the Me-style and I-style in relationship creates a lack of visibility, a lack of authenticity for both parties. When a path is opened to increase visibility, the seen individual feels accepted from an authentic place and then will eschew habits of being that are inauthentic. From this deep connecting point many negotiation paths are available for relationship. This is especially true because our world is one of language and verbal, cognitive symbols so that being heard directly relates to being seen and therefore being real. It is why in the reverse, many are drawn to do things against their nature through words that drag them away from their true center.

By focusing your attention on actively listening and hearing the true meaning and perspective of another you can develop powerful and sustaining relationships as well as avoid those that seem good on the surface but are without sustenance underneath. You can move from a Me or I-style of relationship into a We-style of relationship. Listening and hearing are fundamental tools in the toolbox needed to create a We-style of relationship.

FIGURE 2, LISTENING & HEARING TOGETHER,
OFFER WAYS TO UPLEVEL YOUR RELATIONSHIP
PHOTO CREDIT, CHARLOTTE ELCONIN

MY PERSONAL ADVENTURE:
A MINI CULTURAL REVOLUTION

When I was in college I spent six months studying in *Roma, Italia*. It was a very powerful period in my life. I was immersed in the study of Sociology, paradigms, cultural relativism, and Gestalt figure/ground perspectives. I found these concepts intriguing. Enthusiastic and open-minded with an internal *joi de vive*, I had a secret desire to effect world change; evidently first my world would need to experience change. Initially this change was painful. My Italian experience had all the qualities of adventure: transformation, journeying into the unknown with a sort of insurmountable task, love, betrayal, discovery of internal strength, love again, and immersion into another culture. Here is my story: a personal mini cultural revolution. As you read it, notice if it holds some interesting clues for you about the course of change and relationship styles.

I had not planned to go to Italy. My boyfriend, who was an art major, was going and I thought *'oh I should go too!'* I didn't realize that he had wanted to go without me so he could experience the world unencumbered. In retrospect it would have been more useful to ask him what his plans were before inviting myself along. This discovery was painful. Barely weeks into the trip, finding him happily courting a tall woman from Oklahoma. I mention her height because it was the thing that was so irritating about her, so opposite me; she was like an *Amazon warrior* stealing my boyfriend away from me. He was, of course a complicit and willing partner, no stealing here, I was the only one who was unaware of the situation.

I was stunned, alone in a foreign country and so sad. He and I had been the best of friends for a longtime and I wasn't sure exactly how to proceed. In the days that followed my discovery, I was on autopilot; disconnected, unfocused, just putting one foot in front of the next, I moved through each day cycle. After awhile, I began to re-focus on the beautiful amazing country that surrounded me. I started to identify what I wanted to do, see, accomplish, and experience. In this reevaluation I discovered myself.

There was a lovely young man in our college classes from England. He was polite, handsome, kind, and smart. I liked him and he seemed to like me. His good friend was a young Italian man who was very involved with Roman politics. It was exciting to hang out with them and learn about how young people in Rome spent their days. Quite different from my own experience; they were enormously involved in politics at a very young age. Paolo, my handsome friend's friend, had lost his best friend two years before (when they were still teenagers) to a car-bomb explosion. This was an intentional act connected to his political alliances and embattlements. Paolo had strong opinions and sound arguments to back them up. It was exciting to be in their company and to begin to develop for myself my beliefs about politics in my country and theirs.

My handsome young man, whose care I had fallen into, was even more intriguing. He had gone to school in England but his family was Persian. He was the kindest, most gentle man I had ever known. He had dealt with great tragedy and difficult situations in his life yet he had not let this harden him. We came to be very close and he showed me a fascinating world that I could never have imagined. His gentle eyes had a mixture of sadness and playfulness in them and I felt the safest I had ever felt with anyone when I was by his side.

In the middle of our time together we went to Austria. It was beautiful and magical. I saw Freud's house, which had been a long-time dream for me. It was like a fairytale, but the purpose of our trip was far from the magic and fantasy of Disney. He needed to get a visa to come to America. He had gone before, followed the stealthy steps outlined by whoever was assisting him to do so previously; he had lost money and he had been denied. Half of his family resided in Iran and half was in America. There was still a great deal of wariness about young Iranian men coming to the States and so he had to go through this secret process not knowing the outcome and risking treachery from many angles.

While we were together in Austria, he discovered that he was successful in getting his visa. We celebrated that he would be able to join his siblings in the States.

We had a blissful time together in Rome through the rest of our time in school. After, on my way back to the States I joined him briefly in London and then we separated.

I returned to my home and he to a new home in San Francisco. I visited him once for a brief time after graduating from college, when I went out to an old college friend's wedding in San Francisco and then we lost track of each other.

He once said to me, while we were still in Italy, that his father would never have approved of him seeing me because I was American. His father was no longer alive and his mother was still in Iran. I never thought about how my parents would have responded; they seemed to be open-minded and accepting. But I was aware that to me he was not his country or his culture but rather an individual person with whom I was in love. I had not considered the problems between our countries until he made this comment.

Both these men, the boyfriend with whom I went to Italy, and the boyfriend I met in Italy, had perceived their time in Italy as a time to experience being with someone not accepted in their *real* or *home world*. They each had seen it as a break from the cultural and normative expectations, to experience more fully a deeper self that they would not take with them except in their memories. However positively their experience in Italy may have changed them, the participants in their experience must be left in Italy.

In my innocence, I didn't fully understand any of this until much later upon reflection, yet my experiences with each of them left indelible marks on my sense of self and my character, creating mini cultural revolutions within me about my world view, goals, interior strength, how to partner, and love.

I view the world through a sociological lens and yet even with that, I experience each person individually. Sociology takes the position that one's self is completely bound up by one's culture and that self and mind are really just an introjection of the society or culture within which you live...but my personal experience is that individuals interact with their culture in innovative and unique ways to develop intricately specific and personal selves. The culture and beliefs within another's personality and characteristics are present and identifiable but that self, and character are profoundly personal.

I went to Italy following my boyfriend and in a way following someone else's dream. My boyfriend's betrayal kicked me back into the driver's seat of my life. I chose to see the gestalt of it as a gift: an opportunity to venture onto my own path, and follow my own inner compass. It was through my inner searching, and resolution of that painful betrayal that I was reacquainted with my own heart connection. This infused me with the inner curiosity and strength needed to venture out into my personal adventure. To go against my habit of following and partnering for safety was a mini cultural revolution, and allowed me to discover my own goals, and the strengths, and gifts that I could bring to a relationship. Creating the kind and empowering relationship with my dear boyfriend in Italy, knowing that it would end, this was a shift in my style of relating that signaled an increased maturity in my development away from a Me-style of relationship into an I-style of relationship.

My dear beloved boyfriend with whom I traveled to Italy said to me upon our return that although he abandoned me for this exciting opportunity to be with that *tall girl* he ultimately had a depressing and uneventful experience because she went on to another boy and he was left without either her or me. And I, in my action to respond to his abandonment, had a true adventure.

Sadly, for him this was true. Joyfully for me, he was right.

How you respond to your world is your only true power in the action of life. And perspective is everything.

I think of my dear boyfriend that I met in Italy, living in America, and I wonder how well he is thriving. I wonder if his family that is still in Iran, is faring well through the strife in his country. I am profoundly grateful to these two men for how they cared for me and positively shaped my life and my understanding of relationship.

Using a mindful approach to your previous relationships, you too may see that you have had profoundly positive teachers that have assisted you in developing a more mutually satisfying style of being in relationship. Sometimes, it is the painful events that create the space to change your perspective and venture onto a more growth-promoting path. Take the time to look at what mini cultural revolutions you have endured. Looking at breakups or breakdowns in this way assists you in seeing the breakthrough, and the gifts of the people with whom you have partnered. Looking at these shifts, losses, even dramas in relationships as gifts, shifts the perspective from feeling like it was a waste of time, or negative time in your life into a learning opportunity and something you can feel gratitude toward.

HOW TO CREATE MINI-INTERNAL CULTURAL, REVOLUTION IN YOUR LIFE

The first step is to live. The next step is to apply a mindful, neutral, compassionate, loving perspective to your situation. The *stop, look and listen* method helps to focus you into the present moment in a neutral, mindful, compassionate way. Paying attention to language and meaning, figure and ground, and paradigm shifting are all ways to increase mindfulness so you can act in a present moment way within the context of authenticity and internal strength toward connection and the development of your best self.

Buddhist Meditation practice is based in mindfulness. The natural outcome to mindfulness is paradigm shifting. Paradigm shifting was the central concept of Stephen Covey's book, *The 7 Habits of Highly Effective People (1989)*. His book was written as a leadership development book. I have found Covey's book to be very useful in relationship counseling. His process of personal change offers a strategy to develop a mindful style of relating. If you work through his inner, outer diagram, focus on *seeking to understand* and negotiate from a We-style of relating toward a *win-win* you can shift your personal style of relating and create your own mini internal cultural revolution.

Mindfulness centers you into a neutral, curious, present moment space for perception. Through mindfulness you can develop skills at:

- Making connections and seeing how to integrate disparate views to incorporate a vision of life as interconnected patterns.
- Understanding the subjectivity of how you connect/disconnect and how you view life, the influence of your experiences and your interpretations of experiences in your world view
- Seeing empowerment as a function of personal will-power

- Acting responsibly, understanding that responsibility is the ability-to-respond in the present moment
- Seeing the direct relationship between rights and responsibilities as intimately connected; and that freedom increases your level of responsibility.
- Releasing unconscious habit reaction patterns that do not serve you in the present moment
- Paradigm shifting to create mini internal, cultural revolutions, the result of paradigm recognition, shifting, and integration into a new whole.

Hermann Hesse's literary work *The Glass Bead Game (Magister Ludi) (1943), that deals with the interaction of individual and group needs*, for which he won the Nobel Prize for Literature in 1946, and *Siddhartha (1922, 1951)* which describes an individual's search for authenticity, self-knowledge and spirituality are resources to examine for further insight into this process of the power and importance of mindfulness, and the struggle between group and individual needs in relationships and partnerships.

Other sources that are found under the general section of existentialism and phenomenology offer insight into these conceptual worldviews. *Existentialism* is a philosophy that focuses on how all actions are choices, even no action, and that an individual has power through her responsibility for her choices in the world, and via this responsibility experiences freedom. Jean-Paul Sartre best describes this philosophy in *Being and Nothingness (1956)*. Phenomenology incorporates the effect of the interface of energy, spirit, mind, and physical components in the development of self and meaning. Georg Hegel: The *Phenomenology of Spirit (1977)* and Martin Heidegger:

On the Way to Language (1982) and *The Question of Being (1958)* were strong contributors to this philosophy.

From a psychological perspective the following writers are useful to investigate. The contemporary work by James Hillman who focused on the archetypes of Carl Jung in a transcendent way, and the revolutionary work by Heinz Kohut who developed the concept of dynamic self-psychology which focuses on the development of a sense of worth, well-being, and self-object relationships, primarily in early childhood but continues throughout all stages of development and focuses on internal conflicts and important relationships. These theorists wrote about the integration of spirit into psychology, which offered psychotherapists real tools to help individuals move through stuck aspects of Erikson's psychosocial development stages.

Their ideas are useful to review when taking the journey to incorporate your sprit, mind, and body sensory guidance system, or just to have a framework for how mindfulness assists an individual to uplevel his consciousness which then creates the paradigm shift from a Me or I-style of relating into a We style of relating.

An author who incorporates these philosophies to promote mindfulness and integration of spirit, mind, body and action is Ken Wilber: *Integral Spirituality (2006)* and *No Boundary: Eastern and Western Approaches to Personal Growth (2001)*. Ken Wilber's work has been foundational in the field of leadership, team building, relationship and partnership development from a business, corporate, and group level. He has the ability to show the connecting spaces for large theories, and philosophies, developing a concept of Integrality similar to the concept of Gestalt to explain the way that theories interact and connect. These theories are based in the tenets of mindfulness and phenomenology. In Wilber's work, *Integral Spirituality* (2006), he defines *We- ness as a miracle*, and defines *the look and feel of a We* as incorporating what a We looks like from the outside and feels like from the inside. The power and miracle of the We from his writings is that we can know another at all, an accomplishment extraordinaire that we can have shared understandings and knowings, goals, and values. This is the basis of the concept of intersubjectivity, the study and experience of seeing another and we-ness from the outside and feeling the we-ness and interaction of I and other, from within. It is an incorporation of *meditative inner contemplation* and *neutral, present moment outer observation* (Wilber, 2006). This we-ness incorporates the integration of spirit, mind, and body and allows for a We-style of relating.

In addition to reading some of these source materials, you can also work to shift through physical and energetic endeavors like meditation, inner contemplative practices, prayer, breathwork, Tai Chi, and yoga. Together these practices increase your internal strength and internal will-power, and your capacity to navigate internal needs and external expectations to promote optimal growth and mutuality in relationship.

GIVE & TAKE: WE-STYLE OF RELATIONSHIP CREATES MUTUAL CARE & SUSTENANCE

When dealing with paradigms and working on relationships one important thing to consider is how to remain strong and connected. You want to create opportunities for both qualities to be present. This is an integral or intrinsic component of the We-style of relating.

The Me and I-styles of relating have lesser degrees of connectedness or internal strength.

Being strong is both standing up for yourself through identifying and asking for your needs to be met, as well as supporting the other person while his or her needs are being met. The first is more like taking, or being on the receiving end, and the second is more like giving. Give and take in a dynamic, flexible, responsive fashion is the natural flow of energy in relationship.

Being connected is a function of using your six-sense awareness, *your sensory guidance system*, in conjunction with your communication skills to negotiate your own needs and the needs of the other person. It is a dynamic, ever-changing landscape of primary focus over time.

At any snapshot in time you may find one or the other person on the receiving end of the relationship energy, support, or power. Consider these markers as a guide to evaluate give and take in relationship.

- If, it is consistently the same person who is receiving then, the flow of the relationship is off balance and this may result in problems. This is an indicator of a Me-style relationship.
- If, in order to remain in a relationship you have to give up yourself or your needs then, this is an indication of an exchange pattern. This describes the energy exchange in a Me-style of relationship.
- If, a person is unable to be involved in both give and take in relationship then, the individual's security issues, from the MAAPS concept, is driving the relationship. Relationships are a function of give and take, but the form taken and the style of exchange indicates whether it is a Me, I or We-style of relating.

- If, you find that you are always on the giving end then, you need to reevaluate how you interact with others. You may be inadvertently diminishing your own power in that relationship. Here I am using the word *power* to describe empowerment not power over. Some people think that this makes them a better person that they do not have needs in a relationship, or that they are always understanding the other person and giving in. In reality this is not a stronger or better position, it is actually a weaker position and also a behavior that will degrade the relationship because it diminishes both parties.

Relationships prosper with boundaries. Knowing where you end and another begins is an important aspect of the We-style of relationship. This includes being able to keep a strong sense of yourself and the other person in relationship. This requires the word or behavior of *no* as much as it requires *yes*. With respect to give and take and boundaries, knowing when to say which is a function of an internal balance as well as the qualities of strength and connection. Me-style relationships tend to have difficulty with *No*. And, I-style relationships tend to have difficulty with *Yes*. These difficulties are a result of the inner rigidity based on security issues that result in an inflexibility of how to give and take in relationship. These styles have a lack of dependability, which actually leads to either a lack of boundaries (Me-style) or boundaries that are inflexible (I-style). The MAAPS section of this book delves more significantly into what underlies these problems in relationship and the issues of security that drive the different styles of relationship.

This concept of energy flow in relationship requires balance for maximal health. Give and Take in relationship needs to be in balance if the relationship is to remain sustaining and growth promoting, over time. Here balance is the concept of equity, not necessarily equality. So, under certain conditions one person may actually give more, let's say if someone is sick or in a temporary dependent situation. If, that behavior continues beyond the circumstances then, the behavior may begin to skew its energy and throw the relationship off-balance.

- An effective tool that can assist you in evaluating give and take in relationship is to create a habit of attending to how energy is exchanged and flowing in your relationship
- To maintain balance, pay attention to how energy is dispersed and dealt with in all the relationships in your life.

This evaluation and monitoring behavior keeps you focused on the flow of the energy and keeps you acting in present time. It allows you to observe and notice when there are exchange patterns, or implicit agreements. And allows for an opportunity for you to bring out into the open and discuss with your partner imbalances in your relationship. This keeps the relationship from becoming stagnant or unhealthy.

INSIDE-OUT CHANGE:
THE EQUATION THAT PARADIGMATIC BELIEFS DRIVE BEHAVIOR

Paradigm shifting can occur in an instant when you are looking at a visual representation that has a distinct figure and ground image. Once the two images are identified, seen, and integrated your can see the shift instantaneously.

FIGURE 3, FACE IN TREES ILLUSION IMAGE

Shifting an inner paradigm of how you are in the world takes a longer time and seems to be more incremental. Because of your attachment to how you identify yourself, which is a truism for all humans not a fault or limitation, being different, being the shifted person is more challenging than seeing the shift on paper.

When you internally experience a paradigm shift you can at times feel it instantaneously like the story told by Stephen Covey in *The 7*

Habits of Highly Effective People (1989), about a young man and his children on a train.

> He describes the children acting-out on the train, running up and down and being loud. An observer is annoyed by this behavior. Then the observer discovers that the father is emotionally flat and not stopping the children from their effusive behavior because he wants them to have the opportunity to be like children as they had just left the funeral home and burying their mother, his wife. The observer upon hearing this experiences an internal paradigm shift. His internal experience immediately shifts from negative, thinking the father is a bad father for not controlling his children, to positive, having empathy for the children, and the father, for their loss. He aligns with the father's perspective and agrees with his decision to not squash the children's behavior.

The observer's shift in the above story occurs immediately, which happens with distinct situations. It takes a longer course when the shift is an internal perspective or an internal belief overhaul; having a truly changed internal paradigm shift that changes your actions is a longer process that develops overtime. This can be initiated in response to the immediate internal paradigm shift, or insight trigger.

Covey refers to this as an *inside-out process*. From a developmental perspective all real and sustaining, therapeutic change is an inside-out process.

To shift out of a Me or I-style of relating into a We-style of relating is usually not an immediate *aha* shift. It is something that happens overtime, as you practice mindfulness and meditation. It requires an internal and external shifting of how We looks and how We feels. If you are making this shift within a relationship the interplay of your changes will have reverberations from your partner or vice versa. The process takes the shape of a spiral. You will appear to move forward and backward in your development as you integrate your internal changes into your external actions and release your habitual patterning in behavior, thinking, and expectation. The process requires time to integrate so that when you are appearing to move backward you are actually re-wiring your spiritual, emotional, and mindful paradigms, to create a *new feel* of We-ness in relationship. Movement forward has to do with practicing the action and trying on the *new look* of We-ness in your relationship style. It is an inside-out process of change and integration.

Inside-out change is a function of being self-aware, knowing oneself and then acting congruently with your new internal perceptions, knowings, beliefs, and motivations. This self-awareness increases your personal responsibility in actions and interactions; this is the basis of creating mutuality in relationship. Self-confident awareness allows for action that disregards insecurity, and eschews acting out of habit, thereby increasing the opportunity for dialogue, connection, and understanding in relationship. To help guide you in the process of developing your self-awareness, use these tools.

- Think of the phrase *Be the Change*, from the Mahatma Gandhi mantra *Be the Change you Wish to See in the World*, as a direction for understanding that your only true power to change is to change yourself.
- Incorporate the knowledge through Sociology that you affect those in your group as much as your group affects you. Your self-change can trigger another's choice to shift his perspective or change his behavior of his own free will.

- Beliefs guide values and behavior, what you see is what you believe. If you allow yourself to believe in the strength within you, you can see that strength, and you can be it and live it.

Covey wrote about this as *changing Have to Be.*

If you want to **have** *trust then* **be** *trustworthy ... or if you want to* **have** *a happy marriage then* **be** *the kind of person who generates positive energy and sidesteps negative energy rather than empowering it (empowering the negative energy by focusing on and giving energy to it).*

Being mindful in your evaluations and actions, and applying compassion and lovingkindness, will move you through this process easily and thoroughly. By thoroughly I mean deeply; it will be meaningful and feel real, solid, and strengthening. This is important if you are moving from a Me-style of relating into an I-style of relating. At the core of a person in the Me-style of relating is a hole, an emptiness that drives the person's behavior to enmesh with another to feel whole; this is what is underneath the co-dependent behavior.

A fundamental change in your orientation to an attitude of gratitude can assist any inside-out process. Additionally addressing what security issues drive your paradigm of relating can help you to increase your inner strength, empowerment, and self-confidence.

Insecurity engenders negativity and critical evaluation that excludes compassion. Confidence engenders positivity, harmony, and critical evaluation that embraces compassion. The first is disconnecting and the second is connecting or reconnecting. This is why there is a deep sense of loneliness and isolation, fear and defensiveness in the Me and I-styles of relationship, because they are based on issues of security that separate the two partners, either by keeping them small through co-dependence (Me-style) or by keeping them limited through a lack of interdependence (I-style).

Changing your internal paradigm for interaction from disconnecting (protecting of self, defensiveness) to connecting (knowing one's self, and focusing on harmony, compassion, and love) is a characterological, paradigmatic shift. The We-style of relationship views interactions from an inside-out perspective. Through the We-style of relationships connection in strength and compassion is the guiding focus for conflict resolution rather than determination of who is right. The guiding qualities of the I-style of relationship, competition, defensiveness, and conflict seen as right/wrong, create adversity, disharmony, and separation rather than connection. To shift from an I-style of relationship into a We-style of relationship focus on connection is key.

When your internal paradigm is to be authentically connected, the We-style of relating, then you are drawn to *seek first to understand* as Covey describes it, and look for the connecting threads rather than looking for the places where one disconnects. Successful and effective mediation and negotiation are based on this internal paradigm.

This internal paradigm of connection is a function of mindfulness and a willingness to be balanced in your evaluations and interactions. The We-style of relating incorporates your personal view of the situation and a willingness to understand another's perspective of the situation. This is how the We-style of relationship opens the space for connection, harmony, and mutuality. This style of interaction allows for connection and harmony, and the uplevel of both partners toward agreed-upon goals that do not result in a diminishment of either partner.

The qualities promoted through this style of relating include:

- Self-awareness, flexibility, mindfulness
- Confidence, and a lack of insecurity or need to be right
- Congruence in actions and words with internal paradigms and beliefs; this includes release of beliefs that are incongruent an the development of inside-out change toward congruent beliefs that guide your actions

You can use the phrase *Be the Change you wish to see in your world* as a mantra, to help you shift your perspective when you feel stuck in your relationship; when you are being the change you desire, you will see it in all your interactions and relationships. Or you can practice changing *Have to Be*, as a guide to shift your behavior so that you are creating a *look and feel of We*-ness that is representative of your inner paradigm of the We-style of relating.

USING HUMOR TO SHIFT YOUR PERSPECTIVE TO NEUTRAL

Humor is a useful tool in your tool-box when it comes to paradigm shifting. It allows for the shift to be non-threatening. It has the same energy as an epiphany but with less intensity. Humor creates a conduit for the perception to be seen and released simultaneously. This is especially true if you are attempting to assist yourself or your partner in seeing an over-reaction. Humor can help you see silliness in your thinking or behaving void of negative judgment.

Seriousness can block paradigm shifting; using humor can lighten a situation that may have become too heavy. It's really helpful when you want to sidestep a negative interaction that is steamrolling down a course to opposition or a flat-out stalemate. It can also help when you find yourself in a situation that has spun out of control, because humor has a neutralizing effect. Using humor can result in an instantaneous shift in energy. The key is discerning the style of humor that is most beneficial for the situation and to the individuals involved.

Laughing at yourself when you need to lighten up is an important part of de-stressing, and it helps you get into a mindful state; it can create a paradigm shift, the humorous nature of events opens the doorway into real insight and epiphany.

The mindfulness component to humor is essential when used to deal with resistance. This is something that I wrote about in my book, *Turning No to ON: The Art of Parenting with Mindfulness (2011)*, resistance can look like a NO or just a distraction; it can be present through oppositional behavior, like foot stomping with arms crossed, or more passively though dawdling and delaying with children or even look like passive-aggressive behavior in adults. All of these actions are expressions of resistance and can interfere with the smooth flow of events. Often resistance is actually a cover for something else that is underlying the situation. The underlying issues are blocks, or some sort of obstruction within the individual exhibiting the resistance. Emotions of frustration, powerlessness, anger, and insecurity underlie the behavior of resistance. These are difficult to access, but humor lightens the situation to open a pathway to what lies underneath. Because these emotions are tender, it is important to choose your humorous route carefully in order to avoid injury to your partner. Trust is an important aspect of allowing a shift so if your choice of humor feels mean then the person will shutdown and block access to the underlying issue. Your knowing of your partner will help you assess what humorous action will be most helpful and if you choose unwisely be quick to apologize and explain your loving intentions.

Resistance can be a way of dealing with unwanted pressure, expectation, or structure that feels stifling; strict time schedules or an event requiring attendance, as well as other limits to a person's freedom can result in resistance. By bringing humor into the equation you can uncover the cause of the resistance without getting into a power struggle with your partner. If you are dealing with your own resistance, use the stop, look, and listen method to discern the underlying issue and be open to the humor of the situation.

Humor lightens; it makes the change feel less heavy or more obvious and it allows the shift to be embraced without negativity. Lightening both the weighty-ness of making choices, decisions, and change as well as lightening with respect to increasing the degree of mirth, spirit, and luminosity involved in living and evaluating.

Humor is a useful technique to use when you are processing inside-out change. The change that you are attempting to evolve can feel threatening to your or your partner's security issue underlying your relationship style. When you are addressing a security issue, using humor lightens the information and makes it more palatable. This allows your partner to have increased processing time, so that she doesn't have to react to the information but can mull it over and ultimately offer a mindful response.

Different temperament styles respond most effectively to different styles of humor. Puns, silly gestures, funny faces, self-deprecation, telling jokes are various styles of bringing humor into the situation and they fit different temperament styles and different types of situations. It is most efficient to have a few different humorous behaviors to lighten the scene. It is also important to fit your humor to that of your partner...you may like funny faces and silly voices but she may not appreciate them. If you use a maneuver that is contrary to what your partner finds funny, you will make the situation worse.

Being silly, especially when you are in a position of authority, cuts through the anxiety or the seriousness of the situation. Mirth helps to bring you to mindfulness. Seeing the silly in the situation and laughing can move you to neutral so that you can negotiate more freely. Sometimes, mindfulness needs a little mirth to get the job done.

As noted above, humor is a little tricky; it can create a significantly worsened situation when used incorrectly or at the wrong time. This is especially true with certain temperaments that have a hypersensitivity to being laughed at. In these circumstances it's most useful to allow yourself to be the canvas or conduit for looking silly, allowing your partner to laugh at you and through that, to see his own silliness, on his own and in his own time. If you make the connection too quickly for your partner regarding the humor and what you are attempting to lightly communicate, and he is not ready you may find that you worsen the situation.

Sarcasm can create the opposite effect because it may be giving the opposite message through tone or content. Sarcasm can actually create distance and disconnection, because your partner can experience it as a thinly veiled attack. If you have a tendency to use sarcasm when you are being humorous, make sure it is the best way to lighten the situation for your partner if you are using humor to create a positive paradigm shift.

To develop this style of communicating, practice your ability to listen with your *third* ear (inner, mindful, paying attention) to identify what actions are covert or veiled messages. This helps you to know when to use humor as you are acquainting yourself more fully with your partner. Humor used in a timely manner is an effective tool for shifting paradigms, creating a space for neutrality and mindfulness.

It is the application of a lighter, humorous face to the situation. It lightens it and offers a path to mindfulness. The lightening up of the situation, helps to deflect insecurity, fears, and old patterns of negative relating.

DEFINING BOUNDARIES INCREASES YOUR SENSE OF SPACE AND CONNECTION

Change and growth are adventures into your heart and soul. This can be challenging for you if you are in a Me-style of relationship and you are trying to move into a We-style of relationship.

Relationship styles follow a developmental process from Me-style through I-style to We-style. The Me-style of relating has diffuse and enmeshed boundaries. Which means the boundaries between Me and You in relationship get blurred. The way in which a participant in a Me-style relationship makes decisions is through a need to agree with, or merge into the other to feel the connection. This is how the co-dependence begins. The individual in a Me-style of relating has difficulty saying *No*, when asked to act or be in a way that is inauthentic, because the driving force is to connect at all costs including loss of self. The picture of this kind of relationship is two halves coming together to make a whole. So there is a lack of boundaries between the two participants. ( )

To move into an I-style of relationship requires closing off the boundaries around yourself. Developing a sense of yourself that is defined from within so that you can guide yourself toward your own goals. You need to develop behaviors and mechanisms to meet your own needs and to depend on yourself. This is both exhilarating and frightening. Once you do this, you are freer to develop into a fuller picture of yourself. Rather than two halves making one whole, you are developing a whole picture of yourself so that you can move into and I-style of relationship: two Is walking side-by-side without integration. Connection is through a tally sheet of exchanges in an I-style of relationship. Here competition, defensiveness, and independence drive the relationship so that an individual in an I-style of relating has difficulty saying *Yes,* when asked to create dependence or interdependence. The fear for an individual in an I-style of relating is to become engulfed into the other and lose himself. As with the Me-style of relationship this is a result of an insecure sense of self. Unlike the Me-style of relationship, where the drive to be connected causes enmeshment or a lack of boundaries, in the I-style of relating the fear of enmeshment results in overly rigid boundaries. The picture of this kind of relationship is two *Is* walking side-by-side, solitary selves walking next to each other without integration. 0 0

You have to develop a solid sense of yourself, deal with adversity against your picture of yourself , and create a personal relationship with yourself, to live in an I-style of relationship. After solidifying this experience and developing a sense of trust that you will not sell yourself out, you can begin to move into a We-style of relationship. An I-style of relationship is a stepping-stone to get to a We-style of relationship. This is because you have to develop boundaries first (I-style) before you can be flexible with your boundaries in a dynamic way (We-style).

The interdependence of a We-style of relationship allows for strength of self *and* connection to other, *simultaneously*. The We-style of relationship incorporates support of the individual and collective goals and needs, with dynamic, flux movement between the resources of the relationship toward whatever of these (individual or collective) needs attention at any given time. This requires strong boundaries and flexibility in the interdependence of the two individuals and the third aspect, the relationship or partnership. So that rather than ½ + ½ = 1 (me-style) or 1,1 (I-style) you create a situation where 1+1 = 3, or more than the sum of its parts (we-style). The picture of the We-style of relationship includes two wholes and a third aspect, which is the area the two individuals overlap to create the relationship vortex, **o0o** (view this symbol as two circles overlapping each other to create an inner vortex).

Fear can really be a block to change, embracing the attitude of adventure can reframe your fear into excitement, offering an energy or anticipation to help you to flow with the change rather than block or freeze when faced with change.

Consider evaluating your situation with a focus on self-needs and intuitions first, not in a selfish way but rather, in an honoring, solidifying, bounded way that creates the space for you to see and feel where you end and your partner begins. Whatever *is,* starts at home: this is to say the capacity for forgiveness, love, change, creation, letting go, and acceptance are inside-out processes, beginning within you and then being exhibited in your behavior toward others.. So to gather strength to change and to partner remember the concept that if you want to have something you have to *Be* it first; if you want to have forgiveness, love, change, acceptance, strength, boundaries you have to *Be* each of those first.

It is through the process of forgiving yourself you can forgive others, and through the process of loving yourself that you can fully develop a loving relationship with another. It is in the process of accepting yourself precisely where you are that you can then shift, let go, and change.

This is how boundaries work. Boundaries create a definition. They clarify *this is me, and this is you*, through defining where you end and another begins. This clarification creates a deeper understanding of each individual and also how couples, partners or groups coexist and share goals. From the defined individual space, the boundary, you can create the space for a sense of oneness and togetherness. This definition is dynamic.

Flowing through the process of change begins with gentleness. Boundaries assist in creating an internal container, so that you can move through a process of change more harmoniously. Creating boundaries comes out of self-love, and love toward your partner.

This interior acceptance of yourself frees you from your insecurities and your defensiveness. This definition actually creates expansion. This is counter-intuitive but it is how the energy works. The acceptance, boundary definition, creates the space for expansion into a bigger, deeper, broader you. And it is this same process that allows for a bigger expansion of We-ness. Acceptance is both a gentle and strong emotion and action. It is flexible and flowing in nature, like bamboo in wind.

Part of self-love is self-knowing and acceptance, so that your actions and being are more in sync with your internal, congruent present-moment self. This releases you from the bondage of your history and your historical habit reactions that defined your self in a more limiting way. From this space you can release the structure imposed by your equation of how to deal with your personal security issue. This happens most easily through a loving, kind attitude toward yourself, your habits, your insecurities, and your limitations. The attitude of adventure is a mixture of joy and risk, a sense of exhilaration, a sense of danger and a sheer experience of loving bliss, all at once. By simply applying an attitude of adventure to your quest for change and development, you create the space to move from a Me-style of relating through an I-style of relating into a We-style of relating. Allow yourself to be guided by the look and feel of We-ness from within and without.

CAPTION: FIGURE 4, THE ATTITUDE OF ADVENTURE
PHOTO CREDIT: DENISE BRYCE

SURVIVOR SCENARIOS: CHOOSE THRIVER OVER SURVIVOR

Habit reaction patterns are patterns of behavior that have become habitual reactions. These behaviors are based in the past, in some historical event that transformed you. The event that creates a habit reaction pattern is based in an experience of survival. These behavior patterns express a definition of the world as unsafe, and solidify how you have to act in order to survive. They are the patterns that exhibit your definition of how you perceive you *must* relate in the world. These are unthinking and reactive; the actions are involuntary and without your mindful, present-moment attention. The pattern pulls you into ways of behaving, like a rut pulls a bicycle around a circle. The groove, furrow, or automatic routine of it takes you into the habitual behavior automatically. The reactive pattern engages without your attention to it; it is unconscious, under the radar of your conscious, intentional mind. When you attend to these pattern scenarios mindfully, you can access information about which security issue drives you and whether it is safe to be interdependent.

This unconscious reaction is not intuition. It is the opposite of mindful behavior, which requires a present-moment centeredness where information is experienced and processed in a neutral and multi-dimensional fashion.

Habit reaction patterns are victim or survivor scenarios. They are ways of being in the world where a trigger acts like the groove that pulls you into a set of interpretations and required actions (reactions) to survive. It is an equation that directs action: if this then that. This is to say you have a pattern of reacting in a specific manner under specific circumstances without a consciousness of this equation driving your actions. The habit reaction diverts around your critical thinking skills, rather than mindfully evaluating you react within the confines of the habit reaction pattern. A triggering word, impression, experience, or feeling catapults you into a reaction that is a repeat of an historical behavior that was an original first response to a previous dangerous injury. The first time you acted; it resulted in a successful outcome; the subsequent times you reacted following the trigger and equation, with varying degrees of success. This identifiable scenario set up the survivor habit reaction patterning.

Acting quickly is a useful quality; reacting without thought has a mixed positive outcome. To understand why and how this is true, you have to understand aspects of human behavior.

This human mechanism of creating a habit reaction pattern acts like a shorthand communication about how to be; it is built into your human sensory system. It is based in learned behavior and modeling. This capacity is highly efficient in a dangerous environment; having the ability to automatically act could save your life. However, when this hyperawareness or hyper-vigilance is applied to everyday choices it creates an over-excitation toward protection and reaction. This can result in you developing problems that are unnecessary, affecting your spiritual, cognitive, and physical being.

In the application to relationships the problem with a habitual patterned reaction is when interactions are perceived by way of the trigger as dangerous but, are indeed not life threatening. The reacting from history sets up a habit that is creating a sense of danger that is not there. The key is to be able to use your sensory guidance system and your internal action-response system to ascertain whether the situation just *feels* dangerous because it *feels familiar* or it is *actually dangerous* and needs a quick, proactive, protective response.

To understand the way in which survivor scenarios diverge from healthy action, you have to have a sense of what a useful response action looks like and how it works in real time. I am going to use two different events to describe an activated response system that does not include survivor scenarios.

When I worked on a locked psychiatric unit I often walked a tightrope of danger. On the exterior everything looked as it always did with people milling about, sitting, talking, smoking cigarettes. But when something was off there were cues that I could follow via my sensory guidance system and my experience or history with the people and their typical behaviors. In my experience, intuition is dramatically enhanced by observation and attention to details that are out of place in some way. In addition, the concept of energy is enhanced by intuition. This is to say that subtleties are of great importance.

My first anecdote describes a young man out of control verbally, on the verge of losing control physically. The tenor of his speech was agitated and pressured; he was sweating, and rocking back and forth. These observations indicated to me that he was running too high, like when the engine of your car is revving too high and needs to move into the next gear but is being held back, this young man was revving too high without the energy to change gears. Without direction and assistance he was going to explode. Yet, the content of his speech was calm, focused, directed, and clear. The mistake someone could make with him would be to react by grabbing him; this would push him over the edge and he would lash out physically. A secondary mistake would be to directly focus on what he was doing and comment on it, this would create too close of contact as well, and would push him to lash out. What I did was to invite him to walk with me to the quiet room. He responded by inferring he could 'bash in my head' with an item nearby, in a quiet calm voice. He made no move to grab it, awaiting my response. I calmly responded in a neutral voice that if he were to hurt me someone else would walk him to the quiet room. He accepted the logic of this; the order, the inevitability of it, provided an internal kind of structure, and he calmly walked to the quiet room with me. I walked near him without touching him, maintaining a calm, neutral demeanor. This assisted him in calming himself. He responded to my energy by matching it. My calm demeanor provided a dual purpose, it modeled for him an energy to match and it assisted me in staying in neutral, so that I could read the energy to determine whether others were in danger. Without the calm demeanor I could have interpreted his agitation as more threatening and thereby escalated the situation into a physical altercation. By remaining calm I created the space for him to move into the next gear and release his agitation.

    This next anecdote has to do with reading a dangerous situation and acting to protect without hesitation. When my daughter was very young, she was an explorer, she was a wiggler, and desired lots of freedom. I endeavored to offer her space to move about while maintaining a watchful eye. As this was our habit together, I depended on all aspects of my senses to evaluate when a situation moved from free-play to danger. I listened not only for her to cry out my name but also to the shift from babbling to silence, to excitation, and then on a sliver of occasions fear. The risky time was when I did not hear her or have a sense of her coordinates.

I developed a useful habit of paying closer attention when there was silence. This is a common strategy for caregivers; silence in a generally babbling, happy child indicates something problematic, usually this is a sign that your child is up to something that is off limits.

Another sense that guided me was my intuition or a feeling that something was not right. This served me well when I paid attention to its guidance. The sense that something is off may be logically tied back to what I wrote earlier, a change in what I heard or observed with my child, but the timing of the response is shortened; a knowing or concern pushes through into consciousness, not the knowing of the shift in behavior but an integrated intuition that there is a problem.

The anecdote that supports reading the situation and acting without hesitation happened on a ski slope. Kate was learning how to ski; she was five years old. She loved taking the fast quad-chairlift, which brought us to the top of the mountain at rapid speed. She and I were ski partners. She had on many occasions exited this exact chairlift without incident and without requiring any actual assistance from me. The event that took place on this day was an unlikely set of events that resulted in a very dangerous situation.

As we approached the top of the lift it was windy and blowing snow. Kate moved to the edge of the seat to jump off, as she was very small. I was holding her poles and my poles in my right hand. Then a set of events happened at once: As I was sitting up from the chair, beginning to ski down toward our group, I heard the chair rev up, I saw Kate still on the seat of the chair above me. I instantaneously stopped skiing, reached up and grabbed her foot, and pulled her down off the chair. The change in height of the chairlift from the exit site to three feet in front of the exit site was dramatic, easily eight feet, to allow skiers to comfortably ski underneath the path of the chairlift as the empty chairs rolled by. If I had not grabbed her at that moment I would have lost my chance to grab her off the chairlift. She came down off the chair on top of me; we both landed there on the ground under the path of the chair. The chair lift operator was beside himself with apologies. He had meant to slow the chair for Kate, as he noticed she was small, and he hit the wrong lever and revved it up instead; this threw Kate back onto the chair so she was unable to move herself off the chair on her own.

The instantaneous receipt of all my sense guidance, the sound of the chairlift going faster rather than what I expected, the sound of it going slower; the lack of my sense that Kate was beside me as I expected, and the sight of her moving away directly above me; these senses together informed me as an intuition that there was an emergency that required immediate action. I observed and acted in seconds to protect my daughter from imminent danger. This is the power of having quick responses.

The Art of Partnering with Mindfulness | 73

FIGURE 5, QUICK RESPONSES ON THE SKI-SLOPE
PHOTO CREDIT: LISA ALDON

The problem occurs when the causeway of quick-responses is used for habit reactions. When this happens the outcome is a highway of reactions that create a lack of mindfulness, increased reactivity, and difficulty in partnering within a trusting atmosphere.

SURVIVOR SCENARIOS: SAVIOR, SURVIVOR, PROTECTOR

Survivor scenarios actually take on a number of forms depending on the function that set up the original scenario, *the how mechanism* to survive, or what style developed to survive. Protector (victim)/persecutor, survivor/persecutor, Savior (victim)/persecutor, victim/persecutor, are different forms of survivor scenarios. They share the need for the other (victim, persecutor) to define the self (survivor, protector, savior). These are co-dependent in nature due to their complete dependence on the other for definition.

In order for an individual to define herself as a survivor she must continually create (by way of interpretation and attribution of specific intent) situations she must survive. Thereby actually keeping herself caught in the web of the scenario. This is true for each form of the scenarios.

This is a complicated habit to break due to the secondary gain in being a survivor, protector and savior. Secondary gain is a term describing the benefit involved in the reaction or behavior. The person who has embraced this kind of scenario has actually *survived* something very painful, probably life-threatening or *protected/saved* someone else from a terribly dangerous, painful, or life-threatening situation. So, the individual has a lot of positive self-identity in the habit reaction patterning. In a victim, persecutor scenario the self (victim) is defined by the other (persecutor) but there is not a true secondary gain, nor does the person feel a great sense of self-esteem from the victimization. It may be he feels he is stronger and that is why he can take the victimizing experience, the victim gets stuck in the habit due to a lack of belief that he can live without it or due to an obligation to the persecutor. These feelings make it difficult to break the habit reaction patterning, difficult but not impossible.

What is needed is to *see* the scenario, *understand* what you did to survive, *be grateful* to the scenario for surviving, and then *lovingly let go* or discard the habit reaction patterning for a new way of being that is more fulfilling; this can be a challenging set of actions to undertake. You can accomplish this through mindful meditation, journaling, or counseling about the situation and your feelings, to elucidate the components identified above in this order: identification, gratitude, and release. If you are dealing with a habit reaction pattern you may want to take a moment to review the *Meditation on Lovingkindness* in the reference section. It is a very helpful exercise to increase compassion toward yourself and a difficult situation or person.

SHIFTING FROM SURVIVOR TO THRIVER

In order to get out of the rut, groove, automatic routine, or habit reaction you have to invoke two things, a sense of present-moment empowerment and mindfulness. This is an attitude of a Thriver. Thriving is an action that encompasses more than surviving. Surviving is good, as the alternative is not surviving, which is bad. Thriving is even better. Thriving is developing and focusing your life, actions, interactions, creations, and living toward your best potential and capabilities.

To recognize this difference notice that surviving is a function of creating the best situation possible out of a negative set of circumstances, whereas thriving is a function of creating what you want proactively, creating what you want out of all the possibilities in the universe, not just your current circumstances.

Being a survivor may be the best thing you ever did, and so it may be difficult for you to let it go. You may feel like it is the thing that sets you apart from your peers. As a survivor you have developed special talents, skills, and capacities that are evolved. The problem is the scenario of surviving sets up an attachment to *that style of being in the world*. It limits you; the scenario disallows the open receipt of situations and a sense of being free to choose how to be in the world at any given time.

You interpret the world through your inner paradigm.

We see the world not the way it is but the way we are, the Talmud.

So your survivor scenario paradigm sets up that you are drawn to difficult and challenging situations, requiring you to continually, automatically, invoke the survivor mechanism. This is the rut that pulls you in and gets repeated. You are drawn around the course partially through habit reaction patterning and partially because you receive a secondary gain of feeling successful at surviving. This dual component increases the difficulty to let go of the survivor scenario.

The adage *when life gives you lemons, make lemonade* acts like an inner mantra of the survivor; survivors have a statistically out of the norm set of experiences of having to make something good out of something bad. That in a nutshell is the feel of the survivor scenario habit reaction patterning rut: vigilance regarding a difficult situation needing survival, then *making lemonade out of lemons*, feeling powerful and successful. Power is linked to surviving rather than thriving → linked to reactive rather than proactive behavior.

Through awareness and mindfulness you can choose to see the situation differently and respond differently to shift out of the rut and into a new track. At first you may feel a disappointment at not getting the endorphin response of the secondary gain, but the positive wholeness that comes from thriving will ultimately feel more uplifting and enlivening.

THE POWER OF THE THRIVER ATTITUDE

Being a thriver increases your actual power and responsibility to create what you want. In order to do so you have to be willing to risk defining what you want and then creating the avenue to achieve that desired thing. It sets you into a proactive rather than reactive mode: *I want to create this in my life (proactive, thriver attitude)*, rather than

I can make this situation work to the best form (reactive, survivor attitude). The thriver attitude puts you into the driver's seat of your life.

Certainly having the skill to make a bad situation work until you can create a better one is laudable and to be maintained as a positive skill; however, it is not proactive unless connected with an attitude of focusing your efforts on creating a life that is thriving and reaching your best potential.

Here's how to *decipher* if you are in a habit reaction pattern or survivor scenario.

- Check in with your senses and intuition
- If, you feel that the experience is familiar or a pattern then, you may be participating in a habit reaction scenario
- If, you feel that you have trouble trusting that things can/will go well for you then, you may have a history of having to survive that is coloring your current day choices/actions.
- If you have an immediate feeling of anger, like someone has crossed a boundary and your feeling is charged (the degree and intensity of the emotion doesn't match the situation or boundary crossing), this is a sign that you have been triggered
- When you feel triggered proceed in your actions with caution (interpret caution as clarified attention), invoke mindfulness and centered, present-moment attention to the situation. Be wary of reacting: through mindfulness you can work against the pull of the groove into the habit reaction pattern.

To determine whether to engage the thriver attitude follow these steps.

- Focus and discernment are fundamental
- If you are in danger, use your survivor skills to get out of the situation. This is paramount
- If, you are not in danger but rather caught in a survivor scenario then, focusing your attention on *what you want* rather than what you fear is the best response
- Using mindfulness to review the circumstances in relation to your emotion will help you identify whether this is danger or not. For example, if a stranger is doing something that feels dangerous allow your survivor reactions to move at lightning pace. If however, the situation is with a loving partner, or friend, view your emotion within the context of the relationship in present-time, and with clarity and genuineness

Here's how you can *live from* a thriver attitude.

- It requires a focus on what you want, rather than what you fear.
- Use a neutral, centered stance in the world with a mindful attention to yourself, your skills and limitations.
- Focus on what brings you joy and guides you from an inner empowerment.
- This compassionate, present-moment focus allows the possibility of creating what you want from an unbounded and limitless set of choices. This is the opposite of a survivor scenario perspective, which contains a limited number of choices.
- This paradigm shift from survivor to thriver *allows* for a relaxation of the struggle to survive or fight, and a gentle movement into a balanced flow in living.

The transition from survivor scenario to thriver scenario is a process. It is a gradual awakening to your own triggers and reactions and a conscious choice to shift into proactive action. It is not accomplished overnight. Be kind and patient with yourself, honoring how you survived and how you can now choose to thrive.

At first, you will begin to notice that you are in a survivor scenario, perhaps it will be a function of hindsight, but you will continue to increase your awareness. Then you can practice the steps of paying attention to what you are feeling and consciously, mindfully making a different choice in how you respond in situations. The gift is an inner deepening sense of resilience and strength, a sense of an internal authentic self. Movement from a survivor scenario to a thriver scenario will follow a pattern similar to movement from a Me-style of relating through an I-style of relating into a We-style of relating. Boundaries, a reset regarding dependence, independence, and trust are all major components to assist you in your transformation.

I use the metaphor of the butterfly's movement from caterpillar to chrysalis to butterfly to image the process of movement from survivor to thriver; each aspect takes time to incubate and morph.

FIGURE 6, BUTTERFLY IN CLOUDS
PHOTOGRAPHER CREDIT: LAURA WOLF

THE EFFECT OF TRAUMA IN SELF-IDENTITY CREATION

Identity formation begins in early childhood. It has to do with the psychosocial stages identified by Erik Erikson. How each person resolves the conflicts of each of these stages imparts a special and unique spin on his self-identity.

The use of mindfulness is useful in assisting your child work-through these stages to a confident and positive conclusion or resolution. (See more about this in *Every Twelve Years: Turning NO to ON, the Art of Parenting with Mindfulness (2011)* in the reference section of this book.) The stages that are most often discussed cover childhood, adolescence and young adulthood, however Erikson's stages delineate growth over a lifetime. Although these stages are defined as having a crystallization effect from late teens to your middle twenties, there is malleability during this time period and opportunities to rework missteps you may have made in your earlier development. In some ways you can consider habit reaction patterns as a solution to a stage that requires a new resolution. Applying mindfulness can assist you further in this reworking of your experiences and shift your self-identity at any age.

Crystallization of how you see yourself and the world around you can be hardened and occur earlier when there is trauma, injury, or loss in the early developmental stages. The crystallization process is confronted by different components for different people based on how each resolved the early stages of development. Mistakes or missed interpretations can become hardened into an inaccurate picture of self-identity.

When a person is traumatized while in the developmental process of working-through these stages, the trauma affects how she perceives herself. This may be something that she inputs into the core of her identity. This self-perception can have a strengthening or debilitating effect on her depending on what message is imprinted from the trauma. If she feels she has successfully dealt with the event and perceives the event has made her stronger, then she will be able to incorporate that into her identity. If however the opposite is true she will incorporate a sense of insecurity.

Sometimes these misinterpretations are the basic foundation onto which the person places his desires, goals, and personal expectations. If these misinterpretations do not get corrected they can negatively affect what path an individual chooses and how he goes about completing goals and aspirations. A person with excellent artistic skills may not go into an artistic field because he believes he has no talent. Or a person with a high IQ may not attempt to go into college because she feels stupid. Sometimes the resolution to the trauma leaves the person feeling as if he has no power; in this instance he may have difficulty consolidating his inner sense of self to make any attempt to participate in social, academic, and athletic ventures, and as a result his environment mirrors his inner sense of discouragement. This is an example of how *you see the world the way you are* -the Talmud.

Specific interpretations developed in early childhood are required to help children work through trauma in a successful and affirming way. Children need to feel that somebody cares about them, that they are significant or important to someone, that they are connected to a family that provides stability and belonging. They need to have a belief in their innate, inner goodness, and to experience feelings of mastery, personal power, and control. These are all part of the early stages of Erik Erikson's model of psychosocial developmental stages.

To assist yourself, consider what childhood trauma, loss, or injury may have negatively affected you self-identity. You will find the clues by understanding where you feel insecure and searching Erikson's stages to connect your trauma and your insecurity in relation to what task may have been interrupted or negatively resolved. Once you have identified an etiology for your insecurity, align with your inner child-like self, create an internal loving, safe, and stable

The Art of Partnering with Mindfulness | 83

environment. Give yourself an opportunity to redevelop those earlier of mastery and personal control, without diffuse or rigid boundaries.

You can access this inner space through identification with your strengths; this will assist in the healing process. Journaling and writing are helpful in clarifying your earlier stuck space and moving through it toward healing.

For partnering, this information is also applicable as we age and it can be utilized to evaluate where you or your partner may have gotten stuck in these stages.

By understanding these stages you can give yourself an opportunity to re-work them and find a happy resolution to the stage. Once you have been able to do this the trauma or injury can be put into your history so that you have more psychological and emotional support to apply to living your life in the now rather than protecting yourself from an injury that happened in the past.

This is very important to help you in discerning which of the MAAPS is your security style and how to heal yourself if your security is based in an injury.

Take the time to evaluate if you have built your identity onto a false foundation, a misinterpretation due to an early trauma.

- A cue that this is true is an inner sense of emptiness or loss.
- Notice when you feel defensive, this is a cue from your unconscious that this is where your insecurity or injury lies.
- Find the correlating stage in Erikson's stages; this will help you to heal your injury.
- Use the above techniques to work-through the injury and assist yourself in healing so that you can clearly see your true strengths and limitations.

- A positive *side-effect* of doing this work is that you may discover not only a renewed sense of self but also a passion, skill, or talent that you have hidden or covered over due to the focus on your insecurity or injury. This can open-up an avenue of work or enjoyment that you had closed long ago.
- Review *Every Twelve years, Turning NO to ON: The Art of Parenting with Mindfulness*, (Gineris, 2011) for insight and review in the *Reference* section of this book.

RELEASE OF CHILDHOOD GHOSTS: REVEAL YOUR TRUE SELF

In order to shift the energy of a negative situation so that it will help, (offer you a learning opportunity), and not hurt, (create a blockage in your growth), you have to shift your perspective, and you have to release the power the outcome has over you.

Internal beliefs that lead to habit reaction patterns, or survivor scenarios, begin with inaccurate or incomplete interpretations of how to protect yourself from the hurt **or** incomplete understanding of the etiology behind your injury. These beliefs are misbeliefs that cause an involution within your personality. This involution directs energy inward to cover over the hurt or to protect yourself from experiencing that situation again.

Therapists in *survivors of rape support groups* see this in action. The woman identifies some aspect of the event that she determines caused the event. This develops into a set of actions she believes will protect her in the future. She gains power over the fear and pain of the event by creating a scenario she believes will protect her from ever being raped again. The fallacy is in the woman's interpretation that serves to set the blame onto herself, while simultaneously create an overcompensation for the injury. The goal is to take back her power; but her chosen avenue serves to truncate her sense of empowerment because the driver (cause of the injury) is misplaced. Examples of this misplacement include focus on her behavior as the cause of the rape: she may change her style of dress, stop wearing make-up, dress in baggy clothes, stop eating healthfully or exercising to make herself unattractive; these actions center the responsibility for the rape onto herself. Through this process she is attempting to make sense out of an irrational situation, and create a sense of power where she has experienced powerlessness.

This is inward directed; this is a misdirection that skews and distorts the truth and creates a pervasive shift in the overall development of her personality. The result is a person who develops as if she is missing something; there is a truncation to her personality.

Living as a thriver is reconnecting to your joy through reevaluation of the etiology and roots, of your beliefs, especially beliefs that take you away from your center or make you feel small and disempowered. These are misbeliefs that have skewed your self-identity. Through this process of reevaluation you can right the interpretation and experience a fuller more dynamic sense of yourself.

> *Find a place inside where there is joy and the joy will burn out the pain.*
> *Joseph Campbell*

The best way to do that is to look with a compassionate heart. Sometimes the process can be applied in the present to a present-moment situation so that a misbelief can be avoided. Other times it can be applied to an old situation for transformation, like getting rid of the ghosts from the past.

A ghost injury that has traveled with me for many years was a deep injury in high school. It took me many years to get to the true root and the true injury. The injury was like a ghost in that it haunted me in the background of my life and interfered with my thriver attitude. The ghost metaphor is apt, as the myth states that a ghost haunts an area until an unresolved injury gets brought into the light and the situation gets righted. Historical injures that result in a misbelief at the base of your self-identity structure are like ghosts haunting you, striving for balance and to be set right.

For me, unraveling the complicated scenario related to my ghost injury led down several paths of enlightenment but I still struggled with a set of experiences that indicated I had not fully released my ghost. After many years, I found the root of it and released it. In doing so I have experienced a deep and abiding sense of trust, love, empowerment and success in relationship.

In junior high school I was an outgoing and adventurous girl. I had strong opinions that I was happy to share through monologue and debate, and didn't seem to be negatively affected by conflicting opinions. Often, I would investigate and find out more information to strengthen my perspective.

My personality changed dramatically in high school not because of hormones but because of a longstanding irrepressible bullying experience I endured. This had such a deep effect that I set aside my original focus in career from adventurous, outgoing, risk-taker to inward focus, observant, ever-helpful-to-others therapist. My self-confidence waned and I became unsure of myself and tentative. My joyous, outgoing, trusting nature turned to hypervigilance and timidity.

The way this happened was subtle and occurred over a period of time. I can see now the separate moments wherein I shifted my energy, bit by bit, truncating my inner self and the options I allowed myself to pursue. Although I struggled with what would now be called depression, I was able to finish high school and college with a relative degree of success, good grades, honor roll, etc; the fundamental issue was inner shift away from what brought me joy toward what I interpreted brought me safety. The focus of what to study shifted distinctly.

I turned my attention to existential and psychotherapeutic models to assuage my pain. In doing so I increased my understanding of how groups and people in groups worked. I increased my understanding of mind and mindful processes. This brought me first to center my focus on therapy and then to search out a way of being in the world that included a focus on compassion. And, in the many years that separate me from that time, I have evolved again into the joyous person I once was. But the circuit was long, filled with many diversions, difficult transitions, and unhappy times.

I understand now that I was a target precisely because of my *joie de vive*, my alive and vibrant personality, my lovely looks, and strong curvy figure, which I lightly moved with ease. These things, all attractive and good qualities, were precisely what the girl-collective who targeted me was trying to destroy.

This was probably less personal than it felt to me, as the girls in the clique barely knew me. In research, it has been seen that this targeting behavior is a natural process in social groups and descriptive of how power-energy moves. In retrospect the troubling component was the lack of loyalty from one friend who had connection to the girl-collective and to me. Her disloyalty toward me had a personally injurious effect. Her temperament and psychosocial development was not similar to mine. She didn't have the opinionated *joie de vive*; she avoided conflict acting like my friend while covertly supporting the girl-collective. In retrospect, it was her limitations in her capacity to be a friend that resulted in her betrayal of me rather than malintent. However, her betrayal was far more debilitating to my sense of safety than the bullying from the girl-group, because she did know, *she knew me, she was my friend.* This created a crack in my sense of self and sense of trust, if she could be quiet in the face of the lies and bow-down to the power of the girl-collective clique, then I could not trust girl friends. This was the inaccurate conclusion that I incorporated into my self-identity. This was my ghost injury. Due to my pain, I translated this one girl's actions into an equation: I inaccurately generalized my experience to all girls resulting in the equation that *I could not trust girl friends*, instead of just recognizing I could not trust her.

From a sociological perspective, there is a natural order of things to be in line and homogeneous and my behavior was outside the norm. Simply by existing in that *alive* form I had irritated their interior power issues and insecurities. The girl-collective had come together for the express purpose of wielding power. I had the strength to stand up to them, through being my true self, but I was destabilized by the betrayal of my one real friend. If my internal space had been stronger I would have been able to place the difficulties back onto the girl-group, rather than get injured. Certainly my reaction to this betrayal was rooted in an earlier injury regarding the task of trust and self-worth. Rather than acting from a self-confident internal empowered space I gave away my power to my friend to define my worth; this was due to my fear and my deep desire to be accepted.

The resultant shift within me occurred due to several factors. There was no source near me to assist me through this process to help me realign or remain aligned to my true inner voice of truth and reason. I wanted to be liked and accepted, to fit in the group. I accurately interpreted that being authentic and personally empowered set me apart and made me a target to the girls. I accurately assessed that my friend was in competition with me over the same power issues. I misinterpreted what that meant about how to be in the world, and the safety of the world at large.

In order to feel accepted or fit in I distorted my personality. My survivor response was to change how I enacted and incorporated my strength. Aspects of my authentic self were pushed in and under, and an unassuming, intellectual girl developed into womanhood. This gave me a way to be strong but not be threatening to the girl-group in general. I took to covering my lovely figure with baggy clothes and keeping my voice and truth quiet, listening and assisting others in their growth with little overt focus on myself. I studied and developed my mind, and body in quiet unassuming ways. I deflected that earlier strength and adventure to risk-taking on the behalf of others.

These actions were a distortion of my personality in reaction to my internal fear. I covered over my true self *in exchange* for feeling like I might be safe from attack. Unfortunately, these kinds of exchanges leave marks on a person's interior sense of self. I made that *joie de vive* invisible. I found a degree of peace, but lived afraid to be myself; I lived as a truncated self, always feeling a bit outside the group. The resolution to the conflict shifted the exterior but I felt the conflict on the interior plane.

My response to this ghost injury has made me a better therapist, a better writer, a better observer of human behavior, and a wiser person. Although my original response was to close off opportunities for my personal development, in time I was able to reverse the negative effects on me and grow into a wholly integrated person. The ghost injury limited me in relationship so that I acted in a combination of Me-style and I-style of relating. Once I was able to right the skew in my self-identity I was freed to create a We-style of relating.

Applying mindfulness and compassion to the whole of my experience has opened the door to my earlier youthful joy. It has freed me to feel the joy of my core self as well as the strength of how I turned my struggle into a place to thrive. In linking these two together, I have rediscovered my true full self. I am less afraid to feel beautiful, strong, lithe, and powerful. I once again allow my inner joy to be my guide. Through this I have a better understanding of my pain and the pain of my tormentors. It is quite freeing and enlivening.

Sometimes the ghost injury catches in my heart when I see the aging faces of one of those girls from that girl-collective on the pages of Facebook. I can feel that my pain has been released because although I feel sadness at their image, I feel it less for myself than for the pain I see marked on their faces. I no longer freeze in fear and confusion.

As described by Joseph Campbell, my *pain is burned away by the light of my truth and joy in my true being*. It feels like a happy lesson I pass on to my beloved children.

It is an unconscious reckoning that the interior can show through in the exterior form. There is a concept in Chinese medicine: *Through observation of the exterior you can know what is happening*

FIGURE 7, LIVING FREE
PHOTO CREDIT, RON ROMANIK

in the interior. To assist in releasing your childhood ghosts use these strategies:

- If you observe lines on your face that seem stern and unrelenting, look for what may be unresolved within your psychological, and mindful process and apply compassion to shift the energy.
- If you feel there is something missing in how you relate to the world, go on an internal journey to see if you have left something of yourself in the past.
- Acquaint yourself with your ghosts from your childhood.
- Remember to connect with joy and compassion as you review these.
- Notice this too with your partner; if you notice a subtle involution or repulsion of a talent in your partner, gently point this our to her so that she can look inside to see what is at work.
- Remember to apply compassion and forgiveness toward yourself for the mistakes and injuries you may have caused for others.

The more that you apply compassion to how you view your, and other's, actions, the more you can be free to be your authentic self.

MINDFULNESS AND TIME TRAVEL

Using mindfulness in your interactions and decisions gives you a broader perspective. It gives you a view into the future outcome and allows you to see the ramifications of your actions in a way that is akin to seeing into the future. Through this broader perspective you can see a long way into the outcome of actions today.

Mindfulness allows you to review the past and future to align with a fuller broader picture; this helps to set earlier injuries into a place of history without power over you and to ascertain the holistic outcome of a set of events. This happens as a result of this equation: Logic + empathy + objective observation = mindfulness sight. It is a function of *allowing* your vision to be informed through your sensory guidance system integrated with your mindfulness about the way in which connections happen between phenomena. This can only happen from a neutral, observing, interested, unattached focus. The unattached, neutral focus dissipates the push/pull from attachment to the outcome or historical experience (I want = push forward, habit = pull backward). The lack of attachment allows you to be open to an underlying relationship or interaction.

Here's how it works:

Think about those pictures at the mall with all the different colored dots. When you first look at them they don't seem to represent anything. They look like a field of unrelated dots. But if you stare at them in a relaxed manner, the seemingly unconnected dots begin to connect, and an image appears. If you try very hard to see the picture, you will see only a mass of different colored dots. If you relax and allow the connections to reveal, then you see a ship or hippo or some other recognizable image. This is an example of the mindfulness equation: Logic + empathy + objective observation = mindfulness and paradigm shift. It incorporates the action of allowing, objective observing in the present moment, with interest that is without a preset notion (attachment) of what is there. *Logic* is part of the way in which your brain aligns the various dots and *empathy* describes seeing the inherent patterning by taking the perspective of other. Your brain is hardwired to see wholes, to complete images that are unfinished, and to use previous experiences or previously known images to make sense out of what is presented visually and sensorily. This can happen with respect to a picture as well as seeing the outcome of a behavior or action. The lack of attachment leaves you open to all the historical information, rather than driving the outcome to be a singular expectation.

Observing your own action and the actions of others in this relaxed, neutral, calm, interested, mindful manner allows you to perceive a recognizable pattern or outcome. If, you are trying very hard to see something then, nothing will present itself. When you are open to any outcome and simply follow the thread, then you will be able to identify several potential outcomes or one outcome, and you can take actions based on this information to better create what you want.

Following a thread includes paying attention to word choice and meaning, energy, non-verbal cues, sound, and timing. It includes the actions and speech used, presentation, verbal, and non-verbal.

For example, notice how your partner is responds to your success. Is he able to align with you or does he respond in a competitive way? Is there a shift in his energy, as you get closer to a goal, from being focused on your success to co-opting your actions to create success for himself. The former action is one that comes from a person who perceives himself as successful and whole and is a function of a We-style of relating. The latter action comes from a person who perceives himself as small and needing to fight to maintain an equal position with you (a Me-style of relating), or who feels the need to compete to maintain the upper edge (an I-style of relating).

Observing behavior in this way, and incorporating your observations into an internal mindful perception without judgment allows you to have a view into the outcome, to time travel. It teases out your understanding of the unspoken aspects of your relationships. It provides an understanding of the parameters under which you can depend on that other person in partnership. This allows you to guide and direct your own actions accordingly and without malice, fear, or disappointment. It can also provide a road map for change within your relationship and a change in the style of relating that you choose to utilize.

The concept of *risk* changes when you apply mindfulness to a situation or relationship. This is due to how the logic plus empathy equation above heightens your capacity to analyze risk with respect to your actions, the actions of others, and various situations. With mindfulness you simply have access to more information and more layering of behavior and emotion. You feel more empowered, *more free,* to create interdependency successfully and *less reactive,* dependent, competitive, defensive, or fearful. This assists you to move out of a Me-style of relationship through an I-style of relationship into a We-style of relationship. Insecurities and survivor scenarios function to decrease your risk assessment capacity; mindfulness increases your ability to accurately assess risk. This truth is an example of how attachment negatively drives the outcome, while mindfulness reveals the outcome.

This is the figure and ground concept from a layering and sociological perspective of history and biography that is present in all human communications and interactions. Mindfulness allows you to center yourself, your experiences, and your actions, so that you may have a 360-degree-view of the situation or circumstance. This increases your view into the outcome.

To get started using *the equation of logic + empathy + objective observation*:

- Be willing to observe, take in information, and respond from a neutral, interested, and peaceful perspective →if you feel a pull one way or the other this may be attachment →let the *need for it to be a certain way* be released. See with unattached eyes.
- Look for logical connections and threads and logical outcomes to your and other's behavior. This is the sense that there is an underlying fabric of how things relate. You can tap into this underlying fabric through your objective observation and openness to see patterns.
- Practice allowing rather than pushing or holding.
- Utilize your sensory guidance system to point out inconsistencies in what your partner says and does or diversions from the logical outcome. This allows you to choose to say no-deal or negotiate based on what you discover.
- Allow yourself to be free to choose to act from a We perspective, identifying what you want in the relationship and what you hear the other wants. This guides you to choose Covey's win-win or no-deal. This also creates the space to strengthen your knowing of yourself and your knowing of your partner.
- Choose to act from your own centered self, you centered in your life. Remember this is not a self-centered, narcissistic perspective but rather a healthy sense of wholeness, so that you can develop the We-style of relating wherein two wholes partner to create a third mutually interdependent couple or partnership perspective.

This will increase your opportunity to have a view into the outcome, the experience of time travel, and increase your ability to take an action that is consistent with your observations and your centered-self requirements.

THE 3 DS IN VERBAL AIKIDO CREATE HARMONY

Aikido is a Japanese martial art that incorporates entering and turning movements to engage the energy of an attacker at a stage that throws off the attacker's momentum and then redirects the energy away and down to diffuse the attacker's power and harm. It is very beautiful; when you observe this in action it looks like a choreographed dance.

The art of verbal Aikido is the application of these techniques, actions, and attitudes toward redirecting the harm, negativity, and intensity of verbal attacks to create harmony. This can be accomplished in three steps, the three Ds.

The three Ds - deflect, deflate, define.

1. **Deflect** the tone and tenor of the attacker. Respond to the content from the most neutral, compassionate, and accepting place within your center. This gives the action of stepping into the energy and grabbing it, shifting the negativity away and down to neutralize it.
2. **Deflate** the negativity by reiterating your intended meaning, through clarification and compassionate interest in how your communication was interpreted. This transmits and grounds the negative energy, diffusing the power while staying connected to the other person. Avoid sarcasm, condescension, and down-putting behavior as these escalate negative reaction

3. **Define**, is the most delicate of the three actions; it is the core that creates the container (it shifts the interpretation and creates a space for calm) so that the attacker can release without hurting the receiver (verbal Aikido master), you. Sometimes this third D requires you to go through steps 1 and 2 many times, but over time there develops a recognition or clarified understanding of each other and a sense of harmony. Solutions are always present within the dilemma. Practicing the art of verbal Aikido open the space to discover the solution that brings peace. *Deflect, deflate, define*, these steps together, create peace and harmony. These simple steps can change your world one diffused negative interaction at a time.

To offer an example of how this works, here is a story. When I was a young psychiatric aide on a locked psychiatric unit in Albuquerque, New Mexico, I had a very good friend, also a psychiatric aide, who was a master at the practice of the Japanese martial art of Aikido. He was superb at handling any physical attack, without injury to himself and with the least degree of injury to others. A young man who had stopped taking his antipsychotic medicine began to lose control of his thinking and behavior; his touch with reality was slipping away and he thought he was being attacked. My friend asked him to go into the quiet room (a padded room that protects the individual from hurting himself and others when out of control). The patient felt attacked by my gentle friend's request. He became enraged and began to throw at my friend any thing that his hand touched – chairs, tables, lamps – my friend simply and easily shifted the energy of each piece of furniture and dropped it beside him, protecting the other patients and deflecting the negative energy, lightly and firmly moving toward the out-of-control young man. His movements were gentle, clarified, and precise, lightly deflecting the energy while deftly responding to the needs of the entire room. Once he entered the physical space of the out-of-control young man, he quickly and without harm immobilized his flailing arms and with kindness and gentleness he walked him to the quiet room.

His precision at shifting the energy of the flying furniture had the effect of de-escalating the damage in the situation to himself, the out-of-control patient, and the other patients. It created a sense of calm and control that was soothing. It brought everything to a neutral space so that injury was avoided.

The art of verbal Aikido is a metaphor for utilizing the same strategies in handling verbal attack. The majority of miscommunication and arguments are a result of charged interpretation of the other's dialogue, where another person interprets your statements as barbs thrown and so reacts defensively, or vice versa.

Responding to another's attack via mindfulness increases your neutrality and clarity in the root that underlies the negative communication, simply deflecting the negative statement, and deflating the negative energy, to shift the interaction.

Practicing the Art of Verbal Aikido has Three Steps:

- First, *deflect* the negative tone, and tenor, by simply responding to the actual content with neutral responsive content.
- Second, *deflate* the negativity by reiterating your intended meaning through clarification and compassionate interest in how your communication was interpreted. Then clarify the intended meaning, and take responsibility for not being more clear in your first communication.

- Third, if the communication escalates, continue with steps 1, and 2, with a gentle, kind, precise and light manner. Avoid sarcasm, condescension, and a down-putting tone. Then you are free to find a solution or agree to disagree without malice or charge.

You only have power over your own actions. You cannot change another person's attitude, position or behavior; you can only offer a space for another to shift his perspective on his own. You have control over your own actions, behaviors, attitudes, and responses. If the other person chooses to find you offensive and react defensively, you have the power to maintain your mindfulness.

The most mindful and loving response in a situation where another is angry is to not take on his anger, not react to or join-in the negative interpretation, resist fighting back or a proving, argumentative tone or attitude.

Create a visual image of yourself lightly deflecting the flying furniture and placing it on the ground; create an image of another's charged words as sufficiently solid so that you can observe yourself deflecting them or moving your energy so you are not hit by the negative barb in the words. Think of a Jackie Chan movie. See yourself in slow motion, deftly avoiding what is thrown your way, while simultaneously smiling and gently reaching out an olive branch toward connection and understanding. This is the practice of verbal Aikido and it will increase the level of peace you experience in your relationships.

It is the most healing response to conflicting perspectives and offers a direct pathway to uplevel consciousness. It encompasses a We-style of relating.

TEMPERAMENT AND RELATIONSHIP STYLE

Temperament is that aspect of your personality that is hardwired. Each person comes into the world with a temperament that drives her style of being in the world. The simple styles that alert you to personality traits are easygoing, sensitive, persevering, isolative or absentminded. Temperament styles solidify through interaction with your environment to either, tame the negative aspects of your temperament and create balance or, to crystallize the limiting aspects of your temperament and create imbalance.

Theoretical models of temperament have been developed by the following philosophers - Hippocrates (400 BCE), Plato (340 BCE), Aristotle (325 BCE), Galen (190), and the following psychologists - Dreikurs (1912), Fromm (1947), Myers (with her mother Briggs -1942 and from Jung's work *Psychological Types* 1921) (1956,1962), and Keirsey (1978, 1998). The idea of being born with a temperament and it affecting your health, style of being in the world, how you partner, and your interaction in groups is delineated in Western Medicine (the theorists mentioned above generally divided into 4 types), Taoist theory Five Element Phase theory (5 types), Chinese Medicine: *Requena* (1986) (11 types: 5 constitutions and 6 temperaments), and Ayurvedic Medicine (3 *Doshas*) theories. This idea of temperament is a powerful and highly accepted concept. The process of how to discern the difference in temperament styles is affected by the temperament of the writer. What matters to the author of each of the above temperament styles is incorporated into his theory, and so each of the above theories has a slightly different focus or bias. For the purpose of relationship and partnership, the psychological theorists are most applicable. Myers and Briggs (*Gifts Differing: Understanding Personality Type, 1980, 1995*) consolidated the work of Carl Jung to develop a theory and test (MBTI) regarding temperament (1942, 1956, 1962). Dreikurs work is most applicable to children.

Myers and Briggs identified four continua described below. David Keirsey has made an effort to synthesize the previous theories, using the same continua identified by Myers and Briggs but clarifying relationships differently. Myers and Briggs identified the intersection of the four continua to create the temperament: *sensing/intuitive continuum* identified information gathering, *thinking/feeling continuum* identified decision-making and information transmission, *judging/perceiving continuum* identified a preference in-lifestyle as bounded or spontaneous, and the attitude of *introversion/extraversion continuum* as your attitude of how you rejuvenate, in solitary or group activities.

Keirsey focused on the sensing/intuitive continuum as a functional, defining component to a person's temperament and transformed the continua into a concept of rings to identify how the four continua intersect to create your personal temperament style. Keirsey's work is less linear and more relational. Although, Keirsey and Myers use the same structures, which of the rings or continua matter most and are the defining aspect for temperament differ for these two theorists. Both identify the importance of how you receive and catalogue information, the sensing/intuitive and thinking/feeling components, as the functional aspects of temperament. Myers underscores extraversion and introversion more, while Keirsey perceives judging and perceiving as of higher defining value. These will be described more completely in the next section. Understanding the basic information about how these four continua work together to describe temperament is useful. Whichever theory is most coherent to you will be of benefit to you and your partnership.

Your style of being, temperament, affects how you will be in relationship and in some instances what style of relationship looks most appealing. If you are a parent or a teacher, the idea of temperament is foremost in your mind when you are choosing how to respond to a child. Taking into account a child's temperament increases your chance of connecting to him and creating a space to assist him to move from *No*, inattention, being turned *off* to, *Yes*, excited attention and being turned *On*. Similarly, temperament is considered by partners when coupling; outgoing, structured, laid-back, considerate spontaneous, planner, are all functions of temperament; it's the quality of agreement or attraction that plays into chemistry. Your temperament affects how you interpret and consolidate the information and stimuli in your environment and relationships.

UNDERSTANDING STYLES OF TEMPERAMENT

Your temperament influences your personal style of being in the world, communicating, and learning. To create a successful team the participants' temperament styles have to match in order to communicate and work toward solutions. This takes a combination of focused listening skills, paradigm shifting, and flexibility so that the team members are able to communicate on all eight ends of the four intersecting temperament continua. Successful partnerships use these skills to match each other in communication. Use paradigm shifting and mindfulness to understand the other perspective from these four continua or rings when approaching interactions, this allows for more connecting space. The more you are able to shift out of your preferred mode of interaction and meet your partner mid-way to negotiate meaning and clarify goals, the more success you will enjoy in the partnership. The more you work in a role or capacity that matches your temperament the more you feel at home in your work. Understanding temperament styles is key.

Each person relates on four intersecting Myers continua or (Keirsey rings) of:

- extraverted (*expressive*) to introverted (*attentive*) **important to Myers**
- sensing (*concrete*) to intuitive (*abstract*) **most important for both theorists**; this is a defining difference in temperament and requires mindful acceptance when two parties have differing paradigms.
- thinking (*directive*) to feeling (*informative*) this is an area of miscommunication across poles but great capacity for creating balance in relationship when seen as different perspectives rather than right/wrong.
- judging (*utilitarian*) to perceptive (*cooperative*) **Combined with sensing to form inner ring for Keirsey [SJ, SP – cooperative, utilitarian, which is not discussed by Myers]**; less important to Myers, but useful in relationship evaluation because of the perception of time – planned (j) or spontaneous (p), that can create conflict in relationships.

The Jungian based Myers-Briggs theory focuses more on the extraversion versus introversion component of temperament and viewed this aspect as important in how a person rejuvenates rather than a style of relating as outgoing or shy, which are the more known definitions for extraverted and introverted. Myers and Keirsey both interpret the sensing and intuitive aspect of temperament as a fundamental component. Keirsey clarifies this component as the first inner ring and identifies this as the fundamental differentiation as concrete, observant or abstract, introspective. Myers perceives this continuum as a functional defining aspect that has to do with how a person perceives information though his senses or through his intuitions.

Myers and Briggs added the judging/perceiving continuum to Carl Jung's original analysis, while not directly identified by Jung as part of temperament typing Jung did discuss these concepts in his writings; therefore they focused more on the other three components to identify the core aspect of temperament. Keirsey moves this judging/perceiving continuum into the inner tier of temperament directly aligning it with the element of sensing/concrete (or what he identifies as observant) *slash* intuitive/abstract (or what he calls introspective) continuum. Keirsey sees these as rings that interact to create your inner temperament. This is where Keirsey defines the four cooperative versus utilitarian temperament types: dividing these into two sensing types (concrete plus either judging or perceiving) and two intuitive types (abstract plus either feeling or thinking). This tracks with how Myers puts together styles but diminishes the importance of introversion and extraversion.

The effect of temperament on relationship is most profound when you consider that it affects how you see, hear, attend to information, and use information in relationship to others and yourself. It affects how you work, what style of work you like to do, and how you interact with others and your environment on many levels. Agreement with respect to temperament or matching temperaments increases a sense of being understood, seen, and success in relationship. Lack of agreement creates the opposite, conflict, dissonance, struggle, and obstruction. Because the ideas are opposite each other they have little agreement from end perspective to end perspective on the four continua. Individuals who tend to perceive the world in a concrete fashion have difficulty with individuals who are abstract. The concrete and abstract paradigms are similar to the left-facing duck/right-facing bunny picture. The perspective defines the paradigm. Developing an ability to see from both perspectives is most important.

DUCK/BUNNY FIGURE-GROUND PARADIGM SHIFTING.

This is the same for individuals who gather information in a sensing, fact, tangible (left-brained) way versus those who receive information in a more intuitive, esoteric fashion (right-brained). Keirsey combines together the style in which you receive information, concrete or abstract with the next continuum the way in which you respond to your environment, judging and perceiving; this forms your core stance in the world. This form has four styles, Guardian (SJ- logistical), Artisan (SP-tactical), Idealist (NF – diplomatic), and Rational (NT- strategist). From there, Keirsey connects the roles that are best suited to your temperament with the addition of the third continuum, feeling versus thinking, where the formulating question is informative or directive. Connecting how you will be drawn to act in the world, linking sensing with judging or perceiving to a further delineated thinking or feeling to each; and with the intuitive judging or perceiving with the continuum of feeling or thinking. At this point, there are eight differentiated types of temperament. The additional differentiation of these sixteen groupings, to contain either an extraversion or introversion preference, creates the final differentiating types of 16. This last aspect for Keirsey clarifies whether the style of being relating to your environment is more expressive (extraverted) or attentive (introverted). This component is most useful from the perspective of job choice/success (1998). Here Myers concept and Keirsey's earlier concept of this pole (1978) that it is a function of how you gather energy or rejuvenate is more useful in relationship evaluation. It becomes an important element of how to best negotiate leisure time and space in relationship.

The style in which one expresses information can create misunderstanding if sender and receiver are too far apart on the continuum of thinking and feeling. Here the issue is more of a proactive versus a responsive perspective, using objective versus subjective information to both make decisions and express those decisions (Keirsey, 1978). Thinkers speak in rational directive terms and feelers speak in emotional informative terms (Keirsey, 1978, 1998).

For effective communication to occur, you need to assess your own position as well as that of the other on these four continua (four rings). Some careers value different combinations of these four continua and specific styles are sought. Most people are on a continuum of interpreting and communicating skills from concrete to abstract. Guardians tend to be at the concrete end of the continuum while Idealists tend to be at the abstract end; most people live somewhere in the middle.

How this information is important in relationship has to do with understanding the intersection within yourself and within your partner. In my experience, the preferred mode of interaction on these continua adjusts in different situations and in reaction to your environmental expectations. You may have developed a vastly different temperament style at work than you do at home; which is to say that partnering at work may take a different course than partnering at home. When this is the case, you can experience some confusion that your personal style is so successful in one place and not the other. Once you understand your temperament style you can strive to understand your partner's; this gives you another way to find agreement in relationship.

When considering this information, incorporate how the psychosocial developmental stages can at times lead to a more concrete style of thinking and processing information. You can use this information to understand in what stage you or your partner may be stuck. In relationship and partnering this will assist you in understanding how you may have chosen to partner in a Me or I-style rather than a We-style of relationship.

While right-brained individuals are more on the abstracting end, depending on where they are on the other three continua they may have highly developed skills to mediate along the continuum of abstraction and concretization. This integration and interaction of the continua has multifaceted outcomes. So, although the more diverse or greater the crevasse between people, the less able they are to understand each other as a consequence of a single continuum, when taken together the four intersecting continua can provide complementary balance. This can also happen within partnerships supporting the adage *opposites attract*.

When there is a misunderstanding between individuals at opposite ends of a continuum, it can feel like an assault to a person's character rather than a redirection or teaching when it is related to a difference in information interpretation and consolidation style. This can be worked through easily though with focus on neutral, caring communications. An example of this is the way in which a highly left-brained person might interpret the information-gathering style of a highly right-brained person; she might be seen as flighty or unable to substantiate her perceptions because they come from a more intuitive perspective. A person who tended to be more feeling in his style of expressing information would be seen as subjective and not having an objective reason to feel the way he does, by a person on the thinking end of the expressive continuum. Where you are on the information gathering end defines how you learn and from whom you learn best. For students this is a problem when their teacher is at a different end of the continuum. In work situations, dissonance between supervisor and supervisee creates stress and difficulties. Self-discovery regarding your placement along these four continua will help you to ascertain your personal needs due to temperament. Once you understand this you can assess you relationships to discover if you have a mis-match that you need to shift into a complementary understanding.

The work in relationship is to manage your emotions and increase your understanding of your personal style in relating and interacting in the world. This needs to be accomplished by developing the other aspect of the continuum without deflating your personal style. You can use your understanding of your temperament, to increase your understanding of your partner's position on the continuum, and discuss the differences in a way that is not challenging or competitive but rather inclusive and investigative. The best way to investigate whence your feelings come and to evaluate the objective aspect of your feelings is to use mindfulness: paradigm shifting, objective, neutral observation, and interest. Mindfulness and paradigm shifting help you develop your thinking skills related to your feelings as well as the aspects of the sensing and intuition continuum.

If you have strong intuition you gather information from an observation of subtle changes in behavior or facial cues from the other person. Sometimes this allows you to see information that the other person is trying to hide, or is a part of his unconscious. So, it might look like you are being subjective in decision-making rather than objective, but there is an objective component, observation of real information, in your decision-making process. When you get hidden information and it isn't 'owned' by the other person, consider finding ways to bring this up in a non-confrontational manner to see if you can get to what is underneath the disowned or mixed message.

Individuals who have developed both their right-brained and left-brained style of gathering and expressing information are the most flexible and generally perceived as affable, well liked, and quite bright.

Myers (Myers-Briggs, 1956) developed a test MBTI to discern your preferred style of being in the world from Carl Jung's work on this subject. It is used as a personality temperament test to help individuals understand their preferred style in psychological and business settings. It is used in business consultation and mediation to help build teams and create supportive relationships. Keirsey also developed a test and you can get access to it through the book by Keirsey-Bates called *Please Understand Me (1978)* or Keirsey *Please Understand Me II*

(1998). Both of these theorists have websites where you can review this information further. The Kiersey (Bates) test outcomes are comparable to the Myers (Briggs) test. These tools are useful to increase your understanding of how you fit into these continua and then to apply this information in team-building, communication skills training, and relationship/partnership development. They offer an objective tool to help individuals see where they are miscommunicating and help develop an overall ability in all aspects of the four continua.

When you discover you are in an interaction block with someone you love or a team partner, do some investigation about how each one of you got to specific information. It may be that you are *perceiving* different information or *interpreting* that information differently. You may be able to find agreement if you increase your understanding of each other. This leads to paradigm shifting and an increase in one's mindfulness in interaction.

Your temperament is something that you come in with, the starting point of your paradigm perceptions. Mindfulness allows for you to increase your understanding of your temperament and your understanding of the other paradigmatic temperament styles. Temperament is a powerful core aspect of who you are. As you embrace your authentic sense of self you can see how to work with your partner's temperament in an accepting, complementary way; this strengthens your partnership and increases your interdependence with each other.

DISCERNMENT AND JUDGMENT: HOLDING ON AND LETTING GO

Holding on is necessary in life. It is how the baby gets milk, how the two stay together, and how a tree survives a tornado. It is essential when in the middle of something that requires pertinacity to complete. *Holding on to ideas*, your values, family, friends, and connections *that serve you* is fruitful. *Holding on too long* can stagnate Qi, block progress, and impede smooth flow.

Letting go is necessary in life. It is how the child is birthed, how the seed is set free to find a place to grow anew, and how the adolescent releases into adulthood. *Letting go of ideas*, your beliefs and structures *that don't serve you,* creates space and is fruitful. *Letting go too early* can impede project completion, interfere with focus, or create chaos. Knowing when to hold on and when to let go is a dynamic process of give and take, ebb and flow. It requires intuition, mindfulness, paradigm shifting, strength, and flexibility. Holding on when it is the right time is necessary. Holding on beyond time hinders. Letting go when it is the right time is necessary for transformation. Letting go before it is time is traumatic. Being in sync with the ebb and flow in your environment, actions, relationships, and structures within time and space allows you to know whether to hold on or let go.

Mindfulness is the key. Practicing mindful meditation increases your connection to your inner guidance and aligns you to know what action is best for your optimal growth and development. Mindfulness increases your capacity for discernment and judgment. There is a timing to things. Use your observation skills to evaluate where you are on the continuum of holding on and letting go in every relationship, project, and situation in your life. Pay attention to your guidance within and without. You may notice that something bothers you now that has not previously. This may be a clue to shift in your holding on/letting go process. The more you attend to the whole of your feelings and inner responses, the more you can live in sync with your needs. This is one of the best uses of mindfulness to engage the bigger picture, allowing for the incorporation of all the information that is present in your internal sensory system and cues from your partner in any situation.

Take the time to get into a mindful, accepting, neutral, and open mind-set. Once there, put your attention onto your partnership and each relationship of import in your life. Allow yourself to receive the cues from your internal guidance system and from your partner. This will offer an opportunity to begin a conversation about the progress and process of each relationship. From that space you will be able to navigate along the continuum of holding on and letting go; this navigation may include a change in how you and your partner interact to create a We-style of interdependence in relationship. Use the chapter on developing a connection to your internal guidance system as well as the lovingkindness meditation to assist you in seeing from a neutral, loving space.

The tendency to hold on too long or let go too soon can be a part of your temperament or a function of a habit reaction pattern developed to protect yourself. So use the lovingkindness, compassionate focus on yourself first; increase your understanding of how you relate before making any adjustments to your behavior or asking for change from your partner. Remember that you will shift from a Me-style *through* an I-style of relationship to the interdependent We-style of relating. Be kind and patient with yourself as you learn to feel safe in these new styles of relating.

STYLES OF TEMPERAMENT IN RELATIONSHIP: COLLABORATOR OR INDIVIDUALIST?

There is a language that goes with collaborators and individualists. *Individualists* choose singular pronouns and hold onto information until ready to disseminate it. Collaborators freely share information and are constantly responding to cues from others. *Collaborators* use pronouns like we: they are inclusive and focus on where things connect. Individualists focus on the places of difference. Individualists tend to work in solitary activities and their leadership style is hierarchical. Collaborators tend to work in teams or as support people to others and their leadership style is collaborative and facilitative.

Power for a collaborator is knowledge and the seams at which there is connection and agreement. Power for an individualist is the accumulation of knowledge and a sense they know more than others.

Whether you think and interact like an individualist or a collaborator tends to be a function of nature (temperament) and environment. It is a shorthand way to understanding the paradigms through which you view the world. It can also assist you in understanding under what circumstances you will have conflict with others. In a way it's like belonging to a group because individualists communicate with each other better than with collaborators. Collaborators will continue to collaborate whether interacting with an individualist or a collaborator. However, the collaboration will feel less one-sided when two collaborators are communicating with each other.

Knowing your natural preference as well as developing skills in your less preferred mode, will assist you in relationships. You may have aspects of both modes depending on the situation or the person with whom you are interacting. Also some people interact differently in personal, intimate relationships than in work, career-oriented partnerships.

Look at your chosen field and the kinds of dyadic and team relationships in which you work; this may reveal which tendency is uppermost for you. With the following two questions the first is more collaborative, the second is more individualistic:

- Do you share information easily and work to create a place of agreement?

OR

- Do you tend to observe others and share little until you feel you have an upper position in the interaction?

Do not confuse this with introversion or extraversion. Individualists can be both extraverted and introverted. Their comfort socially is not what defines their individualistic tendency. The same is true for collaborators. It is not their place on the introversion/extraversion scale that defines how they choose to interact in groups.

Once you have a sense of where you are on this scale, observe those with whom you interact for clues to their tendencies. This insight can give you a guide as to how to reduce conflicts at work and home by discussing ways to interact and work together that are inclusive of all parties involved. Being an individualist or collaborator is paradigmatic neither is right, just right for you. Using figure-ground paradigm shifting to bring you to neutral will assist you in having peaceful and successful relationships.

Developing your skill at moving between these two paradigms of individualist or collaborator increases success in negotiations because it means you can speak another person's language to communicate more effectively. The individualist is connected to the I-style of relationship while a collaborator is associated with the We-style.

MAAPS, FIVE GUIDING SECURITY PRINCIPLES OF RELATIONSHIP: MONEY, ACHIEVEMENT, ATTACHMENT (CONNECTION), POWER (FREEDOM), & STRUCTURE

Relationship choices are a function of how you seek security. Whether you seek security through Money, Achievement, Attachment (connection), Power (independence, influence, freedom) or Structure, these five issues of security guide how you choose to partner or the kind of relationship you choose to foster, create, and implement.

To discern which is your driver in relationship consider how you would feel if one of these things was in jeopardy. The driver of these five styles can be the negative insecurity, a fear of lack or deficiency, or it can be a thrust to accumulate the identified relationship driver. Fear, insecurity or a feeling of scarcity drives a Me or I-style of relating. Once you get into an interdependent We-style of relating then the security driver shifts to self-confidence; this shift is from a need, fear, or lack-based insecurity to a serenity or sense of wholeness, inner security, and increase in joy, driving the relationship. In the We-style of relating, you will still focus on one or a combination of the five security drivers as organizing features of what you look for in relationship however you will experience this desire from a perspective of preference rather than need. In order to move through a Me or I-style of relating into a We-style of relating you must first, identify what drives you in relationship and second, identify what drives your partner in relationship.

Take the time to look through each of the different drivers and see which feels highly value-laden to you and which appears to be valued by your partner. You may not have the same driver in relationship. To understand which is highly valued, consider your relationship without each one and notice what happens to your energy. If removing any one of the five results in an interior sense of panic, then you have discovered your core insecurity driver. You may have more than one need-based, insecurity driver. You can begin to work with how to shift from a fear-based connection to your core driver to a joy-based connection to that driver, through paradigm shifting tools and mindfulness.

Understand that the shift is from fear to joy. You may find that you remain connected to a certain set of characteristics as important in your lifestyle or relationship patterns, but the goal is to remove the insecurity or fear, so that you have a greater sense of empowerment, strength, and resilience in how you partner and relate in and to your environment. The idea is that if you set up how you partner or create relationship based on an insecurity or sense of lack, no matter how much you meet the insecurity need, you will never attain a sense of security, and so will continue to feel unstable in your relationships and partnerships. Once you shift your relationship to the specific issue of security (insecurity) from need to preference you have the capacity to fully develop into a fully actualized authentic person and so your relationships will hold a deeper value and degree of sustenance and success.

You can review the survivor scenarios to see how you may have developed a pattern of relationship around a fear-based driver. Remember, you can get stuck in a habit reaction pattern of fear, or an insecurity driver because of a specific event or injury that felt overwhelmingly powerful to you. This happens as a protective effect to respond to a life-or-death feeling early in your life in a significant relationship and continues automatically. In response to this event you moved that security issue into the forefront of your relationship, partnership style so that you could control your environment. You may have even said to yourself, *This is never going to happen to me again!* Over time you become habituated to responding to relationship in this habit reaction patterning. This was probably a very positive choice you made to increase your sense of power and security in a painful and difficult situation. However, once you were out of that situation, the driver began to garner power of its own in your consciousness because of the underlying fear. As such you actually became less in control, because the unconscious habit patterning began to act automatically and reactively, with a sense of unconsciousness, removing your opportunity to respond in the present-time, mindfully in your choice making and relationship making.

The primary mechanism of risk assessment gets disrupted when this happens. Instead of using your personal sensory guidance system to neutrally and objectively receive, interpret data, and respond, you see through your fear-filled insecurity paradigm which skews the information to inaccurately report risk when there is none, and in some cases create the precise problems you are trying to avoid. The core insecurity, which became the driver of your behavior to protect you from risk, overtime becomes a detriment and diminishes your capacity to assess risk accurately.

This patterning is unconscious. In order to shift your style of relating and right the balance the security issue has in your life, decision-making, and how you view partnership, the patterning must be brought into the light, into your consciousness. This is best done through identification, compassionate evaluation in the present-moment, and neutrality through mindfulness. Once you apply a mindful eye to your behavior patterning and how it is connected to your cognitions, your beliefs, and your security issues, then you can make mindful present-moment decisions about how you would like to proceed in relationship. This can create an opportunity for you to shift from a fear-based security driver to a joy-based security driver.

SELF-CONFIDENCE LEADS TO A WE-STYLE RELATIONSHIP

You can think in terms of *need* and *want*. If you *need* to be in a relationship or need the relationship to look a certain way, then you are being driven by a lack or fear-based consciousness. The need to have it be that way gives power to the driver above and beyond your mindfulness. The need drives the relationship form and function. Rather than you choosing and deciding from a mindful, neutral present-moment perspective, you are driven to act a specific way to meet that need. The need creates a hierarchy of action with the need being the primary driver and removes the space for you to evaluate and respond from a neutral, centered place. This hierarchy creates the power for the need to *drive* your behavior, your actions, your perspective, and your sense of safety.

If you have studied Maslow's *Hierarchy of Needs* then you are aware that safety and survival are at the base of the needs pyramid. Maslow's theory describes a hierarchy of needs. The primary needs are required in order for movement to the next level of development.

The base of the pyramid begins with physiological needs, then safety issues, once these are met a person will move on to address, belonging needs, followed by esteem needs, then cognitive and aesthetic needs (identified later in his work) and finally at the tip of the pyramid is self-actualization. Later, Maslow identified transcendence as the final stage and he separated this stage from the bottom seven. He perceived that at this stage an individual has moved beyond an individualistic view of self-actualization to a view of teaching and assisting others to self-actualize.

Maslow described these needs as the motivators of human behavior, and he identified the movement through these various focal points, or stages as developmental. The bottom four needs were identified as deficit needs and the above four stages as *Being* needs. This was a developmental pyramid or hierarchy similar to Erikson's psychosocial stages in that each stage must be efficiently worked through before movement into the next stage. This is to say that if the needs are not met the person remains in that stage of development and his primary motivation in action, behavior, thinking and deed is fixed at that level.

Each level of fixed behavior has a connection to the MAAPS insecurity fear-based style of interacting. Attachment insecurity driver is connected to the physiological base Maslow stage, because this driver is based in a belief/experience of existence, life or death, *without you I do not exist* or *I am at risk of death*. It can also be connected to the second, safety or third needs-stage of belonging.

Money and Power are the insecurity drivers of the Maslow safety stage of needs development. Here the individual is focused on survival from a financial, physical, and limited-resources perspective. Your interactions may be Me-style but are more often an I-style of relating. Power can also be associated with the esteem and cognitive needs stages (four and five). The Achievement insecurity driver is connected to Maslow's need stage of esteem, cognitive, and aesthetic, (four, five and six). This is an I-style of relating. The security need for Structure can be found in each of the Maslow need levels with the exception of self-actualization and transcendence, as in these stages the focus is on unification and transpersonal relationship. Understanding what the injury or event was that solidified this insecurity driver into your specific need hierarchy will assist you to recognize where you are on the hierarchy pyramid.

Maslow believed the stage of self-actualization was the height of possibility for human behavior. He proposed that through self-actualization each person is able to act in a unifying, holistic way to create innovation, solutions, prosperity, and paradigmatic shifts that incorporate a degree of universal altruism. This is the place of the We-style of interaction.

So if you *want* to be in a relationship you are in the self-actualized perspective in how you approach love and belonging. If you *want* to be in a relationship or want to have the relationship look a certain way, then you are in a joy-based relationship. This creates space for you to use your mindfulness and paradigm recognition, shifting, and integration tools to create the best situation for you and your partner. From this space you are free to create a situation that matches who you each are, without requiring one of you to either give up something that you value or become diminished in importance in the relationship.

Joy-based, self-confidence based relationships empower all parties to create together with mutuality and allow for interdependence through dynamic give and take without an exchange balance sheet.

From the space of want you can negotiate a win-win relationship that is dynamic and mutually fulfilling.

Self-confidence leads to a We-style relationship. Ongoing anxiety or insecurity lead to being stuck in a Me or I-style of relationship. The following section describes the different negative forms of the MAAPS security drivers.

SECURITY DRIVERS DEFINED AND CLARIFIED, A NEGATIVE NEED BASE

As described by Maslow, the idea of security drives much of human action and directed behavior. The search for security can take many paths. There are different forms of security attached to financial, physical, emotional, relational, and personal safety. In addition, there is a temperamental component to your security driver choice, specific personalities are drawn to specific hierarchies of security. The intersection of these continua in your personality and world-view creates your core insecurity and gives a view into how you guide your behavior to meet your security driver either consciously or unconsciously. As you go through the definitions recognize that these are along a continuum and you may have a combination of core insecurity drivers. When you have a combination one is primary. Focus on the primary of your combination first, then you will find it easier to right your relationship with your secondary and tertiary insecurity drivers.

Money. If you have a core insecurity of money you focus on making money and creating financial security. The threat or thought of not having money creates an inner sense of insecurity. Money accumulation is a primary focus and it increases your sense of security. If you live here then connection in relationships has a weaker pull on you and wealth creation and savings is of great importance. You will have difficulty giving money away or even spending money on necessary items because of the core insecurity connected to loss of money. Personal connections are less valued and are run through an equation of how to hold onto your wealth. You can survive with few connections but have difficulty releasing the wealth you have created. You may even feel paralyzed by insecurity if you are faced with separating yourself from your money. You will focus on how much money you can retain when involved in relationship development and partnership agreements. You may have difficulty with altruism and charity. The insecurity equation is that money equals safety. Money insecurity can look like a Me or I-style of relating and can have a narcissistic or competitive feel to the overall structure of the relationship.

Here are some statements that indicate a Money core insecurity:

- I am very careful with my money.
- I like to keep my money and earnings separate from that of my partner.
- I like to pay my fair share.
- Saving is a high priority; a lot of my energy is focused on discovering ways to save money and get the best deal for my money.
- I cannot be in a relationship with someone who does not respect money.
- My generosity is tempered by how much someone deserves assistance.
- If there is an unequal portion of money then I feel distraught if I get the smaller portion – even if the larger portion goes to my partner.

- My money is mine; it is not part of a collective pool of money and I control how it is spent.
- I use money to show my love and care for another.

A *Money insecurity driver* is connected to the safety stage of the Maslow Needs Hierarchy Pyramid. This is an I-style of relating. Here the individual is focused on survival from a financial, physical, and limited resources perspective. Because of the way in which money can be like a lifeline, like a source of sustenance, there are connections to the first two stages of Erikson's psychosocial development stages, dealing with an issue of trust, survival, control over oneself, and safety at the most basic level. An early loss, injury, or trauma during these years can create a crack in an individual's sense of security that can skew into an insecurity about money, if there are later experiences in later stages of psychosocial development. It begins as an undefined insecurity around safety, personal power, and getting your needs met, and concretizes into an insecurity focused on the acquisition and accumulation of money as more direct experiences of financial deprivation and personal capacity to create wealth manifest.

The linking has a bioenergetic component; which is to say the intense fear experienced physically and psychologically creates an *imprint* in conjunction with the momentary relief when you increase you financial reserve. Think of an *imprint* as a strong, lasting mark, embedded into your consciousness and belief system. This has a feedback loop that keeps you caught in the pursuit of money as security, with fleeting moments of relief and then an internal pressure to resume the pursuit of money. The I-style of relating keeps you insulated because of the pressure of the core insecurity to keep your money separated from others – since you see it as a lifeline, so that it can create an inability to share or create interdependence

Achievement. When you are driven by the security of achievement you may need to get many educational degrees or move up the social class or career ladder. You may also be compelled to achieve unending athletic success through the pursuit of bicycle racing, marathon/ triathlon racing, strenuous mountain climbing, or other vigorous athletic adventures that require intense competition, training, and accomplishment. This could look like a person who is ambitious to the detriment of connection, often taking on more than his or her partner. You feel the need to keep pressing forward and have difficulty simply being with your partner. You may even eschew relationships altogether or discard relationships once they do not serve your continued movement up the ladder of achievement. The core insecurity when dealing with achievement is a sense that you need these achievements to be seen, that they embolden you and your secure place in the world. Achievement insecurity results in a competition I-style of relating.

Here are some statements that indicate an Achievement core insecurity:

- My accomplishments define me and give me a sense of confidence.
- I feel lost when I am not working toward something.
- I get hurt and angry when I am not recognized for my achievements.
- I feel driven to prove my self-worth, intelligence, and knowledge through my accomplishments.
- I feel competitive and a sense of ownership over my ideas and creation, often needing credit for these.

- I have difficulty in partnership when the credit for an achievement is not clarified.
- I cannot let my partner deter me from accomplishing my goals.
- When I have to choose between my relationship responsibilities and my career achievements, it is difficult to put my partner's needs first.
- Teamwork is challenging for me. I feel invisible in collaborative work.

An *Achievement insecurity driver* is connected to the Maslow Hierarchy of Needs Pyramid stages of *esteem, cognitive,* and *aesthetic,* (four, five and six). This is an I-style of relating. Here the individual is focused on security from an interior perspective of self-knowing, self-acceptance, inferiority, and a lack of safety. Because the issue is an insecurity of inferiority there is a direct connection to the fourth stage of Erikson's psychosocial development stages, dealing with an issue of industry versus inferiority. This stage has threads back to the earlier stages of trust (1), autonomy (2), and initiative (3); therefore, the achievement core insecurity has ties to negative issues in the resolution to these earlier stages. It is as if the individual is stuck in a feedback loop of having discovered a way to feel okay through industriousness, but cannot shut off the need to press on through the next required task and accomplishment, creating a never-ending ladder that needs to be climbed.

An early loss, injury, or trauma during the earlier stages created a deficit in the individual's sense of security. The skew into an insecurity about achievement concretized through subsequent experiences in later stages of psychosocial development. You can think about his like a wobble in development that became exaggerated through each stage until the shift was dramatic and congealed into an insecurity focused on the acquisition and accumulation of awards and achievements.

The linking has a bioenergetic component; which is to say the intense inferiority experienced physically and psychologically creates an imprint in conjunction with the momentary relief when you experience yourself as authentic or real through achievement. This has a feedback loop that keeps you caught in the pursuit of the next achievement, with fleeting moments of relief and then an internal pressure to resume the pursuit of more achievements.

Attachment (connection). If you find that being alone is difficult, or you have your strongest feelings of insecurity around relationships, then it is in that portion of your life that you have a lack of security and a lack of strength. If your core insecurity is attachment, then human interaction and relationship is a focus of security.

Here are some statements that are consistent with an Attachment core insecurity:

- What matters to me is relationship; the money will come.
- I hate being alone; it makes me feel vulnerable and scared.
- When I don't hear from someone right away, I panic; I feel fear and abandonment.
- Sometimes my fear of being left feels like abandonment and it leads to anger. I feel driven to interrogate or act with attacking behavior toward the person who left me.
- I can do anything as long as we are together.
- I have a deep need to be agreed with; I have difficulty when my partner and I have different opinions.
- I feel panicky and abandoned when someone disagrees with me, even when the person is not threatening to leave me.

- I give more time, attention, and money in all my relationships to ensure that the other person feels a debt to me. Sometimes this makes me feel alone and unimportant in the relationship.
- Being in a partnership defines me and gives me an inner feeling of security. When the relationship feels challenged, the need to reconnect in the relationship overrides other responsibilities in my life.

An *attachment insecurity driver* is connected to the base of the Maslow Needs Hierarchy Pyramid, the *physiological* stage, because this driver is indeed an issue of *without you I do not exist* or *I am at risk of death*. Also, it can be connected to Maslow's third stage of *belonging*. This is a Me-style of relating. It can look like a narcissistic style of relating, where the other person doesn't exist except to make the insecure person feel secure. It can be co-dependent. It can also be an I-style of relating based on a deep sense that you cannot depend on anyone and so you bundle yourself and care for yourself, but are unable to trust another loving you; this results in an inner conflict. There is a deep feeling of loneliness in this core insecurity driver. From the perspective of Erikson's psychosocial stages, this insecurity is based at the first stage of trust/mistrust. An individual with an Attachment core insecurity had an early trauma within the first 18 months of life. This is difficult to pin down because rarely do you retain memory from that early in your own life. However, you may be able to piece this together with stories of your birth from your family members. You may have experienced birth trauma, or your mother became very sick just following your delivery and had to leave you for an extended period of time.

The overemphasis on doing for others by an individual who has an Attachment core insecurity is a projection of what she wants for herself, as well as a way to diffuse the inner feeling of terror that she will not be enough to keep her partner. This person may appear clingy, generous, or removed. This is dependent on whether he has developed a sense that doing for others will make them stay, or has developed a certainty that he will be left so is always preparing to not connect fully so as to be less hurt.

This has a bioenergetic component, as with the other core insecurity drivers. In addition, this insecurity is almost second nature to you due to it being with you since you began to have a consciousness about life. This quality makes it more difficult to separate out what is a natural state of authentic trust and what is the fear of being deserted. Very complicated and compulsive patterns can develop with a person who has an Attachment core insecurity, to create a perceived sense of safety when facing abandonment or time alone. If you have an Attachment core insecurity or are partnered with someone who does, a deep compassion and strong degree of patience is required to help re-parent yourself or your partner, and create a trusting space to move away from the insecurity toward an authentic sense of self and trust.

Power. This is a matter of being the smartest person in the room. This security style has a strong competitive tone. If you are driven by power, then you have a strong need to feel that everything you have accomplished you have done *solely on your own*. You do not want to be beholden to anyone and this drives a specific kind of I-style of relationship. This patterning of Power can be about a need for freedom, making sure that no one has any power over you, rather than a need to have power over others. In this patterning style information, assistance, care, and love are withheld to increase the degree of power you feel, and this is done out of an unconscious sense of insecurity regarding your true inner power. This can be a direct need to have power over others in order to feel safe and secure as a need to protect yourself from feeling vulnerable. That is the driver, *the avoidance of vulnerability,* so the choice to focus on the accumulation of power.

Here are some statements that are indicative of a Power Core insecurity issue:

- No one is more important than I am.
- I don't need my partner's help; I can create everything I need on my own.
- I have trouble accepting another's accomplishments; it feels as if they are in direct conflict with my own accomplishments.
- I don't like when I owe someone for their help or what they have done for me. I feel vulnerable when this happens and will change the structure of the relationship to avoid this feeling.
- I do not like feeling vulnerable.
- Others should listen to me and do what I say.
- I put a lot of energy into figuring out the best way to handle things, I do not like it when my hard work is ignored and my partner doesn't do what I say.
- I feel challenged when I have to work within a team.
- I need to be the boss; others do not see what is best and make mistakes, which I have to fix.
- When someone appears to be smarter than me, I feel defensive.

- I create cordings to me so that I can have power over another person when I feel that I want to secure that person remain in my life.

A *Power insecurity driver* is connected to the second stage of the Maslow Needs Hierarchy Pyramid, the *Safety* stage; here the individual is focused on survival from a financial, physical, and limited resources perspective. Power can also be associated with the *esteem* and *cognitive* needs stages, (four and five). When you have a Power core insecurity that is based in Maslow's safety stage, then it is likely you had a significant loss or injury within the first five years of your life, Erikson's first three stages of psychosocial development, *trust* that you would be cared for, *autonomy* in controlling your physical needs, and *initiative* in creating what you want. In some way you experienced a squashing of your sense of personal power. In reaction you cannot trust the environment or your partner to care for you; you fear you will be engulfed. Thus you develop a Power insecurity, shielding yourself in a way to keep others from your authentic self. A Power insecurity driver can also be something that you learned through modeling via a rigid, authoritarian parenting experience in your early years. This overlay of power struggling overrides your movement though the psychosocial developmental stages so that each stage is colored by the need to struggle with overpowering your environment and social group in order to feel safe.

When it relates to Maslow's stages of esteem and cognitive then you have incorporated a skew through Erikson's fourth psychosocial stage, industry/inferiority.

There is a bioenergetic component to this. The deep experience of fear, or vulnerability is solidified into your inner sense of self; connection and interaction with others create an unpleasant trigger, like an electric shock to that core weakness, that trigger propels you to increase your isolation and encasement around yourself. Your relationships are unfulfilling and you are caught in a feedback loop of desiring contact and then feeling the intense fear when allowing another close, leading to a recoiling to an interior isolated stance. The I-style of relating is most common, however there are Me-style relationships with this core insecurity.

Sometimes the Power core insecurity can look like a sado-masochistic relationship wherein you are drawn to a formalized style of physical punishment or abuse, which you endure or are attracted to in order to create a sense of familiarity and connection. This skew allows you to remain separated and have contact that is completely colored by an issue of power. In this scenario the Power is displayed as power-over rather than a search for empowerment. This can have a narcissistic, clingy quality along with a power-tripping component. This is a very complicated behavior style that is covering over a deep sense of mistrust, discouragement, and inferiority. This is linked to an early trauma in the first two Erikson psychosocial stages with an overemphasis of masochistic, fueled achievement.

The bioenergetic component of this style is connecting harm, loss of power to harm. You strive to feel powerful and then need to be punished in order to right that sense of empowerment; this act of putting you in order leads to a feeling of skewed safety. You disconnect power in work and power in relationship, so that you experience a deep level of satisfaction in work and often attain acclaim, yet your personal relationships are filled with a masochistic, needy quality.

Structure. When structure is your guiding principle you may have insecurity around chaos. The avoidance of chaos, spontaneity, or the unknown is what is driving the relationship. Control brings a sense of safety. When structure is your security issue then you are driven to control all aspects of your relationship, partnership and environment so that it looks a specific way. It may be a need to create the opposite of how you feel inside. This need to control your environment is usually a driver that results from an inner sense of feeling out of control, around the lack of predictability and the overall dynamic aspect of relationship. This security driver is reacting to the fact that change is the only constant, and in some way a change created a sticky place for you, and a lack of trust in your own capacity to move lithely through your environment and partnerships.

Here are some statements that indicate a Structure core insecurity driver:

- I need to have things happen in a specific way to feel comfortable.
- When my partner acts in a way that is spontaneous it is frightening to me even when the spontaneous action is a happy thing.
- There is an order to how the universe works.
- When you step outside that order the order of the universe there are consequences.
- I work best when I have the power and freedom to control how things are done.
- I can work collaboratively in teams as long as the structure of the interaction is clear and precise.
- I have to create order in my environment before I can begin a project.
- When I get interrupted, I have to return to the beginning and recreate my steps. This is worsened by anxiety and stress.

- I can't ignore the call to clean a messy area even when it will make me late for an appointment or create problems in my schedule.
- Chaos feels safer than order.

A *Structure insecurity need* driver can be found in each of the Maslow Hierarchy of Needs Pyramid levels with the exception of the seventh *self-actualization* stage and eighth needs stage of *transcendence*, as in these stages the focus is on unification and transpersonal relationship. Understanding what the injury or event was that solidified this insecurity driver into your specific need hierarchy will assist you to see where you are on the hierarchy pyramid. This can be a result of a misstep in any of the first four stages of Erikson's psychosocial developmental stages. Looking at the challenge of the stage and connecting it with your personal Structure insecurity will help you to identify the etiology of your Structure core insecurity. The way it will play out is through a rigid structure that you have developed to help you feel safe in relation to others, food/eating, hygiene, or everyday activities, that requires a set of steps in order to pacify an internal sense of anxiety. This might look like a set of obsessions (things your worry about and need to address) or compulsions (things you have to do in a specific order to feel safe) or both together.

This has a bioenergetic component: The intense fear or lack of feeling safe imprinted onto your physical and sense system, to which you have linked a set of behaviors that assuage that sense of fear. These are triggered whenever you feel unsafe and have to institute the set of behaviors to regain your sense of security. This plays out along a continuum of pressure to act, and intensity. Transitions typically trigger the need to act out the structured behavior(s). It may be that you have to follow a structure to transition from home to work, or work to home. Or it may be less intense and only get engaged under stressful times. You may need to eat the same foods everyday, sit in the same place, or go through a routine before you leave the house, or go to sleep (sleep is a transition of consciousness). You may have an overly rigid relationship to *everything in its place* and not be able to think unless you have put everything away. This may also be played out in your relationship to food, eating (receiving sustenance, nurturance) and purging (disallowing the comfort of sustenance and nurturance).

Occasionally the way in which a Structure core insecurity plays out is through disarray, chaos, and lack of organization. Here the individual is struggling with having been over-structured in a way that was so deeply disempowering that gaining structure is a direct assault on his sense of safety. This is a troubling insecurity style as it results in the individual feeling hopeless whether in disarray or organized.

RECLAIMING YOUR INNER SECURITY, MOVING FROM NEED TO PREFERENCE

How a person develops a sense of insecurity is related to his early circumstances, his place in society, his parent's perspective of security and his personal temperament and skill set. So an individual who focuses on financial security will usually have a story or myth behind it that describes a powerful point in his life when he was without money and the lack of money felt dire, dangerous, and life threatening. The gathering and having of money becomes the object of security. In a different circumstance an individual who focuses on connection or relationship for security will have a story of being abandoned and the abandonment will feel like a dire, life threatening situation. Physical neglect or deprivation and abuse in early childhood can feel like abandonment, and individuals can develop an attachment insecurity in relationship as a result of this. In this instance the relationship, being connected to someone as a transitional object, creates security and the fear is of being abandoned, being invisible, or being insignificant.

The issue of insecurity is an equation of the experience plus the attached story or belief system connected to a feeling of life-or-death; not all individuals that come from poverty or abuse, who have a challenging financial situation, or have dealt with abandonment, will develop this sense of insecurity.

This sense of insecurity is something that shows up along a continuum, from slight to overwhelming. On the slight end of the continuum, supportive groups and talking oneself through the anxiety can be enough to decrease the internal reaction or imbalance. On the more overwhelming end it can be debilitating, interfering with an individual's capacity to function and require a multi-level approach to manage the insecurity and create a sense of authentic safety.

The word security can conjure up many different connotations: a sense of physical safety, inner balance, laws and rules; the meanings are diverse but the underlying concept seems to refer to a sense of balance and safety. In order to create a sense of security, the work needs to begin internally within each individual. The first step is to build an internal sense of security or self-confidence and inner strength.

Child development theorists talk about this as the first stage of development for children. It develops out of trust or mistrust of your caregiver. From there, following Erikson's developmental model, each stage builds on the previous stage. A feeling of trust and confidence will lead to self-confidence, competence, success in relationships and career. Creating this pathway for your child is a function of being present and real with her. Creating this for yourself is a function of returning to neutral, returning to balance, through meditation and paradigm shifting with compassion and lovingkindness toward others and yourself. Mindful meditation is a useful habit to help create this.

A feeling of mistrust can skew the development of these capacities; it can decrease your chance to develop the positive aspects of the stages. It can result in a lack of self-confidence and internal strength, insecurity, timidity, and a sense of incompetence. Ultimately, if enough aspects are negatively affected, this results in an insecurity that interferes with an individual's ability to create sustaining relationships, to make basic decisions, and to deal with nominally stressful situations.

This situation can be positively affected with meditation, prayer, breathing, and reality testing through compassionate paradigm shifting. The first milestone to shifting your internal relationship with security into balance is through the development of self-confidence.

You can have a preference for certain kinds of relationships, one of the five principles of security – MAAPS, without having a negative component or core insecurity. You can think of this as being like your learned security temperament: a balanced relationship with what matters to you results in knowing your particular preferences from a positive, healthful perspective and incorporates the five principles of security – MAAPS. These become core insecurities when you are driven to act in a habitual way to avoid the fear related to an injury in your development. This core insecurity habit drives you to attend to the security issue over and above your own health and/or the health of the relationship. Preferences indicate a preferred style of being rather than a need that drives the relationship. These security principles can be a way of connecting in a balanced, healthy partnership. When you are determining your style and whether it is balanced or an insecurity driver consider whether it is a preference or a dire need; pay attention to the intensity of feeling, charge, panic or triggering quality involved.

The following sections in this chapter and those in the chapter on *Belief systems affect your relationship style and sense of security* are guideposts to help you shift your relationship with your core insecurity driver from a need to a preference. Uncoupling the need to react in a certain way for safety, and shifting your perspective from controlling your environment to create safety to feeling centered and safe in your capacity to respond effectively to your environment and get what you want. Remember, changing your inner paradigmatic perspective and stance in the world is a process that requires several steps:

- First, identification of the problem, skew, belief system that may have served you in your early life but no longer serves you.
- Acceptance, gratitude for how it saved you in some way.
- A choice, decision, and commitment to invert, shift or transform this habit reaction pattern.
- Lovingkindness, and compassion toward yourself as you make efforts to shift out of the old style of relating and habit reaction pattern you have determined to release.
- Practice, increased awareness, and continued reorientation.
- This requires a safe environment and safe relationship to practice.

- Clarification of how you do not need the habit, as well as a soothing toward yourself when you feel triggered to engage the habit – develop your awareness and conscious interaction with your personal sensory guidance system and when you are receiving messages that are authentic rather than fear based.
- A mindful, meditative practice to assist you in reconnecting to your authentic, powerful, secure self.

BALANCE THE POWER DIFFERENTIAL IN RELATIONSHIP THROUGH DETACHMENT

One of the biggest impediments to a healthy and meaningful relationship is an unequal distribution of power between the parties. It can set up an undercurrent of resentment and power plays that inhibit trust and intimacy.

The way in which power is measured in relationship varies. In marriages, money and decisions on how it is spent, sex, how leisure time is distributed, and feeling a sense of collaboration or division of tasks are all areas of power distribution. Even how a relationship proceeds has to do with an agreement on how power is shared in the relationship. These features and equations, in general, determine how power is divided and determines the power differential. These issues can be applied to work partnerships and friendships.

If the differential is too great or not consistent with internal expectations there will be conflict and strife that could upset the continuity, fiber, and longevity of the relationship.

Here the definition of power has to do with an internal sense of empowerment in the style and course of the relationship as well as the capacity to get done that which you feel is necessary or important to the relationship and/or yourself. This includes an internally consistent picture of self by the other. In other words if you perceive yourself to be talented and strong and your partner treats you in a fashion that exhibits that his picture of you is that you are talented and strong – then that is an internally consistent picture of self by the other.

A sense of feeling empowered would consist of a sense of joy, contentment, and strength; together this would feel like a sense of inner control for the person. He would experience shared values with his partner and that he has the ability to direct his life accordingly. Feeling disempowered would consist of a sense of disillusionment and a lack of inner control. In this instance the person would experience that her values are not shared by her partner and that she does not have the ability to direct her own life.

In the former situation, the equitable, empowered relationship struggles are dealt with in a fairly direct and aboveboard fashion, allowing various opinions to be identified and discussed and a reasonable negotiation to be found. Both parties would offer honest and clear information and experience full disclosure of their wants and needs. The outcomes to these conversations would be supportive to both parties' requirements further increasing the internal sense of control for both partners. Energy toward change would be dealt with proactively. Even difficult discussions would be confronted in an honest and compassionate way.

In the latter scenario, the disempowered situation there would be a less honest set of disclosures with ever decreasing identification of problems outwardly. Actions might be taken passively and in an undercover way to avoid directly confronting issues. There would be a tone of reactivity and defensiveness. In this scenario there would also be an internally inconsistent picture of self by other. This is an example of a power differential that is out of balance. An unbalanced power differential can happen in a Me-style or I-style relationship. We-style relationships are grounded in empowerment, open-communication, interdependence, and balanced interaction.

Listening to the language style, tone, and word choice between partners can give you clues to the power differential and if the differential is in balance or not.

A dearth of conversation and interaction can indicate an imbalance. This is especially true if it appears that one member is initiating contact and this initiation is met with silence, or if the lack of connection appears to be one-sided. Other signs of an imbalance are a sense of defensiveness or reactivity in tone or word choice, bickering and side-talking without resolution.

If you notice that you are in a relationship that is out of balance, look for ways to right the balance.

- Observe where you feel resentment or you hear resentment from your partner.
- Try to slow down your interaction and compassionately confront the silence or resentment.
- Work with the words, tone, or silence lightly, directly and with an earnest interest in clarifying meaning and shifting word choice and tone.

If the resentment or defensiveness is within you, try to discern what the original driver of the feeling was. Could it be a longstanding feeling of unimportance or lack of power or a single incident that has injured you in some way? Think of what you need to feel whole again, and then gently ask for that. Try to encourage your partner to reconnect with you on this deeper more loving level.

Try to remember what brought you into partnership and see if you can rekindle the lightness and love. If you discover you have lost that sense of lightness, try to move to a neutral place so that you can leave the relationship without further injuring the other or yourself.

Power is one of the core issues of development. All injuries go to power and all successes are related to power. How you relate to power and how you create a balance of power in relationship is directly connected to the level of joy contentment and strength of that relationship. Begin with your personal relationship with power within yourself.

Review the power differential in your relationship and how power is distributed; consider how this situation has evolved. If you discover that you want a different power differential but you want to maintain your connection to your partner, gently discuss the changes you seek to create increased balance.

Balance is the key. Clarify for yourself first and then with your partner what you desire and what you want to discard. This opens the door to balancing the power differential in relationship.

NEGOTIATING WITH EMPOWERMENT: THE WE-STYLE OF RELATIONSHIP

The hardest thing to do is to stay true to yourself in the face of adversity or in the face of another's desire for you to leave your truth and follow his.

This can be a challenge in social situations and group dynamics. The study of group dynamics identifies specific ways groups of people interact within and across groups and indicates these processes are a function of most aspects of life; blending projects and collaborating in complicated, multilevel ventures in business or social interaction such as bringing together families in marriage or partnering in business are examples of group dynamics. It can be a challenge to remain true to yourself while incorporating another's perspective when negotiating between individual and group wants and needs, as well as negotiating the integration of ideas, theories, and processes within groups.

Knowing your truth is helpful when evaluating how to integrate with another. And because what the other says is not always a true reflection of what the other wants due to unseen or hidden agendas, listening to the whole of another's message and resisting the need to just swallow whole the other's position is important. It is necessary to pause and be mindful in these encounters. Then you can hold to your truth while being flexible with the other.

I have a facility for languages. Not just formal languages like French and Italian, but also personal languages of individuals and groups. It is important to understand what underlies the language of others. This requires understanding what meaning is contained in the words chosen. Words contain *idents* of what matters to people, this is to say each word has a cord to a specific meaning that is more complicated than the definition in a dictionary. Remember the explanation with the word *Grace* in the introduction? That's an example of an *ident*. The style and quality in which people speak give clues to what meaning is held within the words chosen. People may be intentionally hiding their meaning to manipulate or they may be unaware of the hidden quality of their meaning. Listening with a mindful introspection and attention will assist you in discerning the full meaning.

In America you can get the culture of various parts of the country through language. The south, midwest, west, and east have specific qualities hidden within their word choice and sentence structure, even what is or isn't said. The facial expressions, and impressions that assist the verbal language are highly specialized and carry specific meanings. This can be traced to religious, cultural, and personal heritage experiences. Additionally, there are unique patterns within families, working groups, and educational backgrounds. Part of what makes you feel comfortable with another is this similarity or familiarity among and within groups. This occurs immediately through the style in which another speaks, word choice, and non-verbal gestures; you feel comfortable or reactive toward the other based on his or her language and style of communicating.

This whole repertoire of behavior and language has its own manipulative force. There is a push to agree and align, corroborate and connect, underlying the most normal and natural of group dynamics. An example of this is to take on another's distinctive speech pattern. Often people can do this as a way of connecting to the other. Some people do this automatically or reflexively. Having this natural facility is like being a chameleon. The challenge is to be able to see, feel, and understand the other's perspective without loses a connection to your own authentic truth. The balancing agent to this is to have a strong and secure sense of who you are at your core. This allows you to have the capacity and freedom to enter another's world and still remain true to your authentic self.

Holding to your truth is an interesting process of being connected with an even hand-strength: too strong and you are inflexible, not strong enough and you can get lost. Being overly flexible leads to instantaneous understanding and connection but when overly expressed it can dilute authentic purpose or self. I find the best thing to do is to remain in a mindful state, an open, observing, interested curiosity. The use of a mantra or phrase, which allows you to tether yourself to your authentic self so you don't lose your way, can be very efficient.

- I am interested in your perspective but I don't have to accept it as mine.
- It is okay to disagree and be in relationship.
- I don't have to give up myself to be loved or accepted.

This allows you to explore with others their world without losing your own center. It's like a safety rope that frees you to explore and negotiate openly.

MINDFUL SPEECH, MINDFUL ACTION

When you are speaking you are creating. Words have energy. The power and energy within words is described in spiritual and religious texts, clarified by many philosophers, and evidenced in the power of a persuasive argument.

My favorite book that describes the power and distinctive aspect of words is called, *Words as Eggs (1986)* by Russell Lockhart. The idea behind this title is how eggs are a whole universe; the complete components of a life. You imbue meaning and images into words and they then mold your perceptions. Words are symbols, and they have both universal and personal meanings, which is to say they are multidimensional in their meaning causing both clarity and confusion in their use. Clarity derived from the universal meaning and confusion from the personal meaning.

I find this is a useful concept in communication. Communication happens intrapersonally, speaking with yourself and interpersonally speaking with others. When speaking to yourself often the style is to get down on yourself, to say negative things that create a negative internal sense of yourself. An example of this is to say *things never go my way* or *I am going to do a bad job at my presentation* or *I can't do anything*. These statements send out a negative energy vibration. They shift your internal position from neutral to negative, thereby giving power to the words to create the negative expectation.

A better, more mindful way to deal with fears and anxieties is to say *I am afraid that I will not perform well but I am going to do my best and believe in myself*. This allows for the fear to be acknowledged and the negative power of creating that which is feared, to be neutralized. This speech, when combined with specific examples of previous times of success in the past, allows for the negative energy to be dissipated.

A word may have the universal dictionary meaning attached to it, as well as charge from your own experience with the word. This can create a dissonance in communication if you assume that all others fully understand the word choice.

This is important from the perspective of mindful speech, especially when in a position of leadership, parenting, and relationship. Look for feedback from the person with whom you are communicating to determine if your communication has gone in the way you intended. If it has he will be on the same page with you, if it has not his response will seem to be out of sync with your intended communication. You can then retrace with him what word or thing you said, or did, that caused him to go in a different direction than your intended communication.

The best way to remain in mindful speech is to be both descriptive and empathic when speaking, pause and consider how you are presenting the information. From a parenting perspective, it is helpful to consider setting boundaries by saying what you want to see from a positive perspective for example: To a young child in a store full of breakables you might say *Be gentle* rather than *don't touch*. The first identifies a way in which to be that sets a careful boundary but allows the child to develop her skills at touching and not breaking. The second sets a boundary but gives the child nothing to do but stay still. This may be what you want under certain circumstances, but as a rule it doesn't provide guidance to developing an internal boundary and skill at touching without breaking.

In relationship, mindful speech allows for the continued development and negotiation of the relationship without blaming or divisiveness. Providing information in a positive and inviting way is better than a negative and blocking style.

An example of positive, collaborative, mindful speech is to say *I am having difficulty with something about how we are interacting. I would like for us to work on this together to resolve the problem rather than take opposite positions that push us further apart*. Following this, it is best to describe with non-charged words what you experience as a problem in the relationship. Using description and inviting collaboration to create a mutually positive resolution is best.

Mindful speech is an attitude and communication style that you can develop over time. Keeping your attention on mindful speech will help you to focus your energies to create exactly what you want with the least amount of strife and the most ease.

Once you are doing this in a natural fashion, you can create a shift for those around you to remain neutral or refocus the situation when things go awry. Mindful speech leads to mindful action through the natural flow of a drop of water rippling out; your choice to be mindful shifts the energy of any situation to increase the chance for increased understanding and an upleveling of consciousness. This benefits all partnerships.

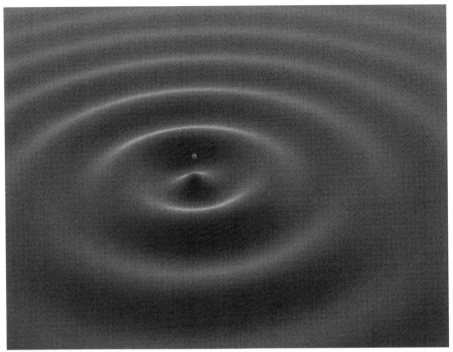

FIGURE 9, THE RIPPLE EFFECT OF MINDFULNESS

TRUST CREATES SECURITY

Trust is a funny combination of belief, intuition, proof, and alignment. What makes a person trust can be something as simple as a feeling within, an inner response to the way a person feels, how a situation clicks, or how something looks right.

It's like a song that's in key →things flow and there is a sense of the direction. When it's out of sync it's like there is a blip in the energy→like a skip on a CD.

Have you ever listened to someone say something and you knew he was lying or withholding some bit of information, because as he spoke something was off in a subtle way. Your being, your internal sensory guidance system, is like your own personal lie detector: it picks up on these subtle shifts in energy. That feeling is something that is related to intuition or detailed, close observation. When you trust that, then you are developing a deeper, cleaner, hyperawareness that can guide you efficiently in your decision-making.

Trust and security are functions of what happens when there aren't a lot of blips in the energy between two people; it builds on itself so that when you have a long time of even, positive flow you can weather something being off.

Your senses are connected to your brain to offer a set of stimuli that help you judge which path is correct. This is true for both mundane and profound tasks. The more you allow the information from your senses into your decision-making, the more effective your decisions can be. Part of the trick here is to recognize when you are feeling a habit reaction pattern based on fear rather than your personal sensory guidance that can direct your way. Meditation, prayer, and breathwork all allow quiet, breathing space, and time to maintain a strong connection to centered self through your sense awareness. These tools are important for being able to maintain clarity and tell the difference between fear stimuli that are the product of habit reaction patterns and true sense awareness stimuli that offer a direction in your decision-making.

Trust is both trusting yourself, and trusting others in relationship. Trusting yourself is listening to the sense awareness information and acting on it. Trusting others is a function of looking for congruency between words and actions. Trust heals insecurity through a response to the underlying fear that leads to the security issue: it offers a knowing, an internalized self-confidence, and a confidence in your partner due to your past mindful evaluation and intimate knowing of her.

A wonderful exercise to develop your connection to your sense awareness in real-time is to ask yourself *what am I feeling right now*. The best way to develop this is to have an attuned ear to when you are feeling *this doesn't feel right*. This is a subtle feeling like the hair on the back of your neck standing up or an internal sense that something is off. This is information that is not verbal but feeling in nature.

Your right brain takes in information as wholes and within context, like image imprints, which is why we can feel something is off but to describe it verbally or analytically, takes longer processing time; that verbal description is a left-brain activity.

Trust is a right-brain activity that is then translated into words and left-brain concepts. It is a sense-knowing, and complete when received. Your right brain informs you that something is in sync or out of sync; it is immediate, a calm, sense-feeling. Whether visual like a painting, musical like a symphony, olfactory like a lovely perfume, or tasty like our favorite recipes, what makes it work is how you take it in from your right brain. To get a deeper understanding when something feels off, focus on it and bring it into your consciousness, then engage your left-brain analytical ability to evaluate what is off and how it is out of sync.

To increase your speed in interacting, you can short-circuit this right-brain activity that lets you know something is off, focusing more on the left-brain activity of verbal and analytical analysis. This is fine until there is a misread or misstep. The short-circuit interferes with your sensory guidance system, disabling the connections between what you pick up with your right-brain and interpret through your left-brain. It removes access to your internal communication to make a decision; or disregards the information presented through your right-brain. Later you notice you were not paying attention to your intuition or inner sense that something was off, saying — *oh I should have paid attention to that weird feeling I was having when that person said/did x,y or z.*

The more you develop a space for meditation, prayer, breathwork, and focus on your sense awareness, the less you short-circuit your connection to your right-brain activity so that you can trust your actions and feelings in making decisions.

Belief, intuition, substantiation, and alignment are the processes that develop, support, and maintain trust. These create and support your actions and responses, your willingness to trust yourself, and others or to take action to realign with your inner self. These are integrated right and left-brain actions.

When you are faced with a difficult decision, using mindful meditation and direct observation skills will help you to make the best decision. Trust that it will bring you forward on the best course of action. Engage your sensory guidance system and incorporate information from both your left and right brain.

HEART-LED ACTION TRANSFORMS THE EFFECTS OF LOSS IN RELATIONSHIP STYLE

You cannot control outcomes, but you can control your actions and how you connect with others in the present-moment. Allowing your heart to guide a relationship is the first step in developing a We-style of relationship. This is heart-centered, heart (spirit) leading mind and body. Here the idea of heart-led is not the idea of emotionality disconnected from mind and body; it is the idea of an internal sensory guidance system: using your senses and intuition through the lens of compassion and lovingkindness to take action and to analyze the situation.

The perspective of experiencing the whole of a relationship can allow for the joy to balance the sadness of loss, injury, and misunderstanding. Through a heart-centered connection, you apply compassion toward yourself and your partner so that both of your experiences, wants, and perspectives are incorporated into the relationship. This is a We-style of relating. It is relating from a centered, balanced, secure self.

When there is a loss of a relationship, allow your heart-centered connection to reveal both the positive and negative aspects of the relationship. The idea is that the outcome doesn't diminish the importance of the connection while together. Each relationship has the capacity to enrich you whether the relationship is longstanding or short-lived; it is through your appreciation of what was powerful and life affirming about it, that enriches you. This means you acknowledge the negativity of the lost relationship while you incorporate useful, positive lessons from it.

This is a tenet of energy: when you focus on the light or positive, that brings more light; focus on the dark or negative aspects brings more of that. So, choose to have your heart be the guide and you will experience more joy and happiness in your life even if you still have to deal with adversity.

Each relationship has its own timing. Emphasize the value of the lessons, beauty, and importance of what was shared over the ending and dissolution. This attitude allows for time together to be powerful and honored rather than reduced in importance to the end result only, like a math equation. Experience the multidimensional components of relationships; avoid seeing them as linear: this + this = that, wherein only the end result is valued. We-style relationships are not reductive, where the sum can be reduced into its various components. There is something that is synergistic about the shared aspect of the relationship that stands alone as important. That aspect is connected to the outcome, but the journey, interaction, growth, progress, and support during the space of time, and between people, has value beyond the outcome itself.

Each contact and connection in our lives has power. Sometimes the information gathered is to redirect your behavior or attention (when your response to the relationship is *I need to learn not to do that in relationship*), other times it is a picture of a perfect moment of how to live. Both experiences matter, and serve relationship development positively.

This is where the concept of mindfulness and paradigm shifting help to bring balance to your focus and living experience. In a dissolution of a relationship, or loss through death, you can be caught in the sadness or anger so there isn't any space for your heart connection to be incorporated. This disempowers you; it interrupts your ability to smoothly move through the loss as a transition onto another path, or along a continued life-path. This lodging in the sad or angry emotion can cause a dam wherein you are caught and unable to move. This can cause blockages and stagnation in all aspects of your life – relationships, career, even health.

Hold on to the beauty, comfort, and positivity of each relationship while transforming the negative aspects that may have led to a dissolution, or in the circumstance of a death, flowing through the deep, profoundly painful emotional aspects of loss. This idea harkens back to the essential issue of holding on and letting go. What you embrace and what you release requires discernment. It is the essential question in integrating loss, in relationship and into your general being and worldview. Be kind to yourself as you move through this process. Let your heart guide you through all your emotions, continually bringing yourself back to the joy, light, and happiness present in the relationship while releasing the pain, negativity, and injury in the relationship.

Embracing connections fully brings the most joy, security, and strength into your life experience. Practice discernment. If you are feeling discouragement, insecurity, or fear in connecting try these steps to realign with your heart connection.

- Think of recent losses, what was truly beautiful about the connection.
- Do an inventory about what you have difficulty releasing.
- Use focused meditation to release held sadness or anger: Breathing in light and joy, Breathing out fear, stuck sadness, anger; With each breath feel increased freedom to bring the essential aspects of that relationship forward into your present-moment; Release aspects out of your control.

As you move through this process, you experience an inner sense of security and develop a stronger sense of trustfulness in yourself and your relationships. Through revealing heart connections you develop trust in yourself and your partnering capacity.

GRACIOUSNESS LEADS TO INNER STRENGTH AND OUTER DURABILITY

Graciousness is doing the right thing under pressure, which is usually when you are most challenged to act without grace. Graciousness is the embodiment of *Grace*. It is showing character and compassion when you are being attacked or threatened, rising above or transcending the conflict, and acting from a centered, compassionate place.

Graciousness is a behavior that accompanies mindfulness. I am using the term *grace* to refer to your beneficence, goodwill, kindness, and compassion. Using mindfulness to analyze a situations, being mindful in the present-moment with neutrality, interest, and caring, results in gracious behavior. This requires a change in consciousness. It is a transcendent way of being in the world. It requires moving out of a dualistic style of being in the world, from a Me or I-style of relating into a We-style of relating.

You have to move out of the duality of right/wrong, victim/persecutor perspective and into a transcendent consciousness of compassion and mindfulness, a sense of oneness; taking action to promote peace and grace rather than proving you are right, or punishing another for their mistakes, shortcomings, or perspective.

True dialogue can only occur when people are interacting from this perspective. Dialogue is a negotiation and discussion where there is give-and-take through an attempt to understand each other. Stephen Covey's book *The 7 Habits of Highly Successful People* (1990) prescribes a specific style of interaction for real negotiation to take place. Each party must take the position to *Seek First to Understand*. This means you must use a mindful approach to understanding, not a litigator or debater approach wherein you are looking for the flaws in the position, but rather a mindful approach where you attempt *first* to understand whence the person is coming and then offer your own perspective; clarifying the position of the other fully before identifying what your own position is. This behavior allows for a paradigm shift through mindfulness so that a true negotiation and dialogue can follow, where each attempts to resolve the situation or conflict to meet the needs of *both* people. Covey calls this a *win-win*. The action of *Seek First to Understand* leads to neutral openness, mindfulness, and paradigm shifting; it is graciousness in action.

Conflicts in relationship derive out of two personal perspectives or paradigms that are in conflict with each other. Both parties are right from their respective perspectives. The conflict arises through the restrictive perspectives. The act of moving through paradigm recognition, shifting and integration is required for negotiation; this removes the restrictions and opens up the space for open dialogue. To get to this space of dialogue and negotiation graciousness, seeking first to understand, and desiring a win-win is needed.

The block to win-win in relationship or dialogue stems from searching for a winner or victor rather than seeking understanding. Each party sees from his or her own limited perspective, unable to negotiate beyond that view because they cannot hear or see each other's distinct perspective. When this continues over a period of time, each party digging in of his or her heels, each requiring the other to acquiesce, a stalemate ensues. The conflict becomes solidified as each marshals forces to prove the rightness of his or her position rather than moving to understand the position of the other. If you have experienced this, you know how this happens, and you can remember how difficult it is to extricate yourself from such a conflict. The key is stepping back, the *stop, look, and listen* technique; using mindfulness or querying your partner about what he means seeking to understand. You get to what matters, when you understand the other person's point of view. This offers the space for *win-win*. The win-win process is veiled by the emotion of proving the rightness of a perspective, a dualistic tendency. Me and I-styles of relationship get stuck in this dualistic arguing. All the insecurity principles that focus on limited resources and dualistic worldviews also get stuck in proving right/wrong. Stress magnifies the reactive quality involved in fear, dualistic, and insecurity based paradigms and increases the difficulties in focusing mindfully and acting with proactive, compassionate behavior.

Graciousness as an action creates an inner concentration that allows for you to rise above or transcend that push/pull to conflict and be mindful, compassionate, and understanding.

Wait to speak; listen with neutral interest; seek to understand; breathe; these actions create an inner openness and strength to choose graciousness action in conflict. Being right in relationship is often less important and less constructive than connecting and understanding; unless what you are sorting through is a basic incompatibility in the partnership, then the rightness can be seen less dualistically right/wrong, and more from a perspective of *right relationship* for you, something that is not in sync with your best interests from an integrated spiritual, mindful point of view.

Set your attention and intention on connection and understanding. Graciousness is healing and instructive, especially under stress; in relationship and team-building focusing on a We-style of relationship is optimal.

FIGURE 10, SEEKING UNDERSTANDING, SHIFTING PARADIGMS, FINDING AGREEMENT

BELIEF SYSTEMS AFFECT YOUR RELATIONSHIP STYLE AND YOUR SENSE OF SECURITY

As described in the earlier chapter *Quick Review of Sociology and Relationship* and *What matters* at the beginning of the book, you have your own personal sociology and personal primary guiding values that direct your beliefs and behaviors. Understanding how your history and biography together define your relationship style and what matters to you in your hierarchy of needs in partnering and relationship can give you helpful insight into your relationship style. MAAPS and the five security principles delineate the relationship between your core insecurity driver, your belief systems, and your specific kind of Me, I, or We-style of relating. Your temperament plays a role in how you choose to relate, however your belief systems are the primary foundation for which of the security principles drives your style of relationship.

Social development evolves through stages. Your experiences and your primary agents of socialization (family of origin, heritage/culture, ethnic/racial status, social class status, spiritual/religious group, gender status) and social group connections define what is the right behavior for you. These agents of socialization give you your biography, teach you what is valued, and lay the foundation for your belief systems. Your location in time (ie: the milieu in 1950 or 2010) informs you about what is acceptable behavior, how to develop socially, what to believe, how to think about your environment, how to behave and act in the world, how to work through problems, how to partner, and what roles to play. For example, if you were raised in the 1950s, your view of the world would be different than if you were raised in the 1990s. So the location in time affects how you develop through these psychosocial stages. Your experiences, biography, and history together, affect who you are and how you act. Understanding your group connections and socialization helps you to change habits that are inefficient and ineffective in partnering and are not inherent but rather part of an ideology or group-think that you have introjected (taken into your thinking as a belief whole, without mindfully considering) from your primary groups.

If, you were raised in a family where there was strife around money then, you might be driven by the money security principle. Or if you had an early abandonment, you might be driven by the attachment security principle because you are stuck in that early trauma. Or you may be driven by the achievement security principle through a connection to a primary group that valued achievement. You can review each of your primary socialization groups for the underlying ideologies and how they interface with each other to create your inner belief system network. Although these feel hardwired, in reality they are not. They are modeled and learned, introjections of social structure based on what you observed, experienced, heard, saw, and did as a young person going through the psychosocial stages of development.

Think of it this way. You have to manage your temperament style; it is an integral aspect to your personality. Temperament can be fine-tuned and modified but it is in a sense hardwired. The aspects of how you see the world, your belief system, and what you perceive as the rules of social engagement that come from your socialization are *habits*. These are completely malleable and changeable, so that once you understand the history and foundation behind these various beliefs you can choose to let go of the unproductive habits, paradigm shift, uplevel, and socially develop into an interdependent We-style of relating that is at a higher level of consciousness.

So, when you defined the following words earlier in the book, you were getting a clue to what belief systems were running your life. Now you can use the next few chapters to determine whether you are daytime-sleepwalking or using your mindfulness to approach relationships.

You can shift your beliefs by inverting them, by looking at what underlies the belief, and then make a conscious decision about what or how you want to change in your relationship style. Jot down a few notes about these following words again and see if things have changed since you began reading the book; get a sense of what your foundational beliefs are about relationship, partnership, and any core insecurities.

Partner
_____

Lover
_____

Spouse
_____

Breadwinner
_____

Homemaker
_____

Strength
_____

Powerful woman
_____

Powerful man
_____

Empowerment
_____

Security _____

Happiness _____

Success _____

Good person _____

Reasonable _____

Remember to pay attention to what makes you feel fearful, insecure, weak, isolated, joyful, powerful, confident, strong, and connected. These feelings are cues to what matters to you in developing social relationships and partnerships. Remember what matters to you is connected to where you are on your hierarchy of needs, and your belief system. You can discern what matters to you or your partner through your actions. Actions align your best interests according to your core belief systems. So, when a person says *I don't want to do this* yet acts in a way that is incongruent with his speech remember, you will discover the truth of what matters through the person's actions. Knowing yourself is a function of knowing what matters; when you increase your inner self-knowing, you can always act in a way that is empowering for yourself. When your or another's actions do not agree with, or are incongruent with, what you or another says matters then you want to *trust the actions as the actual thing that matters*, rather than trusting the words.

You stay in relationships that do not serve you by *trusting words over actions*. When you do this, your *relationships are serving what matters in your belief systems* but are not truly supporting your authentic, whole, congruent self.

To increase your self-awareness look at figure and ground, stay present in the moment, pay attention to your sensory cues (what bothers you, causes feelings that something is off, or feelings of anger, hurt, and fear), and be willing to let go of habit reaction patterns and survivor scenarios. Be flexible about how you incorporate your belief systems into your behavior. It requires a vigilant eye to maintaining an internal consistency in actions, words, and beliefs.

Listen for inconsistencies to discover if you are out of sync. When you find yourself saying that you are doing something that you don't want to do, then either your beliefs or your behavior are not in sync. The best response is to stop doing it; if you feel you can't stop doing it then delve deeper to find what is actually driving that situation so that you can act and speak in a congruent manner. Knowing what matters to you and acting from that space allows for self-confidence and increases your capacity for success toward your goals. Knowing what matters to your partner equally creates success toward your established goals or clarifies that the relationship is not worth pursuing. Getting out of a stuck situation takes a lot of energy, but once you are living in a congruent fashion you will have more energy available to you to live fully and to partner in a mutually fulfilling fashion.

TURNING OVER A NEW LEAF – INVERTING A BELIEF

The intentional act of looking at something from a different perspective can result in a feeling of transformation and illumination. A powerful way to shift your perspective is to turn something upside down → invert it. That 180-degree difference is even more dramatic than broadening and narrowing your vision as you do in figure-ground perspective shifting. When you want to look at your beliefs and see if you are operating from a misbelief, then this inversion concept is key.

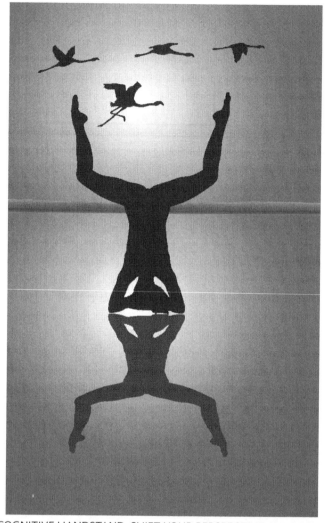

A COGNITIVE HANDSTAND, SHIFT YOUR PERSPECTIVE 180-DEGREES

Turning over a belief requires a voluntary consciousness plus a willingness to see anew or rather through new eyes. You are shifting your perspective to change the lens of your internal vision in the same way you zoom in or out on a subject with a camera, focusing and refocusing, but you are also looking at what is underneath the belief. This deconstruction of the belief assists you in determining which aspects of the belief are helpful and consistent with your true inner self, and which may be limiting you in your relationships and growth.

In Gestalt therapy, turning over a belief is used to see what is under the belief, the etiology of the belief and how it is driving your actions and cognitions, especially in relation to anxiety. Fritz Perls had many techniques to get underneath a belief and to move you to your core self. One technique was to exaggerate a small discharge behavior like tapping your foot; he would have you really kick it up and down to see what came up, in order to get you to access your feelings. Albert Ellis talked about beliefs as ways to direct behavior and avoid unwanted consequences. This is very useful in getting to the thinking equations that drive behavior. These techniques were mindfulness tools to increase your understanding of your introjected beliefs and your authentic self. Increasing your awareness reveals what underlies your beliefs and the function of the belief in your world-view. You can determine if the belief still fits into your overall core value system or if you need a more functional belief once you have developed your self-awareness.

Beliefs are the things that guide you. They are based on your core values. Some beliefs are a misconnection of core value and action. Similar to the survivor scenarios or habit reaction patterns, the core value and action are tied together in a thinking→action = equation. These beliefs need to be investigated and understood at a deeper level. To determine if you are acting from a belief that doesn't serve the purpose you think it does, pay attention to your feelings. To identify which beliefs may be not serving you, look at how you feel in certain circumstances. Notice when you feel anxious or a sense of urgency that seems out of proportion to the situation, this dissonance is a clue. It indicates you have a belief that is driving the situation. Many beliefs keep you tied to others in an energy draining way; these are usually tied to a core insecurity; you are driven to act in a specific fashion to maintain the connection, but it diminishes your core self. The actions you take to maintain that habit can be automatic and unconscious and are tied to past circumstances rather than present-moment circumstances.

You must change the world within to change the world without.

The action of making a change for the better, of *turning over a new leaf*, requires the mindful action of reviewing and turning over the belief that is at the center of your situation. This is a cognitive inversion. Once you understand the etiology of the belief you can then reset how it drives your behavior. You can reform the belief, align with it, or shift the way in which you interpret the belief to create more of what you want in your relationships. Your actions and thoughts are linked; together they define how you see the world and how you act in the world. Using the action of inversion gives you a different understanding of how the belief colors or biases your doing, saying, and seeing; this clarification allows you to shift your words, actions, and beliefs into alignment.

- Look to the underlying beliefs that guide your behavior.
- Listen to what you report as fact determine if some of that *fact* is ideology.
- Notice your assumptions – this is when you connect threads that are not actually connected; this may be the result of a belief system.

A simple technique to turn over a belief is to get two pieces of paper and cut these into the shape of two large leaves.

- On the front of the first leaf write the feelings that are bothering you and the habits you feel are destructive or not healthy that you want to change.
- Then turn over that first leaf and write what beliefs drive those habits. These will be deep inner feelings about yourself and your style in relationship. Issues of lovability, survival, fear, and loss are strong motivators for actions.
- On the front of the second leaf – the new leaf – write down changed actions, describe how you want to act in the world.
- Then turn over the second leaf and write down the opposite belief of the information you wrote on the back of the first leaf (so if you had written *I am unlovable* then here you would write *I am lovable*).
- The simple action of righting the belief will not only give you greater strength to change your behavior but is actually the first step in changing.
- With this task, you have created a path to change. Turn over a new leaf and begin to live in a way that is more in line with your core self.
- To further solidify this path, you can write down a set of actions you are going to take to realign your actions with your true beliefs.

Effective change happens when beliefs and actions are in balance. It is an act of mindfulness, with a focus on congruency and balance.

APPLY THE METAPHOR OF SPRING CLEANING TO GET RID OF MISBELIEFS

Just as you can accumulate clothes and items that are no longer useful, you can accumulate ideologies and beliefs that clog your thinking and growth. This stagnates the smooth flow in relationships too. When you clear out the cognitions that are worn out or no longer useful you realign your words, actions, and values. This allows beliefs that no longer fit to be discarded and replaced with more authentic beliefs.

This process is similar to spring cleaning with your clothes. You see that a suit or dress doesn't fit, maybe your shape has changed or the item is out of style, in each case the clothes and you don't match. This is a metaphor for how certain beliefs or paradigms can become out of date or a mismatch to your core self. You may find an outfit that doesn't work in its current shape or style but with altering can remain in your wardrobe; beliefs can be like this, too. The whole belief may be off in some way but with altering and a makeover it may be just right. Think of this as a metaphor as a guide for evaluating which aspects of your beliefs are a good fit and congruent with your authentic self and which need to be discarded or altered (unlinked, separating out the part of the equation or the belief that doesn't serve you).

If you are stuck in a Me or I-style of relating using this metaphor to sift through your beliefs can help you discover what is driving that style of relating and give you an opportunity to shift it into a We-style of interaction in relationship.

To apply this metaphor consider what pattern in your life repeats itself in a way that is discouraging or bothersome. Once you have identified that look at what belief underlies that pattern. For example, if the pattern is that you seem to always be a giver in relationship but not a receiver, look at what *your* belief might be to promote that (not the other person's belief). You are evaluating your belief because you are the constant in the pattern, so in some way you are contributing to always being the giver and not the receiver. You have the power to change yourself. Sticking to the metaphor of spring cleaning with your thinking, look within to see how the belief matches your authentic self. This introspective action will result in more happiness and less conflict. Beliefs that fit, like clothes, accentuate your best aspects and diminish your limitations. Making adjustments helps to create seamlessness in how you move through life.

In the above example you could find that you have a core belief of feeling like you are not enough, that you have to give to others to be loved; you have linked together the requirement to give and be loved so that receiving makes you unlovable. This could have developed from an early childhood incident that gave you this impression; look to your early memories and beliefs you have about your early life with your primary caregivers or significant others. Without blaming that caregiver or other, or getting stuck in that old memory, try to view the event from a more objective, compassionate perspective both toward yourself and the other person. You can use the idea of inverting the belief to see if you can get a 360-degree view of what was happening at the time for both you and the other person.

From this bigger perspective, see how you can unlink that belief and your behavior; look for what doesn't fit, and see how the belief works once you discard the untrue or habitual pattern that is misbelief.

- Start with an affirmation, that is the opposite of the misbelief, like for the example above, *I am lovable.*
- Then identify proof of that affirmation by looking at your experiences and your behavior from a neutral present-moment

perspective; investigate what the words mean to you and how they may be linked to an historical negative experience that created a habitual reaction pattern or survivor scenario.

- If you can only identify proof of the feeling that you are unlovable, go deeper and apply more compassion toward your being.
- Ask for some proof from people you love and trust about your lovableness; document it.
- Keep written information that you can go back to for reference and redirection so that you can begin to incorporate your changed belief.
- Keep working with this until you can feel an inner peace or sense of grace regarding the earlier situation, your present day relationships, and your self-identification.
- Organization experts suggest when you are going through items to determine what to keep and what to release you make four bundles: items that have meaning and fit in your life in the first bundle, give away in the second, throw away in the third, and items that need altering or fixing that you want to keep in the fourth. So, think of this in reference to your beliefs: the middle two are discard as a whole, and the first and last help to clarify your inner beliefs with your stance in the world.
- This work results in a new you from the inside out. You feel differently about yourself and others and you act differently in relationship.

The result of this kind of action and focus is feeling competent and content with your self. It creates a strong inner core that is evident throughout your interactions and relationships.

Think of how you feel when you wear an outfit that fits perfectly and is in style; that is the same feeling as living inside the paradigms that best fits you, too. This is a powerful process. It can result in amazing growth. Have fun with it and be kind toward yourself. Keep the spring cleaning metaphor in mind.

Sometimes you know something doesn't fit but you want to hold onto it for some other reason. That can happen with beliefs too; be gentle with yourself. It will work out perfectly over time as you apply the different steps above to your process.

Sometimes clearing out the space physically performs the function of creating an internal space for change. Other actions that can help create that internal space are mindful meditation, yoga, focused breathing, prayer, writing about the issue, and active listening, to both others and yourself. The latter is a modality you can use all the time in relationship and interaction. Listening to the non-verbal components in conversation, the tone, and the language or word-choice all offer ways for you to increase your understanding in communication. Through these techniques you can see or hear where you are out of sync with reality or how you are acting or thinking based on an inaccurate belief system.

The most difficult space to create is the space within to change thinking and behavior patterns. Changing habits requires identification of the problem as a first step. The space creation to change is like a stretching out so that you can observe from a different perspective. Identifying you need to do some spring cleaning and create inner space for change can come from a comment from a partner or from a nagging negative feeling within you. This can be an enlightening experience or it can be insidious, a slow developing awareness over time.

Creating that inner space starts with the questions,

- *What is at the center of this thinking or behavior?*
- *What is the underlying belief or value that drives it?*
- And then once discerning the answers, defining if that value or belief is consistent with what you actually believe and value.
- This requires a slowing of actions and a reworking of your perceptions.
- Allow for an increase in awareness and delay action to allow for reworking your thinking with a renewed perspective.

Recently, I was struck by an internal belief that I had been using to organize my behavior and thinking. It was not actually an accurate description of reality, but rather a picture of a misunderstanding from my early childhood. It had been frozen in time and since I had not incorporated new information or critical analysis as I grew, it became a stuck and rigid insecurity-based belief that drove me to act from a position that I must prove my worth and my intelligence in order to be liked or in order to be in relationship (attachment, achievement insecurities). It was as if I had to bring something extra to a relationship because just being myself was insufficient for friendship (Me-style). This was the opposite of what I taught my children and patients, and yet here I was acting from this inaccurate perspective. This was an astonishing revelation! It was powerful and a bit disconcerting to discover. Seeing it, recognizing it, and understanding its etiology allowed me to apply a little spring cleaning to create the internal space to let it go. Immediately, I felt a shift in my perspective to incorporate the whole of my life experiences, not just that one event that birthed my earlier inaccurate perception. As I incorporated my new belief I felt lighter and more solid, stronger and more flexible. My awareness of this issue, first allowed me to change my thinking followed by my behavior.

Mindful reflection and paradigm shifting create internal space so that change can happen. Using methods of reflection, yoga, deep breathing, clarification, mindful investigation, and journaling open a space for you to view and review your internal systems and create a space for internal change. Develop a habit of practicing these mind and heart opening practices. This will increase your recognition of, and freedom from, a restrictive belief system that is not an actual representation of reality. As you observe problems in how you are behaving in relationship you can realign with your core self and open a space to shift from a Me or an I-style of relationship into a We-style of relationship.

DAYTIME SLEEPWALKING THROUGH YOUR LIFE, WAKE UP!

Sleepwalking is an activity where an individual in the middle of the night, gets up, walks around, speaks, even interacts while seemingly awake but is actually asleep. It is a strange experience for both the sleepwalker and the observer. Incidents of sleepwalking described by the observer tend to be unavailable in the memory or wakeful experience of the sleepwalker. It's a bit scary but for the most part harmless. It is understood that the sleepwalking individual is in a "hypnotic-like" state. If fully awakened he will be surprised by his circumstance and deny the activities ascribed to him, as he has no memory of them.

The unconscious, security driven, habit reaction is an automatic and without conscious attention behavior that is quite similar to sleepwalking. You are pulled along by a habitual system and a lack of questioning acceptance; it is as if you are in a hypnotic state. When caught in this unconscious, insecurity driven, habit reaction it is as if you are sleepwalking through your life. In this way you are not wholly conscious of your behaviors, the effect of your behaviors and actions, or the foundation of your habitual reactions. When you are questioned by another regarding your behavior, you respond similarly to the sleepwalking person in the middle of the night, denying your consciousness of your actions, behaviors or the consequences therein. This can result in a break down in relationship and partnerships. Without an awake, aware consciousness of what drives your behavior, you can act in a sideways, unhelpful, and irresponsible fashion (irresponsible in that you are unaware of what your responsibility is for the situation). In order to awake from this daytime sleepwalking state, you need to increase your awareness and attention to all situations in a mindful, present-moment fashion. You cannot change your behavior until you are conscious of it. First, you need to develop an understanding of how and why you utilize your security driver in relationship; and then second, what it's etiology is; and third, institute a shift so that you can consciously choose to act in a way that best meets your healthful, mindful, balanced inner self.

To consider how you may not be fully conscious of your actions, and what you may need to do to wake up and fully respond in the moment to your life and situation, requires a detached perspective and a willingness to observe the whole of the situation. The best way to increase your consciousness is to notice the responses and behavior of those around you with whom you feel close, whom you trust. Notice when there is a bit of information or a snag between what you think and what you hear them saying, try to see if you can get into the present-moment to get a full picture of what they are trying to communicate. This can be both painful and enlightening.

The idea is to awake to the full experience of living responsibly and ethically.

One thing that impedes this is a group-mind. Group-mind is the experience that you need to agree with the group perspective without question or investigation. Group-mind interprets experiences to prove a paradigm of thought, a belief, but this thinking is not an objective representation of the situation or problem. Group-mind requires agreement. Mindfulness is the opposite of group-mind and allows for understanding of the group-mind perspective while perceiving all the elements in the situation; mindfulness creates a more balanced picture of the situation. Group-mind requires daytime sleepwalking. Think of the image of a zombie movie, each zombie is mindlessly walking toward his goal; this dramatic and funny image helps you get into the spirit of waking up – *you don't want to be a zombie; you want to be a dynamic, living spirit-human.*

This mindfulness in the present-moment is rejuvenating, freeing, and empowering. Holding on to past habitual reaction patterns is limiting, stagnating, and constricting. Because it is habitual it may appear easier at first, but the drain it takes on your spiritual and emotional well-being is great. This style of unconsciously sleepwalking through life can limit your prosperity, internal sense of empowerment, and success in relationships. When you eschew group-think, and you wake-up from your unconscious, insecurity driven, habit reactions you have more energy to proactively create what you want in what I call the triple play of your life: your career, family and personal development. When you are acting from a conscious, mindful perspective your spiritual and emotional well-being is lifted up. Use the *MAAPS, Survivor Scenarios,* and *Paradigm Shifting* chapters to assist you in waking up from your unconscious patterning to make a conscious choice about how you want to move through life and interact in your relationships.

YOU IN THE DRIVER'S SEAT OF YOUR LIFE
One way misbeliefs can drive your behavior is when you have lost sight of your life-purpose or meaning. This happens insidiously. It is a function of how you mediate between your inner wants and needs and the outer expectations of society. As you attach to important groups you interpret the group expectation as paramount for you to be accepted. This can pull you away from your authentic center, so that the choices you make about how to act, what to study, how to interact in relationship, even what will bring you happiness is colored by these connections. When this set of choices causes you to disregard your authentic self, you move into a passive position →into the passenger seat of your life.

As a child you were free to focus your playtime toward what was attractive and fun. As you developed, you were drawn to specific structured activities where you exhibited talents or skills. In school you further developed those talents and skills. This process guided you in choosing which career you found interesting or supportive to your personality style. Your experiences built on each other to get you where you are today. If, you had successful resolution to each stage, and what guided you was from an internal connection to your authentic self then, you will say that you life's work is following your bliss. Yet, this process gets interrupted when things happen in your life to take you off this course of development and put you onto a path that takes you away from your center and creates a survivor scenario. This can be a result of injury, it can be a result of a mis-match between you and your caregivers, or it can be a result of an influential outside group. When your experiences shift you away from including actions and behaviors that are joy-driven, you develop a core insecurity driver in relationship to assist you in feeling safe and to deal with survival issues. Happiness is set aside in favor of safety and security. This anchors back to Maslow's Hierarchy of Needs Pyramid and the safety and security stages at the base of the triangle. You stop being the driver of your own vehicle from an interior centered, integrated space and the structure, expectation, or needs of others starts to move into the driver's seat. Instead of your skills and talents guiding you to the perfect bliss-filled job, other people's expectations, the group-mind, societal propaganda, and others' desires push you onto another path not guided from your internal centered self. You feel out of control to change this process. This leads to a lack of satisfaction in your life, to depression, disillusionment, and a lack of motivation. Since you are not connecting to life through a truly centered inner self, you feel the disconnection, you feel flat, disoriented, or lost. Your own life feels uninteresting; it provides no pleasure because it isn't derived from an inner state of joy. This disconnection from yourself, can look and feel like daytime sleepwalking; you are disconnected from your behavior, actions, and goals. You feel powerless, as if someone else is in the driver's seat of your life and you are simply along for the ride.

Finding yourself in the passenger seat in your life happens overtime. It's a subtle pernicious shift of energy; giving away your power to managing outside expectations over inner needs. To shift back into the driver's seat of your life focus on fun, joy, or bliss. Bring back a sense of internal meaning and passion into the equation. This seems like a simple suggestion, even obvious but it is harder than you think. It is because you are habituated to your routine, perhaps you feel cornered into your job or career choice. You suffer the unhappiness and boredom because you do not feel you have the capacity to change your situation. This is something you can see in others more easily first, because you have created a blindspot to your own situation. Usually though you can feel the dissatisfaction, depression, or lack of meaning in our life. Sometimes, it is just that you do not understand how to get back into the driver's seat of your life. Change, even change for joy and fun, can be deeply resisted.

The best way to move over into the driver's seat from the back seat or passenger seat of your life is to start by simply observing when you feel good and when you do not. Don't take any action at first. Just notice and document what you are noticing. The following examples help you to define where you are in guiding your own life. Read these and think about how you may be acting in this way, then consider how to shift into the driver's seat.

- Do you wait for others' goals to be presented and then fit your needs into their goals? If so, you're in the **back seat**.
- Do you observe a problem secretly or privately solve it for the other person before identifying it to them, while simultaneously doing your required work? If so, you're in the **passenger's seat**.
- Do you not take the lead even when it is offered? For example, "Where do you want to go to dinner?" "Oh, I don't care; wherever you choose is fine." If so, you moved yourself from the driver's seat into the **back seat**.
- Do you plan for and even push for your desired goals? If so, you're in the **driver's seat**.

The awareness from this exercise may cause you to feel stuck or panicked because you have an inner insecurity that is keeping you caught in the passenger or back seat of your life. You can review the MAAPS section to work with your insecurity driver.

Notice how you go about your days, your interactions with others at work and in your personal life. Are you consistently putting yourself into the back seat of your life, even removing yourself from the driver's seat? If so, you may want to consider what is driving that habit within you so that you can choose to move into the driver's seat of your life. Remember to notice and document first, then once you have enough information you may be able to re-choose what action you want to take in a given situation.

If your change is going to upset another's expectation of you, then you may want to let her know about your plans for change first, and to involve her in the process. This is especially true in your relationships and partnerships. These are interactive systems, so when you change the system changes. Although this is good in the long run, it can be scary for your partner, so keep him involved as you shift.

This is an enlightening process both in how it can open your eyes to your actions (bring light to the picture) as well as free you of some burdens (lighten your load). Being in the driver's seat of your life has its own responsibilities, but what it allows you is the opportunity to connect with your authentic self and live the life you want. This is a foundational component of moving from Me or I-style of relating to a We-style of relating. Insecurity drives the Me and I-styles of relationship; confidence drives the We-style of relationship.

INNER GUIDANCE: INTEGRATING SPIRIT & MIND

You can access a network of your internal guidance system, intuition, sense awareness, and beliefs that directly connect you to your authentic self. When you listen to cues from your internal sensory guidance system you create a direct line of communication to your authentic self. This directs you to act in ways that are in your best interest. It is like your personal GPS system that guides you to take the best path in life for health promotion, happiness, and prosperity. When you are driven by a core insecurity your capacity for assessing risk is diminished, because you are assessing danger through the feedback loop of the security driver. When you are being guided by your personal internal guidance system you are responding directly to the interaction of your being and the environment; this results in an amplified capacity to identify, assess, and respond effectively to risk. Your inner guidance increases you strength, security, and empowerment.

Your internal guidance system is an internal network that integrates your spirit, mind, and body responses through your 6 senses; the five senses of sight, touch, sound, taste, smell, and your sixth sense intuition. These are personal and wholly connect you and source energy; this is the place of spirit within your body. Because this is a personal system there is no need to learn someone else's language. The subtle sensory cues from within yourself meaningfully guide you to act in your best interests. Just listen to what you hear, feel, know from within yourself. You can be directed to avoid negative situations through an inner cue that something is off, and guided to move forward in a positive direction when your inner cues indicate you are on the right path.

TRUTH WITHIN: RIGHT RELATIONSHIP

"No meaning that comes from outside of ourselves is real. The Buddhahood of each of us has already been obtained. We need only recognize it – Thus the Zen Master warns his disciple: - If you meet the Buddha on the Road, Kill him!" (Kopp, 1976).

For Sheldon Kopp in his book, *If you meet the Buddha on the Road, Kill him!*(1976) the Buddhahood is enlightenment, the sense of living in alignment with spirit through the eight petals of proper living: *right understanding, right attitude (thought, emotion), right speech, right action, right labor or livelihood, right relationship(effort, vitality), right mindfulness,), right consciousness;* embracing your connection to spirit so wholeheartedly that you are able to walk the your authentic *right path*. Kopp was entreating his readers to look within for their truth rather than looking outside. This comes from his understanding of the Eight-Fold path from Buddha's Fourth Noble truth, in his teachings of awakening to your authentic self connected to spirit. The most effective and personal guidance is within.

Over the years a number of programs designed to assist you in becoming more successful and happy have popped up. This includes an interest in yoga and meditation as a means for spirituality and stress reduction. These can be useful when you focus the teachings to align with your inner guidance. The focal point to discern your true path remains within. The promise of becoming more successful and happy is hollow when the center of the program is without a direct connection to your personal, spiritual center. Any program that assists you in becoming more in touch with source connection and your heart-centered guidance is a profound gift.

Some of these programs have a quality of indoctrination. Indoctrination is the opposite of reaching a deeper connection within. If you use your inner sensory system and listen to your internal responses then you will know if you are being led away from, or into, your center. Indoctrination leads you away from your center and creates a layer between you and yourself.

Truth doesn't belong to the guru or the giver of it – truth is. It is available to anyone who seeks it. If you have to learn someone else's language to speak to yourself, you may be creating a connection that is not direct and there can be a skewing in the information you receive. There is already a clear and direct communication available to you within. Truth is present within you through your integrated spirit/mind/body sensory guidance system; through this heart-led system your connection to source is direct.

To find the truth of your path, go within and reacquaint yourself with your heart, your spirit-self communication. Prayer, meditation, breathwork, yoga, personal journaling, dreamwork, therapy, or any other method that is attractive to you can provide a pathway for you to develop a deeper understanding of your inner truth. The language of your truth is personal, idiosyncratic, and unique. As you pay attention to your internal sensory guidance system you develop a deeper understanding of what matters to you and aligns you in your life. You may discover that you have some habits that cover over your personal truth, some belief systems or interpretations of truth that may need to be broken through and rearranged. As you shift through these patterns you get a clarified perspective of your inner truth. Use the chapters on *Survivor Scenarios*, *MAAPS*, and *Belief Systems* to identify and breakthrough these barriers. Use the tools in those chapters to go under the habit reaction patterns you developed from your life experiences that contain the "should" and "should not" introjects (ideas and beliefs swallowed whole by you from your primary socialization groups) that do not serve your inner truth. These are elements of indoctrination. You can assess whether they are truth or indoctrination by attending to whether you feel clarity or dissonance within you. That is what you pay attention to, the light strange, odd, funny feeling that something is off; that is the aspect of knowing deep within.

Truth is something that rings clear, like a song on key, throughout your senses. Listen, feel, attend to the subtle internal cues as you move through your life and all is reveled in your own heart-centered language.

REBALANCING: EMPATHY, EGO, AND SPIRIT

The word ego has a number of paradigmatic meanings. These various meanings create confusion about how to use your mind or psyche to assist in rebalancing your thinking and actions. Buddhist writing, alternative healers, and spiritual guides use the word ego to name the bundle of power-control driven aspects of human behavior. This separates out the ego aspect of the tripartite mind (id, ego, and superego) (Freud, The Ego and the Id, 1923) and *incorrectly attributes the power-control issues of the mind in humans* to the ego. (Although some of the core insecurity drivers are from the ego-defense mechanisms, for the most part the role of the ego is to balance not to seek power and control – these aspects belong more to the id and superego aspect of the mind.) This paradigmatic misrepresentation dissociates the core role of ego in self-development from mediator and redefines the role as egotistical (I-style relating that focuses on competition and avoids empathy) and narcissistic (Me-style relating which focuses on narcissistic needs, without empathy).

The role of ego mediates between your personal wants disconnected from society (*id*: me, my wants, needs; I, power) and your belief systems swallowed whole from society (*superego*: should, should nots)(Freud, 1923). The role of your ego mediates between individual wants or needs and the needs or wants of the group. From this perspective, ego is a neutral, helpful aspect of your personality. It is the part of you that can be objective, empathic, compassionate, and mindful. Your ego aspect has the capacity to see self and other on the same plane.

The bundle of power-control driven aspects of human behavior referenced by religious and alternative traditions as *ego* are actually *id* and *superego* aspects of the tripartite structure of psyche. The Me and I-style relationship styles utilize these worldviews and it is these styles that you need to rebalance with your ego mediation to shift into an empathic style of negotiation and We-style of relating. In reviewing your core insecurity drivers you may find that you or your partner are dealing with aspects of narcissism or egotism. Developing empathy and working with using a neutral, balanced approach to neutralizing your core insecurity driver helps you move from narcissism and competition (Me, I) to collaboration and connection (We).

Engaging your conscious ego to evaluate and mediate mindfully the whole of your situation will help you rebalance. The connecting issue here is empathy. The conscious ego aspect of your mind is the aspect of your psyche that has the capacity for empathy. Without a strong conscious ego your style of being in the world becomes imbalanced, too much unmediated id or superego and you develop narcissistic and egotistic behavior.

Narcissism is a truncated me-focused style of being in the world, a skew in personality away from mindfulness, neutrality and objectivity. Narcissism is problematic in relationship because individuals who are narcissistic focus solely on self needs and wants, can be petulant, intolerant of negotiation, manipulative, and have no capacity for empathy. A narcissist is in a continual Me-style of relationship, and has difficulty taking responsibility for how his actions negatively affect another. Partners of narcissists will feel unseen, unheard, and invisible; they will feel as if their own needs are unimportant.

Egotism is an inflated I-focused style of being in the world, a skew in personality away from mindfulness, objectivity, and neutrality. Egotism is problematic in relationship because individuals who are egotistic refuse to utilize empathy, place self needs and wants above anything and anyone else, and can be overpowering, forceful, intolerant of negotiation, competitive, and manipulative. An egotist is in a continual I-style of relationship, and has difficulty taking responsibility for how her actions negatively affect another. Partners of egotists will feel inferior, unseen, unheard, invisible, and attacked and will feel as if their partners do not care about them.

Empathy is paradigm shifting→putting yourself in another's position and understanding that other's perspective. Mindfulness and compassion require empathy. Lack of empathy disconnects you from society and others both personally and globally. Narcissism and egotism instigate you to take actions without regard for how you may hurt another and focuses your actions on self, alone, without a connection to society as a whole or your relationship partner. To interact in an integrated spirit, mind, and body you have to have your mind be informed through your heart-center, (spirit) which is to say through your personal sensory guidance system. This centering creates the space for empathy and paradigm shifting. It is through the ego aspect of your mind that you can access the guiding quality of spirit, because it is the conscious ego that can incorporate empathy in decision-making and action taking.

Groups that teach you their language and then have you act by that set of symbols and beliefs are having you work with your mind disengaged from your integrated spirit and body. This can include referencing your ego from this egotistical or narcissistic perspective. When you feel or notice this is happening, translate their language back into your own sense of self, and integrated spirit, mind, body sensory guidance system. Trust your internal sensory guidance system.

A guiding principle for empathic action is the golden rule, *do unto others what you have done unto you*, or the silver rule, *do not do unto others what you would not have done unto you*. Both incorporate ego in this mediating way: mind informed by spirit, integrated into action, in balance. Both require an attitude of empathic lovingkindness to guide your action. The second directive seems easier to apply, to know what you do not want done to you and then apply it. The set of everything you want is idiosyncratic and unwieldy. The negative rule, *do not do unto others...* creates safe, healthy boundaries in relationship. Guidance from without must be filtered through your inner guidance to experience its truth. You have an integrated knowing when something is not truth. Something doesn't ring true, look right, feel right. There is a catch in the information or a blip or bump. If you are paying attention you know it. The tricky part is paying attention.

If you are simply on automatic and going through life as a passive receiver, you may miss the information present in every interaction, in each dream, and story, and connection you make or have. This includes how you react to the story of your politics, your family, your ethnic group, your partner, and your peers, the stereotypes you allow to guide you rather than the personal information you feel, hear, see, and know from within.

With empathy and listening to your sensory guidance system you can move through your insecurity drivers in relationship and move through the hierarchy of needs to develop a We-style of interacting in relationship that allows for both aspects of your and your partner's unique personal paths to be heeded and integrated.

LOOK WITHIN, FIGURE 12

MULTIDIMENSIONAL SIGHT: RIGHT MINDFULNESS

Paying attention to the vast information available to you through your internal guidance system is essential for mindful, comprehensive communication, and right action. This is a natural, instinctual process; it can be eroded in early childhood due to a push to conform to group rules and beliefs. When you want to recapture your connection to this internal guidance increase your awareness and practice paying attention and responding.

The words *intention*, *attention*, *perspective*, and *perception* increase your awareness and focus you onto the space in a multidimensional way. Each word embodies a specific energy or vibration that stands alone, but when the energy of each term is linked together, the whole process creates a multidimensional picture and style of interacting mindfully in relationship.

You can feel into the meaning of each of these terms for yourself. An image of the vibration of the word interacting like an equation with the other words gives the internal image dimension through color or shape as an imprint. It is a moving picture of how you experience the words interacting. This will allow you to create your own understanding of how to focus yourself in relationship. The interactions between and among the vibrations are as important as the word meanings and the whole equation.

An image of how these words intention, attention, perspective, and perception might interact give the feeling of *a spear* and *a target*, then *a circling or container* and then finally *something that shoots to a height and then grounds like an anchor*. Imagine the words in all directions and energies; not a blur of color that becomes murky but energy and color clarified, interacting and adjusting in real time, dynamic and organic.

- Intention focuses you in, on what you intend, what you want or what the other intends, wants.
- Attention focuses you on the tone, loudness, word choice, meaning, and emotion as well as whether you and the other have the same meaning for words and actions – it pulls you into the present.
- Perspective gets you into the figure/ground aspect of the interaction and allows for paradigm identification and paradigm shifting.
- Perception has aspects of the previous three. It allows for mindful understanding and mindful action. It is organic and dynamic, like looking at a situation, relationship, or problem from a 360-degree perspective, breadth as well as depth, multidimensionally.

So, when you are thinking about a situation or a relationship, start to use these words as guideposts to increase your mindful awareness of yourself and the other(s) involved. Pay attention to your internal guidance through your six senses, to see if you can get a multidimensional picture and understanding of the situation or relationship. You can use your intuitive sense, observations, questioning skills, and willingness to listen and act in a mindful present-moment way. This will have two effects: 1) increase your personal degree of compassion, and 2) decrease your personalization of the information. By personalization I mean taking something personally, with some sort of negative attachment, rather than seeing the information more objectively or mindfully.

Paying attention to the quiet voice within and clarifying your intention will increase your understanding of your inner guidance and give you direction about your best right action. It can also help you know when your best action is non-action, allowing or going with the flow, remaining in a waiting, allowing space. Being mindful opens the door to seeing in multiple dimensions and distinguishing different currents of information simultaneously, which creates a space to understand each separately and see how each affect the other. This is the required state for relating from the We-style of relationship. It is through this multidimensional equation that you remain internally powerful and able to negotiate openly to create a win-win in your relationship decision-making.

You are directed through your inner guidance when you feel like something that someone says is off; that is a message from within. Paying attention to these messages through your intuition, inner hearing, seeing, knowing, and feeling is the easiest way to rebalance and most effective way to get onto your path and create your life fortune.

If you are not doing what you want or living at your highest potential, go within and reconnect through your internal guidance system with yourself. You can use any integrated spirit, mind, body action. Prayer, meditation, yoga, running, walking, dancing, writing, journaling, dreamwork, toning, and therapy are all activities that can connect you with your inner truth. The key is that whatever you use, your guide is within, not without, and the answer is personal, empathic, and loving.

When you begin to listen, pay attention to the subtle, gentle messages in the background. The angry, emotional loud messages in the foreground are fears and insecurities, habit reaction patterns. Your personal inner guidance is quiet and calm not anxious and loud, unless you are about to have a car accident, then you may hear a firm strong impression to **pay attention**. Your internal guidance has a firm yet light message or vibration: *turn here, let go, trust, believe, and ooh that doesn't feel.. sound,.. look... right.*

INNER GUIDANCE IV: INNER TRUTH INFUSION

In medicine, an IV refers to an intravenous infusion and I think that is the whole thing in a nutshell. *Infuse yourself with your own inner guidance and your cells will swell with joy, strength, and the necessary resources to create what you desire.*

Your best tools to increase your capacity for joy, strength and prosperity are the use of mindfulness, compassion, and love. You access these through your inner guidance and following your inner guidance supports you and your community.

- This is an opposite notion from *scarcity of resources,* where competition for resources is required.
- *The notion is inner guidance will increase opportunity for all.*
- The idea of taking from another to fill your pocket, keeps you in the duality that results from the concept of scarcity of resources.
- Opening to your inner guidance increases trust and faith; this reveals you are able to see how you and your community can prosper and uplevel together, not one over the other.

Here is how the notion *that inner guidance will increase opportunity for all* works:

The more you can see another person's point of view through mindfulness–> the more increased your understanding –>-> and the greater your understanding, the greater your capacity to see the other as yourself –>-> see how you are similar –>which increases your capacity for compassion and love –>->-> through this increased compassion war, conflict, and those activities that spawn from misunderstanding will diminish and an overall upleveling of consciousness and prosperity for all is increased->->the more you can see another person's point of view through mindfulness...and this upleveling process continues.

These steps connect you to your inner guidance.

- Draw your strength from within and *source* (source as spirit, god, the universe, the Tao). Envision yourself surrounded with love and light; feel gratitude and compassion toward your community.
- Listen to your inner guidance above the propaganda around you. Focus on your spiritual connection. Shift away from negativity refocus your energies on gratitude, love, and forgiveness. Smile, and 'do battle' by living in that light with spirit. Think of the battle as not against human forces but against mistruth.
- Remain steadfast in your inner truth. This can be like an armor or coat of truth of light and love; surrounding yourself with that energy helps you feel more protected. See through the lens of compassion and love.
- Believing *is* seeing. Let your heart and faith lead your seeing.
- Question the assumptions in propaganda. Listen internally. Focus on making each choice from an integrated, spiritual connection. Feel strength from your feet all the way up your spine to the crown of your head, surrounding your waist like a belt, and spilling out around your chest and heart center.
- Walk in the truth of what you know and remember to always be in gratitude and love. Consider the power of the swiftness

of truth to spread through a community. Truth spreads more quickly than propaganda; especially when you listen with your heart and sensory guidance system first, without glitches or questions.

- Through everything have faith and be faithful.
- Face your fears, acknowledge them, then stand in your faith inverting the fear.

Be educated about what is happening around you in the day-to-day earth-plane, yet act from your inner truth and inner guidance. See the way. Know live, and feel your truth. Standing in your truth while infusing yourself with inner guidance, disperses insecurity and allows for the kind of interaction that is a We-style of relationship. This focus moves you through Maslow's Needs stages, away from fear-based interactions toward joy-based interactions and transcendence.

TOWARD A UNION OF WE: SHIFTING YOUR CONSCIOUSNESS

When working with relationships one of the first necessary steps is to look at how the parties relate.

- Are they defensive and competitive?
- Do they maintain a balance sheet of exchange patterns?
- Do they spend time and energy listening to their partner's point of view?
- Do they seek understanding or are they waiting to find the flaw in the argument?

How partners relate gives you information about what is *driving* each person and the underlying foundation of the relationship. Once you have a sense of this, you can develop an integrated picture of each individual's underlying needs, exchange patterns, belief systems, paradigmatic structures, connections, and security structures.

Narcissism and competition in relationship are forms of relating that disallow interaction and interdependence. These styles of relating are part of a singular, need-focused structure. Narcissism is part of a Me-style of relating and a co-dependent relationship structure. In this structure, the parties utilize an exchange pattern and the paradigmatic structure is *you take care of me and I'll take care of you*; each exchange is noted and weighted and the parties require an equal exchange for each action of care. Need underlies the tie to each other and there is a lack of independent action or thinking. This style of relating may appear collaborative on the surface but in actuality the giving is highly conditional. The insecurity in this type of relationship is that the other completes him and so abandonment is feared; there is a high degree of separation anxiety. These partnerships require intense agreement on everything and do not respond well to independent thinking. Intensity can be the marker of intimacy rather than a sense of trust and security. From a financial perspective, one party may have all the financial responsibility and the other party may have all the emotional responsibility. The exchange is money for support. In this style of relationship, the two persons are halves to the one whole: there is no individuality, only couple.

Competition connotes an I-style of relating. It results in a pairing that is independent without interaction or interdependence. Each party is in a wholly enveloped structure. There is no dependence or co-dependence, as you might see with a Me-style structure, but there is no interdependence either. Each party stands on his or her own two feet. It is as if the two people are walking side-by-side. There is no integration or mixing of the two beings. Fairness and rigid boundaries are the characteristics of this type of relationship. There can be an exchange pattern balance sheet, but this has more to do with winners of the competition and proof of being right rather than what each brings to the partnership. The financial structure of this relationship is independent; each person pays his or her way, and if there is a need for a money exchange it is set up via a contract, similar to a loan, with some set of conditions and plan for payback. This I-style of relationship may be a marriage, yet all work done for the couple is parceled out equally, if there is an imbalance then financial compensation is doled out for duties that are maintained for the home, or the couplehood, ie: the yard work, gardening, maintenance. The emotional structure is equally self-contained. In this style of relationship the two persons are two persons: there is no sense of We-ness or group, only the two selves walking side by side. Here the insecurity centers on avoiding dependence and connection as this is seen as a way to stay free from bondage; there is a fear of engulfment.

Collaboration and connection are a third wave of partnership. In this We-style of partnership the two parties have an interdependence and integration without a loss of individual selves. The two persons maintain a sense of self and have individual beliefs and experiences, while also enjoying an integrated participation with each other. In this We-style of partnering there is space for two Is and a We: interaction incorporates a tapestry of flexibility, a weaving that results in a rich experience of collaboration, connection, and a sense of expansion. This We-style of relating offers enhancement of each party, without a loss of freedom. It is flexible, accepting, and interdependent.

Security is derived through a sense of support and connection without a loss of individuality. Conflict in this style of relating offers a way to work through issues toward a higher level of understanding and connection to each other that incorporates each person's core desires, needs, and beliefs. It is a function of negotiation rather than a compromise. Financial and emotional structures are interrelated and integrated so that both parties are flexibly participatory, flowing easily in a responsive, dynamic fashion.

Once you have found your style you can begin to shift your attention in the relationship. Embrace your fears and your insecurities and embark on a journey to move from narcissism and competition to collaboration and connection.

These styles of relating are developmental in nature: you can move through these various styles or structures by focusing your loving, attention to your own security and individual fear-based patterns, to transform them. Mindfulness is a useful focus of thinking to assist you and your partner to evaluate and transcend your personal blockages in relationships. Development of your personal sensory guidance system will be highly valuable in this process. You can use these models to determine what kind of relationship structure you are in and then use mindfulness to uplevel your style of relating. If you discover that you are in a Me-style relationship, turn your love toward yourself so that you can be the best partner to yourself first. This is a beginning step to moving from dependence to independence. If you find you are in an I-style relationship, trust yourself and your partner to risk giving and receiving in an unconditional way. Create a belief that being connected can be fulfilling rather than disheartening. This will open your heart to create a path of connection with your partner.

Mindful, loving, attention toward yourself and your partner opens the door for a conscious shift in how you relate to create a union of We.

CONSCIOUSNESS EVOLVING: I

Phenomenology, mindfulness, and paradigm shifting interface through the evolution of consciousness. Through the process of phenomenology, awareness, and mindfulness, paradigms are identified and can shift. This shifts your perspective and awareness as well as how you feel about something. As perspective shifts, your feelings about a situation shift and as your feelings shift your perspective shifts, so that each can affect the other. Consciousness shifts through this process→ your consciousness as related to your awareness. This is a multilevel event. As you become aware of your feelings, your paradigms, your values, and your actions, you have the opportunity to evolve your consciousness through a shift in your perceptions and actions. Awareness is subtle and profound. It is not simply awareness on a sensory level but also cognitively and mindfully. So when you are developing your mindfulness and applying this to your actions, thoughts, and perceptions, you are actually shifting your consciousness. You are changing your perceptual world both subjectively and objectively.

This is an evolution of consciousness that takes the form of an inner and then outer spiral. First you observe a shift, then you internalize this observation, and then instantaneously you feel an internal shift that guides your outer movements and behavior.

Consciousness refers to the interrelationship between the mind and the world with which it interacts; it is an awareness, understanding, or a sentient clarity. The origin of the modern concept of consciousness is often attributed to John Locke's *Essay Concerning Human Understanding* (Locke, 1960). Locke defined consciousness as "the perception of what passes in a man's own mind."

The literary author William James is usually credited with popularizing the idea that human consciousness flows like a stream, in his *Principles of Psychology* (1890). According to James, the "stream of thought" is governed by five characteristics:

"(1) Every thought tends to be part of a personal consciousness. (2) Within each personal consciousness thought is always changing. (3) Within each personal consciousness thought is sensibly continuous.

(4) It always appears to deal with objects independent of itself. (5) It is interested in some parts of these objects to the exclusion of others" (Principles of Psychology, 1890, William James).

A similar concept appears in Buddhist philosophy, expressed by the Sanskrit term *Citta-satāna*, which is usually translated as *mindstream* or "mental continuum." In the Buddhist view, though, the *mindstream* is viewed primarily as a source of noise that distracts attention from a changeless underlying reality. For our purposes, the *mindtream* is anything that is ongoing as in consciousness, attention, or awareness.

Stream of consciousness writing offers the experience of being within the person's perception of events, in her mind or thoughts. In psychological counseling this type of journaling allows a person to see or review how she experiences another or a situation and recognize habitual reactions that are not useful. It is a form of writing meditation that allows for a shift in perspective or an internal paradigm shift.

Phenomenology is a method of inquiry that attempts to examine the structure of consciousness in its own right, putting aside problems regarding the relationship of consciousness to the physical world. This approach was first proposed by the philosopher Edmund Husserl, and later elaborated by other philosophers and scientists. Husserl's original concept gave rise to two distinct lines of inquiry, in philosophy and psychology.

From a philosophical perspective phenomenology has largely been devoted to fundamental metaphysical questions, such as the nature of intentionality ("aboutness"). From a psychological perspective, phenomenology largely has meant attempting to investigate consciousness using the method of looking inward or introspection, looking into one's own mind and reporting what one observes. These methods of phenomenology are simply a type of mindful, meditation and are very useful in reviewing your behavior and what causes you to act in a specific way.

Introspectively, the world of conscious experience seems to have considerable structure. Immanuel Kant, a phenomenologist, asserted that the world as we perceive it is organized according to a set of fundamental "intuitions," which include object (we perceive the world as a set of distinct things); shape; quality (color, warmth, etc.); space (distance, direction, and location); and time. (This is developed more fully in the chapter on *Seeing in 4D in this book*). It is through these processes that you develop your sense of self, time, place in the world, goals, and success and failures. The idea of mindfulness then is using these processes to assist you in your own internal development to meet external goals and aspirations, which change as you focus your mindfulness, incorporate shifting paradigms, and respond to the world in the present moment.

Despite the large amount of information available, the most important aspects of perception remain mysterious. A great deal is known about low-level signal processing in sensory systems, but the ways by which sensory systems interact with each other, with "executive" systems in the frontal cortex, and with the language system are very incompletely understood. At a deeper level, there are still basic conceptual issues that remain unresolved.

Mindfulness is about working with the energy of your perspective and then shifting that perspective to see anew. It can have this universal quality wherein the individual becomes increasingly interconnected in his or her understanding of others. Through this it can lead to what the Buddhists refer to as the One. This means that what you do to others you do to yourself and that other and self are not divisible and so that 2 plus 2 equal not 4 but *One*.

The evolution of your own consciousness is about shifting not only your perspective but also how you perceive and enact your values. This is a powerful thing.

If consciousness can evolve, then this evolution can be effected through meditation and mindfulness. *Evolving consciousness: II* offers understanding about how to evolve your consciousness through perception paradigm shifting.

EVOLVING CONSCIOUSNESS: II

The concept of evolving one's consciousness in an intentional, distinct, and proactive method is what therapy offers. You can shift your spiritual consciousness to perceive the balance of spirit, mind, and body to bring about the highest degree of health, understanding, and prosperity. The multilevel shift in consciousness allows you to align your actions, behaviors, and statements to your inner and uncensored values. As you become aware of your feelings, paradigms, values, and actions, you have the opportunity to evolve your consciousness; to shift your perceptions and your actions so that in essence you are living in a completely different world. The issue of awareness is subtle and profound. It increases your awareness on a sensory and cognitive level.

Your consciousness is your awareness on a physical, wakefulness arena, as well as your multilevel understanding of time and space and the concept of dimensions. Individuals who have access to a knowing of information or events before they occur, a future-knowing, now, are living in a dimension, beyond third dimension, that includes time on a continuum → fourth, fifth or sixth dimensional awareness is another type of consciousness. This is for most part outside a normal experience of time and space which appears to occur in a linear third dimensional fashion.

Alignment means acting or speaking in an integrated fashion consistent with your spiritual, moral, and perceptual core values. So, when you are developing your application of mindfulness to your actions, cognitions, and perceptions you are actually shifting your consciousness. You are changing your perceptual world both subjectively and objectively, as well as changing how you interact with your environment and the people with whom you relate. This is an evolution of consciousness that takes the form of an alternating inner and outer spiral. First you observe a shift, then you internalize this observation, and then instantaneously you feel an internal shift that guides your outer movements and behavior. Visualization and mindful, meditation are useful tools to elucidate your core values. You can also use these tools to begin to create new patterns in how you relate in the world.

Visualization is a type of meditation that incorporates an inner picture of what you desire to shift or create. You begin the visualization process by going into a light meditative and peaceful state. To practice use the meditation diagrams in the *Reference* section of the book.

Using your breath, you can consciously calm and balance your conscious awareness and being. When meditating make your inhalations shorter than your exhalations; breathing-in for a count of five and then breathing-out for a count of seven is a good start. The visualization part is what you see on the inner plane; what you put your attention on in a visual way; like seeing a beach, a forest, something that can increase your sense of peace.

To use a visualization to shift your perspective you may use the internal feeling you get from viewing a picture of someone with whom you have a supportive, compassionate, forgiving, and loving relationship to shift your experience of another negative, difficult person or situation. First, gaze upon the face of the one with whom you have the positive, internal feelings, and sensory awareness. Once you are firmly experiencing this individual's love and kindness, you can replace the image with the problem person or situation. The loving feeling or sensory experience from the first person can elicit a feeling of compassion, lovingkindness, or forgiveness in you so that you can see the other from a different perspective. This will allow you to have a shift in your consciousness of that person so that you can more effectively and less harmfully (personally) deal with that person or situation.

Another way to use visualization is to picture the shift in the person or situation. For example, if you are feeling unheard by another you can go into a meditative state and picture the other person listening to you. This helps to clear the negative imbalance around the event. If you are feeling lost you can use the visualization to experience finding your way. This turning the problem upside down offers a paradigm shift and the viewing of the change offers a change within your sensory experience and consciousness. These visualization and mindful, meditation techniques have been called other things in the therapies of Fritz Perls, *Gestalt Therapy*, Albert Ellis, and many cognitive-behavioral therapies. They are powerful techniques in reworking difficult injuries to reset a person's *habit* of being in the world to neutral because they offer effective strategies for shifting your awareness and evolving your consciousness. These techniques are intentional, distinct, proactive, self-directed methods for releasing trauma, shifting paradigms, and smoothing out habitual reactions. Therapy offers this, but you don't need to go to therapy to make these changes, you can do it through visualization, mindful meditation, and the practice of breathwork and yoga. These processes can shift your spiritual consciousness and increase your sense of oneness and connection to others, and your environment, in a positive way and create an opportunity for you to choose a different style of relating. The value of using visualizations to heal your relationship is very powerful. You can return to these techniques time and time again to release misbeliefs and shift into a We-style of relating in partnerships.

LEADERSHIP THROUGH INNER STRENGTH OF WILL: CREATING SPACE FOR WE

"The quality of everything we do: our physical actions, our verbal actions, and even our mental actions, depends on our motivation. That's why it's important for us to examine our motivation in our day-to-day life. If we cultivate respect for others and our motivation is sincere, if we develop a genuine concern for others' well-being, then all our actions will be positive." Dalai Lama

Leadership and will are strongly connected. How the will within is communicated and utilized is different with different leadership styles. Will without heart can lead to a hollow and disconnected success, and it is also the way to dictatorship. This can look like a person who drags others forward toward a goal regardless of the consequences. Propaganda, divisive rhetoric, and *shoulds and should nots* are some of the mechanisms involved in this style of leadership.

Heart without will results in partially developed ideas that swirl around a person but cannot be fully manifested; this can look like anarchy. This leadership style has a tendency to be reactive and emotional without a deeper understanding of the complicated factors encompassing the need and end result required. Will is the element that simultaneously presses-on, pushes-through to create the change as well as sees the bigger picture that incorporates the whole of the problem. So heart without the will component results in a lot of emotional smoke without a real transformation. Think of the picture of the Peanuts character Linus surrounded by the gray cloud → all that this leader can see is what is inside his head. He is unable to transform his concerns or ideas into something that can create change or move a community beyond the vague sense of discontent.

Will and heart together are the best aspects of a powerful, intentional, and transformative leader. These together allow for both individual needs and community needs to be attended to in equal measure: this is collaborative and consensus driven; it is not a dictatorship or anarchy. So, what matters in this heart and will connection in leadership is attention (present-mindful-focus); intention (compassionate, loving win-win motivation); care for others, even those with whom you disagree; and a focus on mindful, present-moment dialogue and action together, toward the enhancement of all.

Leadership via collaboration is something more than facilitation of others' needs. It is not just a separate role of listening and divining what the group desires, it includes an inner strength of will, and an inner set of principles that are at the heart of the need and the solution. It is a spiraling process of involution and evolution allowing for the various aspects of the problem and solution to be identified and incorporated.

Leadership is a natural human action. It incorporates a person's ability to be altruistic while simultaneously incorporating individual needs. Hermann Hesse wrote many novels in which he offered insight into the human condition. In *Siddhartha* and *Magister Ludi (1968)* (also published under *The Glass Bead Game in 1980*) he described the individual search for authenticity, self-knowledge, and spirituality. He emphasized the issues of individual needs versus needs of the group in *Magister Ludi*. His work has important information to develop an internal strength of will informed by a powerful, heart-based internal guidance system.

Understanding how and in what ways individual and group rights and responsibilities interplay is a foundational aspect for effective leadership. Mahatma Gandhi, Abraham Lincoln, and Martin Luther King, Jr. are representative of this kind of leadership as were the actions ascribed to Jesus and Buddha. These men demonstrated a way of thinking and being that were will and heart integrated, to assist in the evolution of the spiritual consciousness of the environments in which they lived. These are not the only leaders who have integrated will and heart to create change. Daw Aung San Suu Kyi of Burma (Myanmar) has been practicing this type of leadership to help transform her country throughout the last thirty years. This idea of change is a way of thinking and being that is directly guided by an integrated inner strength of will, strongly influenced by a heart-based internal guidance system, and unbiased by any ideology that is not connected to a genuine, caring, compassionate, mindful, lovingkindness toward others, self, and community. You can create the change your group or community needs by integrating your heart and will so that you act from an inner strength of will informed by your heart-based internal guidance system. You can develop your powerful leadership skills by simply focusing on listening and hearing in an open, evaluative, interested way, guided by your inner strength of will and heart-based internal guidance system, with the goal that best serves the community and the individual together, the We-style of relating in partnership. Start today by refocusing your attention and intention to create what you recognize you and your community need for health and success: 1/ Develop your internal guidance system; 2/ Develop your listening and hearing skills; 3/ Develop your responding communication skills to reduce defensiveness and reactivity; 4/ Practice mindful, paradigm shifting with a focus on understanding, discovery, collaboration, and areas of connection and transformation. Practice *being the change you wish to see in the world* in all your interactions, so that you can be a leader in your community.

LESS ATTITUDE, MORE GRATITUDE: INCREASE ALTRUISM AND EMPATHY

Mindfulness offers a way to shift attitude into gratitude. Routine meditation can shift the way your brain functions and communicates, transforming how you perceive your environment; this allows for increased connection and a sense of gratitude. This may explain the power of prayer described among healers and healthcare providers. It allows for paradigm shifting not only cognitively but physically too. It can transform a sense of *attitude* into a sense of gratitude. *Attitude* is defined here by a sense of negativity, rigidity or defensiveness.

If focus is on what isn't working, one's limitations or injuries, then an attitude of neediness, negativity, self-centeredness, discouragement, and self-pity develops.

If focus is on what works, strengths or gifts, compassion, and connections, then an attitude of gratefulness and gratitude develops;

you feel more in sync with the environment around you. This has a relaxing and opening effect.

Buddhist monks who practice *Metta* or compassion meditation, a Lovingkindness meditation which includes focused deep breathing, have been shown to modulate their amygdala, along with the temporoparietal junction and insula, during their practice (Lazar SW, Kerr CE, Wasserman RH, et al., *Neuroreport* 2005;16(17):1893-1897).

In *The Winner's Brain: Eight Strategies Great Minds Use to Achieve Success (2011)*, Dr. Mark Fenske identified how: *Brain scans of individuals performing mantra repetition show an increase in activity in the frontal and parietal lobes, which are associated with the control of attention. Drawing your focus away from distressing signals reduces activity in the areas of the brain that regulate emotion, such as the amygdala, which is associated with the fear response.* The act of focusing on a mantra may serve as an emotional regulator, making you more persistent and resilient.

In an MRI study, more intensive insula activity was found in expert meditators than in novices. Increased activity in the amygdala following compassion-oriented meditation may contribute to social connectedness (Lazar SW, Kerr CE, Wasserman RH, et al., *Neuroreport* 2005;16(17):1893-1897). So meditation and mindfulness increases your ability to play well and interact positively, and helps to focus on a We-style of relationship partnering. Amygdala activity at the time of encoding information correlates with retention for that information. However, this correlation depends on the relative *"emotional quality"* of the information. More emotionally arousing information increases amygdala activity, and that activity correlates with retention. Amygdala neurons show various types of oscillation during emotional arousal, such as theta brain wave activity (linked to increased creativity, relaxation, intuition, right-brained activity, emotional and subconscious connectedness). These synchronized events could promote synaptic plasticity (which is involved in memory retention) by increasing interactions between neocortical storage sites and temporal lobe structures involved in declarative memory (Pagnoni G. Cekic M., *Neurobiology of Aging* 2007;28(10):1623-7.). Review the Lovingkindness meditation in the *Reference* section of this book to practice this kind of daily meditation.

Smiling creates a relaxation of your shoulders, jaw, and neck muscles and increases neuron firings in the connected areas in your brain that regulates emotion, memory, and cognition (amygdala, hippocampus, and hypothalamus). Breathing deeply increases this sense of openness and relaxation. These same areas are negatively affected by stress; furrowing your brow leads to increased tension and strain on your shoulders, neck and jaw and a reduction in firing in these same areas in your brain; this can lead to increased depression, fibromyalgia, migraine headaches, a sense of isolation and disconnectedness, and memory issues if it goes unabated.

During stressful times people tend to decrease their breath to shallow breathing. Simply focusing on deep breathing can decrease these negative effects. Then attending to the positive elements of a situation, its benefits, lessons, positive outcomes, or its attributing gifts, can shift your perspective from negative to positive, from feeling sorry for yourself, defeated, or fearful to a sense of gratefulness and positivity →from attitude to gratitude,

These simple actions infuse your brain with positive sensations that allow for creative resolutions to your challenging situations and problems.

Create a daily practice of meditation, mindfulness, smiling, laughing, and deep breathing. This creates the space internally in your brain as well as your heart and mind, to shift from a Me or I-style of relationship to a We-style of relationship. These practices shift you into less attitude and more gratitude, giving you all of the above positive properties to shift your style of being in the world. Practicing this daily strengthens you further. This process and positive outcome builds and grows through attention and intention of action.

FIGURE 13, STRENGTHENING YOUR CORE THROUGH GRATITUDE, THE TREE POSE IN YOGA

LOVE HEALS, LOVE BINDS, LOVE FREES

Love is a profoundly powerful experience. Really loving or feeling loved opens your heart to forgiveness and unending strength. Sometimes that strength is the strength to let go with love. Feeling loved embodies the qualities of acceptance and feeling seen. Really loving another exemplifies the qualities of acceptance and understanding.

A desired outcome of relationship is to feel loved and accepted. The best way to feel love is to love another. A book by Eric Fromm called *The Art of Loving (1956)*, is one of my guiding sources for how to love. This book offers a paradigm shift from the traditional concepts of loving and seeing. It's loving from the perspective of acceptance, care, and compassion. His ideas are echoed in Thich Nhat Hanh's book, *Peace is Every Step (1991)*. Both of these books identify mindfulness as an integral component of a loving relationship and offer useful guidance in how to develop and maintain a We-style relationship as a way of being and interacting in the world. This is the shift in paradigm. It is a choice of how to respond in the moment toward both positive and negative interactions with others.

When I get triggered, by another person's negativity toward me I feel anger or sadness or some other drop in energy. If I respond from that angry place, I find that a wall or block is created that interferes with conflict resolution. If, I come from that reactive paradigm then, I am not open to discovering how to resolve the conflict. I am focused on the argument, or defending my position. This only creates a defensive reaction from the other person, which leads to a standstill and no resolution. If, I choose to respond with a connecting energy then, I begin to feel my energy rise and fill me positively. That is a function of love or compassion; it allows for the space to be expanded so that both paradigms can be evaluated, and a place of understanding and acceptance can be created to experience a paradigm shift and connection between and among individuals.

The love energy required for this to happen is not romantic love, but rather lovingkindness and compassion, the sense of Agape from the Greek, meaning selfless love. This universal love is spiritual in nature, the love described in various religious and spiritual traditions. It is a position of being in the world, a style of lovingkindness which incorporates forgiveness, acceptance, and compassion as basic components of being and interacting. The Buddhist tradition talks about a concept of *Right relationship*, or *Right action*, not right as in right versus wrong but right as in correct, correctness in balance of spirit, mind and body, in sync with the situation, the environment, and within one's being. Opening to love in a way that is consistent with right relationship allows for evaluation from a neutral, compassionate, accepting perspective, so that the *best* aspects of all involved are incorporated into the relationship style and solution.

To determine whether or not you are in sync, scan your emotional and physical sensations. Increasing your awareness of your own inner senses helps to give you information about how to respond in a given situation. Experiences that cue you are reacting to the situation include: if you have a drop in energy, a negative attitude, a loss of hope or a feeling of fear/anger; you may be breathing shallowly or holding your breath. Cues that you are in a responsive, loving perspective: if you notice a feeling of warmth or heightened sense of understanding, an attitude of gratitude, or a feeling of generosity or openness to a compassionate, lovingkindness perspective. You can shift into a compassionate, loving responsive stance by focusing your intention and attention.

To shift into this stance focus on your breath. Breathe-in and breathe-out, this creates the space to be open to love and compassion, and increases your capacity to view the situation from a balanced perspective. Love opens your heart, and breath opens your space for love.

Love heals. Loving yourself first allows you greater access to your internal strength and diminishes your insecurity. This creates an opportunity for you to develop your responsive right relationship and mindfulness, because it decreases your defensiveness and reactivity. By increasing your self-confidence and sense of competence you are more at peace and can access neutrality and compassion. You do not feel as if you must protect yourself from imminent injury, so you can be open to receiving information in a neutral and mindful way. Love is healing toward yourself and your partner.

Love binds in that it creates connection. When that binding feels restrictive it chokes your inner sense of strength and interferes with your capacity to trust and create interdependence. When the binding is like a sweet connection so that you feel strengthened then it allows for development of yourself, your partner and your couplehood or partnership.

Love frees through acceptance, understanding, and care. When you see your partner fully without criticism she feels accepted and loved. When you feel seen and accepted you feel loved. From this space you can then interact about changes you each desire, if this is necessary. First love and acceptance, then shifting for care of each other; when the necessary shifts are injurious to one or the other of you then release of each other through love without negativity or criticism.

WE-NESS: WIN-WIN OR NO DEAL, AND A WORD ABOUT PSYCHOPATHS

The evolution of consciousness toward the concept of one world is the *way through* dualistic interactions that are driven by scarcity of resources, fear, or insecurity. The outcome of a continued focus on mindfulness in relationship is a *one-world* concept as an evolution of spiritual and cognitive consciousness for the embracement or inclusion of all of humanity and the planet.

Global change begins small between two people and in groups. It is a shift in seeing, acting, knowing, and being that shifts consciousness in this way. It is an inside-out change that is directed through the heart by gratitude and the energy of inner knowing and connecting through spirit. It is not a shift that can be driven from a fear/insecurity-based cognitive perspective. It cannot be ruled into being; it is not an outside-in change. Simple shifts in focus, simple decisions to trust, open, connect, and be interdependent create a wave of change in human consciousness.

This is movement from the Me or I-style of relating to the We-style of relating. Mindfulness, compassion, and paradigm shifting, with sincere, open-minded interest, and focus on looking for a way to honestly create a consensus, driven by love, care, and understanding, is the most effective way to create success in partnerships; this is the way to embrace the space of *"we"*.

When you are developing your skills at mindfulness, compassionate action, and focus on a We-style of relating, you are assisting in a global wave of change in consciousness. But not everyone will uplevel; this is a function of unique personal capacity. There are those who cannot do this; it is a function of how you choose to be in the world and how you choose to see and act in relationship. This choice is guided by the synthesis of your temperament, your primary groups, your early life, and how you resolved the psychosocial stages. There are instances when the integration of these factors results in a person who is, at his or her center, incapable of empathy or interacting from a We-style of relationship. There are individuals who use mindfulness, and the words of compassion or understanding as a manipulation others into vulnerability. Therapists use the term *psychopathic* to describe this kind of behavior. A psychopath is an individual who is devoid of a conscience. Psychopaths manipulate the chosen target to act in a self-injurious way; this can be physical as well as emotional. The psychopath has no real internal experience of guilt or shame, but manipulates the normal aspect of guilt in others to trick them to act in ways that suit the needs of the psychopath. Individuals with this style of relating in the world can shift their exterior behavior, countenance, tone, and words to appear as if they are something they are not. This type of personality structure does not have the interior flexibility to develop into a We-style of relating; his actions are imitations of what he has observed. Discernment of whether you are in a relationship with a psychopath takes a few steps. You want to observe whether s/he has the capacity to take responsibility for his/her behavior, and negotiate equitably. Pay attention to your personal sensory guidance system, you will feel like something is off in some way, even if you cannot identify what it is. Notice if you feel seduced into doing something that is outside your typical behaviors. Be wary of cues that you are being manipulated, especially if it seems too good to be true. Psychopaths do not have the capacity for empathy, or negotiation. Also there is a high level of blame and guilt to get his/her needs met. When you are dealing with a psychopath it is best to follow the words of Stephen Covey in his book *The 7 Habits of Highly Effective People (1989)*: "win-win or no deal." This is to say when you are interacting with a psychopath the concept of win-win is unattainable, as a psychopath is unable to move into a true We-style relationship.

Covey wrote when "*... you cannot find a place of win-win then it is most effective to choose no-deal*" (1989). So you can use your mindfulness to assist you in discerning what another wants and *seek to understand* the other, but once you understand the other is unable to create a *win-win* (a negotiated perspective that includes both parties needs/wants) you are best to choose *no-deal*.

This no-deal concept can look like a termination of the relationship or, in the case of someone with whom you must continue to interact (like a divorced parent of your child) it can look like an acceptance that there can be no "we", so negotiation is from an "I" to "I" experience, where you seek to simply create what is most effective for you and any other party involved (like your child). Do not get into a discussion of an integrated "we" with the psychopathic personality.

Once you have discerned you are dealing with a psychopath, you must take care to not let him play on your emotional fears, concerns, or feelings of guilt to manipulate you toward his goals. This is a different form of mindfulness; it uses compassion and understanding so that the actions, words, and behaviors you choose are without malice, but incorporate the full and complete understanding of the other person's true lack of capacity for "we".

Here are a few simple guideposts to assist you in discerning if you are interacting with a psychopath:

- He or she acts dramatically different in specific situations.

- She or he has a chameleon quality, and can take on a persona that is expected, in order to be accepted.
- He or she uses your feelings of guilt, or your desire to be kind and helpful against you, to get you to forgive him or her and extend another chance.
- When a third party is involved in mediation or evaluation, she or he is able to manipulate the third party to agree with her or him against you, even after you have shared your concerns.
- He or she takes no responsibility for any negative behavior inflicted upon you and deflects such to some element of you.
- She or he changes her or his countenance to get her or his way including mimicking words and emotional behavior of kindness, compassion, mindfulness, and forgiveness.

Finally, it is important to use your internal guidance system, your neutral, mindful observation powers to discern whether you are interacting with someone who is honestly and sincerely communicating with you. Notice whether her or his actions, behavior, and words are in congruence.

Pay closest attention to the subtle, small things, as this is where the psychopath's true consciousness and intentions will be shown. Look for a lack of the natural side-effects of mindfulness and compassion, such as a softness in her or his eyes toward a situation, an energy of lovingkindness, or a release of the need to always be the winner. These are aspects of a true internal shift toward We that the psychopathic personality cannot fake.

There is a growing shift on the planet toward a higher consciousness of partnership and relationship. The energy of how partnership and collaboration is evolving. It is moving toward a higher degree of spiritual oneness. It starts with love, compassion, open-minded neutral mindfulness, and focused attention toward harmony and balance. As this shift continues to develop focus your energy on interactions that will be fruitful, loving, and increase the value of your small world, the world of your relationships. This will wave into global change as the power of this loving, equitable, interdependent We-style of interaction moves through communities.

Give yourself permission to use your mindfulness to discern the capacity for partnership and focus your energies on those who are also working toward the thread of compassion and love and We-ness. Allow yourself to release partnerships where this is not a possibility so that you can focus your energies on developing the best, most healthful, and mutually fulfilling relationships. This will carry through your world and across communities like wildfire and shift the consciousness of the planet toward collaboration and the idea of one-world.

Those individuals who lack the capacity for this kind of We-ness will find their way; however their power over others will be greatly diminished, as you and others make the choice of no-deal in relationship with them. This is the best, most loving response to include them, without being overtaken by their disabilities.

MINDFUL LIVING IN THE WE-STYLE OF RELATIONSHIP: HOW TO INTEGRATE YOUR PERSONAL GUIDANCE SYSTEM INTO YOUR DAILY LIFE

The power of intuitive understanding will protect you from harm until the end of your days. – Lao Tzu

As discussed earlier in the book, your personal sensory guidance system is fine-tuned to assist you in making decisions and responding to your environment successfully. It is an integration of your five senses of hearing, touching, seeing, tasting, and smelling plus your intuition. It informs you via cues about your environment and your actions. When you pay attention to these cues you receive powerful guidance; it's like your personal GPS unit. Helpful questions that increase you attunement: Do things feel off or right on? Does something feel clear or askew? Does the information go in with veracity or in a sticky fashion? Do you have a bad taste in your mouth or does something not smell right? Does the information ring true or does it fall flat? Is there congruence or incongruence in another's statements and behaviors? These questions orient you to listen, feel, see, and know through your personal guidance system.

It is in the quiet, light, notions and intuitions that you can feel and know. These represent the direct and ever vigilant guidance of your personal guidance system. Truth is revealed from within, via your integrated sensory guidance system. When you get information from an outside source translate it through your personal guidance system. Pay attention. Apply mindfulness. Focus your compassion and lovingkindness toward the whole of the situation and pay attention to the messages you receive from your sensory guidance system. Delay immediate, reactive-responses to loud, forceful, manipulative messages from without, especially when you receive contradictory information from your personal guidance system or you experience these as out-of-sync. Here are some tips to develop your relationship to your sensory guidance system.

- Incorporate a daily breathing focused meditation practice.
- Use your third ear to listen→Listen, pay attention, hear with your whole being, to the content and the non-verbal aspects of what is said.
- Practice daily yoga; this doesn't have to take a lot of time, even a ten-minute focus on breath or the sun salutation can bring you into your integrated spirit, mind, body vehicle.
- Question from a mindful space the basis of others' beliefs while listening with your sensory guidance system.
- Treat yourself with the same love and kindness you use to treat others.
- Pay attention to the whole of how others treat you.

These actions allow for increased understanding of both other and yourself and increase your direct connection to your integrated, personal, sensory guidance system. The focus within helps you to support and align your beliefs, statements, and actions. When you maintain this connection daily you will find you have a stronger capacity for seeing the full picture of any given situation. You will also increase your balanced relationship with yourself and develop your resilience. All of these qualities help you to shift from a Me or I-style relationship to a We-style relationship; you are developing an internal self-confidence and sense of yourself so that you can effectively assess risk and create mutually powerful and happy relationships.

MODEL CRITICAL THINKING, ESCHEW PROPAGANDA

Inherent in human behavior is a strong pull to follow the group. You can observe this in action with toddlers in preschool, young children in elementary school or through witnessing the popular movement of music, clothing, and behavior of high school and young adulthood; the in-group in society telegraphs to the human psyche how to be, what to think, who to follow and what will keep you in the clique. This is built into the developmental structure of humans.

This pull to follow the group-mind and to be inculcated into belief systems is the basis of societal strength. Unfortunately, it can become the downfall of society over time or become a tool to control people without their overt knowledge.

In the 1950s, psychologists studied university students to discover if an individual will follow the group and conform under various conditions. It was called the *Asch Experiment*. What they found was that '...when students were presented with a group of peers who offered the incorrect response *they conformed to answer with the incorrect answer 75 percent of the time for at least one answer*' (Asch, 1951).

Also in the 1960's psychologists studied whether a person would act against his or her own inner sense that something was wrong when told by an authority or person in a power position that it was necessary to act in this way, against that subject's inner sense that something was wrong. This was called the *Milgram Experiment* (Milgram, 1974). This study's results provided serious information: that *'seemingly "good people" with reasonable skills to evaluate the serious negative effects of an act would still follow through with causing harm to another person when told by an authority person (person in a position of power) that it was necessary and deferred responses to the effects of their actions'* (Milgram, 1974). These studies indicate there is an inherent pull to go against your inner guidance system when pressed to do so for acceptance into the clique, or by a person in a position of power or authority.

The best way to avoid being manipulated by group-think or propaganda is to use *critical thinking* in all of your decision-making. Critical thinking questions the basis of your belief systems and the underpinnings of powerful people's opinions and positions. Rather then saying 'I agree with that icon, hero, politician, or cool person,' *critical thinking encourages an inner dialogue that questions 'why do I agree* and what does that statement, philosophy, or belief system mean down and up-stream.' This increases your chance to be congruent in your beliefs and it increases the freedom and empowerment you can experience in your life course and development.

When you are questioning, consider this: *What is popular is not always what is best for a society.* Because of the above-mentioned inner push to be accepted and part of the *in-crowd*, those in power and seeking power, get their message out through subtle coercion using these group rules of inclusion and exclusion to manipulate you. They use this human goal to feel included, liked, accepted and specifically to be part of the cool in-group to control you by creating propaganda that supports maintenance of their power while diminishing groups and values that they want to destroy. It's important to recognize that you are pulled to follow propaganda, while developing a good way to stay connected to your sensory guidance system for your inner truth.

A great critical thinking tool is the *stop, look, and listen method*. You can stop, look, and listen to the whole of the situation, the underlying beliefs, and what might be the contributing factors when you feel you are being pulled along a current to do or agree with something 1/ *as if* it is the only answer, 2/ and that pressure is from the outside, cool in-group, and 3/ not connected to your internal sense of knowing from within. This is a cue that you are caught up in something that may have propaganda in it.

When you become overly stressed or forget to use critical thinking you accept propaganda as truth, swallowing it whole (introjection). This is a shortcut due to stress, or lack of time. Sometimes, it is due to an *unearned* trust toward the group or those in power. You aren't assessing the risk because you are swallowing whole that those in power are indeed going to direct society to the best interests of society.

Sociological theory and psychological theory both, have shown that those in power want to maintain that power. This means that their desire to maintain power can override their stated intention to act in societies' best interest. One way this power principle plays out is through the means to make money, or owners of production (as opposed to the workers in the production); those who own the means to make money want to stay in power to control this. This power principle can be applied to any system where the person or group in power wants to maintain power. When the balance of power diverts to those in production through unions, if the people in power of the unions become focused on maintaining power they can then be like the owners of production and create a skew away from their stated goal of caring for their fellow workers. This can happen in politics, too. This power principle and the use of propaganda to maintain power and control is part of the structure of human groups. One of the tools for promoting and disseminating propaganda is through media, marketing, television, and movies. The passive way in which the propaganda information is viewed and experienced short-circuits critical thinking and the various agencies are able to promote their agenda to maintain power by linking their agenda into what is seen as *cool*.

The best response to your environment is to use your own critical thinking skills to evaluate the truth of what is being said. Examine how you know it is true, without accepting whole what someone says whom you perceive as a guru, leader, hero, or cool person. There is power that comes with fame; this is related to the latent pull to follow the leader of the group. Following what a famous person says or does gives your psyche the sense that you are somehow connected to them, which feeds that hidden inner pull to conform and align with the group. This is precisely the process that allows for *odd or different* children to be bullied in school. The *cool* person or the person perceived to have power is followed. She is using her power in a power-over way.

An individual standing up and saying that it is wrong, or simply standing with the odd or different child can deflect this effect. This requires critical thinking. It takes strength to go against the *cool* person, as her focus may then be redirected toward you. The latent quiet allowing of maltreatment for fear that the maltreatment may be directed at you is *a way the in-group wields control*.

Choose to go outside of the norm and follow your inner sense of what is right and you can stem the flow of the propaganda. Although the risk of attack from the *in-group* to this action is possible through a negative spotlight on you or an effort to discredit you, this is the best opportunity for like-minded people to collaborate or dialogue about other ways to behave. This is critical thinking; this is right action; and this is the basis of the We-style of relationship. Your critical thinking skills connected to your internal sensory guidance system can best guide you. And the more you use these and model their use, the more those around you will use them. It is in this way that bullying, subtle power coercion, control through group-mind, and propaganda will be extinguished. This can help you interact in a We-style of relationship. Group-mind and propaganda are counter to the We-style of relationship. Neither is collaborative. Both are controlling to meet a personal, power-insecurity goal.

Innovation is a natural by-product of critical thinking. It comes as a result of questioning:

- Is that statement true?
- How do I know the belief or statement is true from my own experience?
- What is the other side's argument and how is it true?
- What might be the reward for the person in power to deny the truth?
- What is wrong with the statement or belief?
- What needs to be changed in the situation or environment?

Critical Thinking is Mindfulness.

The intensity of another's statement does not make it truth; that is just another propaganda technique.

Truth is.

Truth can be felt in your heart; it rings true; it has an internal alignment, not in the agreement of the words to the belief but in an integration of the truth of all the positions and how that truth lines up. It is an internal heart sense and has a lightness to it, not a loud booming voice. The latter is just a technique of coercion. The more punch, charge, or loudness in the argument the less critical thinking exists therein.

Critical thinking allows for the truth of all the sides to be accepted and incorporated into the solution or belief system.

Subjectivity is loud, forceful, emotional, and pulls to accept. It blocks mindfulness and the critical evaluation of all sides.

Objectivity is quiet, light, and non-emotional. It has an opening to reveal the truth of all sides.

Discover your truth through critical thinking and mindfulness. Model this behavior and thinking style for your children, your partners, and your peers. This will result in bringing to light propaganda so that real solutions can be found to the difficult problems facing you.

FINDING YOUR WAY: CULLING THROUGH THE PROPAGANDA

"The giant was a terrifying enemy; even the best warriors of Israel trembled at the thought of fighting him. David was merely a young shepherd and a musician, yet he was the one to defeat the giant. How did he do it? He had three smooth stones in his slingshot, and he hit the giant between his eyes. THE GIANT HAS NO DEFENSE WHEN HE IS HIT IN HIS THIRD EYE. He cannot defend himself against these three things: *truth, virtue and love*. So that's the message for us: to *speak the truth*; to *work on our own virtue*; and *to act with love*. At this point in history, all three take courage..." Marianne Williamson 2012

Marianne Williamson has authored many books on spirituality and mindfulness. My favorite is *Illuminata* (1994). The above quote from a seminar where she retells an old story from the Bible in a way to encourage spiritual empowerment and healing provides a description of mindful living.

The essence of truth, virtue, and love are so powerful they create a space for you to be impenetrable, solid, and strengthened, to see your way through the propaganda that is all around you.

From a metaphorical perspective the idea that truth, virtue, and love are the powerful forces that work through the third eye is similar to the concept of standing in the light of spirit. This is the power of standing in your heart center. This happens effortlessly when you open yourself and create space in relationship for truth, virtue, and love. Your best lessons about truth occur when you are challenged to not speak the truth, not act from the center of your true self, your heart-center (virtue), when you are not acting out of love for all the parties involved (including lovingly acting toward yourself), or simply when you are acting out of fear.

Consider this: *evil* is *live* spelled backwards. Perhaps not living is evil and living incorporates the opposite of evil, experiencing light. Fear seems to open the door to evil through the concept of not living in your true or full light. Love seems to fill you with faith and trust, so that you can go toward your truth and virtue, not avoid them out of a sense of fear. Faith promotes living; fear promotes not living.

When I was a student living in Italy, these lessons came to me experientially in my awareness of the difference between my truth and that of my beloved boyfriend with whom I had traveled to Italy, as well as my perceptual awareness of national and political "truth" seen from my new lens of outsider in a foreign country. I learned that there are different kinds of truth and that truth had a *time-stamp* or perspective to it that shifted its relativity. This is to say that at different times or in different places or cultures, different things were held as true.

    I sought the way to find authentic or universal truth. Carlo Levi in his book *Christ Stopped at Eboli* (1945) dealt with many issues of figure and ground when defining truth. This book helped me identify there was a personal truth and to discern the difference between what is *true* from a perspective point of view and what is *truth* from a universal, spiritual point of view.

    The first step in finding your way through the propaganda that surrounds you in the media, in your cultural and political affiliations, and in your world is to *discover your truth, your personal virtue,* and *what love looks and feels like to you*. Love from the compassionate, accepting, non-attached, mindful perspective that connects all as one.

    This can be an effortless transformation. Simply notice, accept and feel gratitude for what is working in your life. Open yourself to being rather than doing. Rise above the perspective of right and wrong and into the concept of living (faith) and not-living (fear); this will assist your ability in seeing, feeling, and knowing the truth and developing your virtue.

    Through simple acts of lovingkindness and mindfulness, you are strengthened. Smile more, laugh more, accept more, feel the pain of others more, love yourself more, forgive more, release your fears more; all these actions increase your capacity for truth, virtue, and love. The first step is through the use and active mindset of compassion. The best way to get there is through a daily practice of meditation, yoga, and/or prayer, and the constant companion mantra of the attitude of gratitude.

FIGURE 14, FAITH NOT FEAR, RIGHT RELATIONSHIP
PHOTOGRAPHY CREDIT: RON ROMANIK

PIERCING THROUGH SEDUCTIVE LOGIC TO TRUTH

Seductive logic that pulls on your *neurotic* structure (the incomplete solutions to your early psychosocial traumas) makes you want to believe; like a con-artist manipulating you through reactive stimuli and reactive nerve pulse firings. Think of this like a puppet pulling on strings in your brain. It is a trick. It's not the truth or the way.

Trust yourself and use your personal sensory guidance system. If information isn't going in straight, then there is probably something crooked about it. This is delicate because for a lie to be believable there has to be an element of truth in it. It's the interpretation of the meaning of the truth that is at issue. Using terms that are vague or heavily laden with emotion allows someone to imply meaning without really saying the whole truth, which usually belies the implied meaning. This enables the person to hide his meaning underneath the inference. It is through this implication of meaning that one person can manipulate the other person to agree, follow, or believe him. This kind of communication is not indicative of a We-style relationship. It creates deception and dulls trust. This is the complicated part of language; advertisers, marketing agents, and politicians use this ambiguous aspect of language to manipulate you, the listener or target audience, to hear just what they want but not necessarily the whole picture. To avoid being fooled you have to be willing and responsible to use your mindfulness in analyzing the whole experience of the situation to make the best decisions in purchasing, voting, and action. This requires thinking and feeling through your sensory guidance system. This is the complex aspect of partnership. Hearing the truth to evaluate risk and clarify the level of security and trust that the relationship is truly offering. Part of the seductive component is that as a partner you want to trust and believe what your partner says, so you are more easily seduced to accept the implication of the truth rather than use your mindfulness to evaluate the whole picture. This is why people you are in conflict with, like an enemy or someone who you are in competition with, may have a keener ability to see when you are manipulating and you can see through his or her half-truths.

Your closeness can be a barrier to being objective in your assessment. A person who is more distant from you, when focusing her observation skills, is able to see, feel, hear, and know when something is missing in your presentation; this is accomplished by attending to inner cues from her sensory guidance system. This is an attractive component of the I-style of relating; because the two *I*s do not have an interdependence, they are less connected and less likely to be seduced by propaganda or partial truths.

Just as you have access to information through your personal sensory guidance system, that system integrated with your observation and thinking skills can assist you in *reading* others so that you can assess whether or not they are telling the truth or hiding something. The key element is this: you, and others, *telegraph* what matters to you through how you dress, move, and speak through life; all humans have *tells*, through observation, neutrality and mindfulness you can read those *tells*. Everything that you say, wear, or emphasize is about communicating what your group alliances are, your belief systems, who you admire, or distaste, and what matters to you. You cannot hide this from someone who understands the symbols, is looking for them, and is not attached to any of the beliefs, groups, or hierarchies that structure your life. This is how the con man is able to use your self against you. It is also how you can catch him. This is to say you have the equal capacity to read others, as others have to manipulate you, simply by paying attention to your personal sensory guidance system and looking for congruence and or *tells*. When you are responding mindfully in the present-moment with neutrality and curiosity, and trusting your internal sensory guidance system then you can easily avoid being conned and will be able to see through seductive manipulation to the truth.

Your best defense is to trust yourself, to listen to your inner sensory guidance system, and to be a neutral mindful observer. You can develop a deeper understanding of your partner through the same methods if you are willing to objectively observe your partner's behavior and pay attention to your sensory guidance system.

This system of using perception to assess the congruency of a person's beliefs, actions, and words is the basis of the therapeutic relationship. The therapist is outside another's system such that he can understand not just what is said but also verify what is unsaid through what is communicated through mannerisms, word choice, gestures, silence, intonation, and other non-verbal cues, to get the whole picture. The therapist is using his perceptiveness and observation to see how the puzzle fits together or the mystery can be solved. He observes with interest, neutrality, and mindfulness to activate and inform his intuition. Therapy isn't an equal sharing relationship, it is not a We-style of relationship per se; the unequal give and take in the therapeutic relationship could look like a Me-style relationship where only the needs and assumptions of the client are evaluated and addressed, but it is mindful and based in compassion and lovingkindness so it isn't a typical Me or I-style of relationship. This inequality is useful to assist the therapist to remain objective and attentive to help the client see how his habit reaction patterns keep him caught in a loop. Therapy creates a space to question and invert assumptions to shift those paradigms and allow the client to really respond in the now, in a mindful way, so that the client can live more happily and more fully.

The idea of boundaries is significant difference between a therapeutic relationship and Me-style relationships. Therapeutic relationships have clear, well-defined boundaries. Me-style relationships do not have effective boundaries. The partners don't have a good sense of where one partner begins and the other partner ends, because the Me-style of relating is the style of relationship based on a need to feel connected and completed by another; each partner truncates himself or herself into half of a being to come together with the other to make a one whole. The Me-style relationship has difficulty setting boundaries and the I-style of relationship has too rigid a boundary. Both styles are based in on a core-insecurity and are fear-based.

Responding from a heart-centered place, using the instinctive emotional sensory guidance system with mindfulness to act in an empowered and truly connecting, collaborative way, sets the person onto a path of moving out of a Me-style of relationship, through an I-style of relationship, and into a We-style of relationship. *The truth will set you free.* What comes with freedom is response –*ability* and responsibility. This is the ability to respond in the moment as well as ownership of what you want. This is a We-style of relationship. In order to create what you want, first you have to identify what it is you want and then make a commitment to create it. In relationship this includes clarifying what you want to create together and negotiating how to create it together.

To have a successful We-style of relationship you have to develop your skills at piercing through seductive logic so you can see what the person is trying to communicate from a manipulative perspective as well as what the potential outcome of the information may be. Unlike a situation where you are consciously being conned or manipulated, in relationship you use this practice to help to uncover what is subconsciously driving yourself or your partner so that you can move from a Me or I-style relationship into a We-style relationship. This allows you to increase your clarity about a situation and act with integrity. The mindfulness and neutral evaluation of the information detaches the emotional meaning from the words so that you can determine whether you actually agree with the information and how you want to respond.

Congruent information and actions increase trust. Incongruent actions and verbal statements decrease a sense of trust. In negotiation use your sensory guidance system cues as you are listening to a seductive argument that just feels off somehow, to determine if you can trust what is being said or if there is more to discover before you make a decision regarding the situation. This is what Malcolm Gladwell described as a *blink response* in his book *Blink* (2006). A *blink response* is the inner sense you get at the front end of a meeting or interaction that communicates that something is off; when your sensory guidance system is responding to the incongruent information or some non-verbal element that says *this doesn't feel right*. In order to pierce through seductive logic to the truth, you need to be willing to have your own inner sensory guidance system and mindfulness steer your evaluation system rather than the power of the outside source providing the information.

Trust yourself, use your personal sensory guidance system, if it isn't going in straight then there is probably something crooked about it.

SHIFTING THE SUBSTRATE: CREATING CHANGE WITHOUT DRAMA

Identifying what you want to change is challenging. It is easier to identify that things aren't working than it is to identify the etiology. Discovering the driver for change is a little bit like conducting an archeological dig through a person's belief systems, internal paradigms, and accepted misperceptions. Language and words are laden with personal meaning; dissecting that meaning can provide invaluable insight into the etiology of a problem.

You may feel discomfort or a lack of happiness, but for the most part this doesn't move you to change. Usually you ignore it or misinterpret the reason behind your discomfort. After a while that uncomfortable feeling, ennui, or angst causes you to do something that really shakes up your relationship or your environment. If, it shakes it up enough then, things can fall away and change is possible.

When you discover a need to change in this way, through a crisis, it is generally very painful.

To change without drama requires an active relationship with your sense of comfort and your sensory guidance system, similar to responding to cues that you are hungry, tired, or in need of exercise. There are cues that can direct your response efficiently. For example, when you are hungry your first cue may be a loss of energy or focus, or it may be irritability (hypoglycemia). If you ignore these early signs, you may get a stomachache, headache, confusion, or super-irritability. You can follow this trajectory for other physical needs like sleep deprivation or lack of exercise. The earlier you pay attention to the clues, the earlier you can right the course. Things that need changing in your personality, work, or relationship follow the same course.

Developing mindfulness and compassion as a style of being in the world increases your capacity to pay attention to the cues and necessary information. Sometimes what obstructs your change is exactly what needs your attention.

Often the thing you want to hold onto is the thing you need to let go. This is not an absolute rule, but rather a guideline. When you want to hold onto a situation or relationship because you interpret it defines you in a positive way, but to keep it you have to deny your authentic self, this situation becomes an obstruction rather than an asset. This kind of equation results in negative habit reaction patterns, self-sabotage, even destructive behavior. This is an equation for a Me or I-style of relationship. The process of discovering what you want to change and moving into a We-style of relating is sometimes bumpy.

Paying attention to those cues, listening to your quiet inner voice, and allowing your instinctive knowing to lead the way will get you to the necessary information more quickly and with less drama. This intentional and deliberate process is the most efficient way to allow a peaceful and compassionate change to present itself to you. Through this process you can shift your perception, paradigm, or habit to fully meet you true need.

Facing your fears is the often the fastest way to bring about change. The idea that the thing you are afraid to change may well be precisely what you need change is a bit counterintuitive. Your knee-jerk reaction is to run in the opposite direction of your fear, to avoid it, but facing your fears is the most healing prescription and results in lasting change. You hear the words *catalyst for change* to describe an event that shifts you so that you can change. A catalyst for redefining yourself in a more authentic and true way shifts the substrate of your patterning so that you can be your authentic self.

LEAD THROUGH JOY: FOCUS ON CONNECTION AND EMPOWERMENT

Follow your bliss and the universe will open doors where there were only walls

— Joseph Campbell.

Leadership is about having the ability to fully see and understand a problem *and* define and communicate the solution. It is also about power and energy.

There are positive leaders who negotiate power from an interior source, and there are negative leaders who manipulate power from an exterior source.

When you can ascertain a solution quickly, you feel an internal sense of "rightness" and can communicate it efficiently, then you have power for others to listen to you and you will be able to be a positive leader. It is not the leadership in and of itself that will result in success or well-being. Leading toward something of value is a key component to making a difference as a positive leader. This is the energetic component of leadership and power. Negative leaders have lost their internal sense of bliss and joy and are focused on the enticing allure of power in and of itself.

Think back to a leader in your childhood who had power, quick thinking and a powerful style of motivating the group. What do you know about that person's life course? Was he or she able to translate that powerful, quick thinking into success? Only some of those individuals focused their energy onto a meaningful and successful path. Some got lost in the effervescence of power itself. For some, their charm and ease in directing the group caused them to lose their way and get caught up in the power, like the swirl of a rapid that just circles around a rock rather than moving the water down the river. This stuck energy can be hypnotizing. The whirl feels so strong that you don't notice you aren't actually going anywhere, just spinning in this feeling of power with no result or movement toward a goal. Individuals caught in this whirlpool find that others move on while they are stuck in the same position. Sometimes this spiraling energy can be destructive, much like a leaf caught in a swirl rapid around a great boulder in the river; constant swirling in the same place with great force and energy destroys the leaf. The best way to get out of this spiraling situation is to employ mindfulness: First, recognize your circumstance; second, focus your energy to not follow the current and truly shift your energy. When you're stuck the best way out is like *jumping the curve*, refocusing the energy to move into a different perspective. Shifting your perspective away from the energetic pull of the whirlpool and onto a neutralizing perspective gives you the energy to jump the curve into a different consciousness or mobilizing goal.

The most effective way to do that is to discern your inner and undeniable bliss. If you follow your bliss rather than that feeling of power, you will shift the current such that you can be guided out of the whirlpool and into the true current of life and source energy. Focus on gaining power pulls you away from your central sense of joy. Caring for others and giving energy to many through a sense of obligation depletes your energy. To determine whether you need to refocus your goal from power to bliss, ask yourself:

- Do you feel energized or depleted in your energy?
- Do you feel emotionally drained or do you feel exhausted when you receive disapproval?
- Do you feel pulled away from your goals due to responsibilities to others?
- Do you feel that you are not the guide of your own path?

The answer to the first question above will be most useful. This lack of energy, a sense of depletion, exhaustion, depression, and inner sadness or loss can indicate a long-standing focus away from your internal sense of bliss.

How do you find your bliss? Seems funny, but some people have lost their internal knowing of bliss. They don't know or remember what brings them joy. They are focused without instead of within. If, this describes you then, the answer is to go within, to be still, to listen, to observe, and to pay attention to energy.

When your energy wanes, you are moving away from your bliss.

When your energy swells and grows, you are moving toward or with your bliss and allowing it to guide you.

To get out of the whirlpool of swirling, circular energy that simply depletes you, you need to first identify your circumstance. Observe what brings you energy and what depletes you. Identify the activities that increase your internal sense of well-being and inner joy. You may not have a memory of doing something joyous or being in a situation of joy. You can do a little inner research by reviewing what activities brought you joy, that were fun and playful, in your early childhood. Once you've identified these patterns, and have reconnected with activities that bring you joy, begin to adjust your life course so that you're guided by your sense of joy. You may develop a habit of a single activity or a more diverse set of connected activities. Your sense of vitality can be your guide.

Sometimes these changes in you create fear in others and they may respond negatively. This is simply a fear-based response because they have not yet connected to their bliss.

Kindly, gently redirect them away from feeding off your energy. Encourage them to discern their circumstance and find their inner bliss.

Following your bliss opens your world to many beautiful opportunities. It increases your energy, expands your awareness and capacity for love, compassion, and acceptance of yourself and others. Your joy will increase your well-being. It can have a positive affect on those you love.

The way of mindful, loving leadership toward fulfillment, success, and peace is leading through joy. This leadership style is empowering and powerful in the most enlightening way. This is movement into a We-style of relating in partnership of all kinds because it is inner directed toward meaningful, enhancing group and personal goals. The loving behaviors of boundaries, mindfulness, lovingkindness, and mutuality are the powerful outcome of this style of leadership.

FORGIVENESS AND CURIOSITY RATHER THAN DEFENSIVENESS

The key to staying in the present-moment, acting, and interacting from a We-style relationship is mindfulness. You avoid reacting defensively, combining acceptance and forgiveness. With mindfulness, *You are shifting from No to Yes and Off to On through these actions (NO to ON, 2011)*. To connect you have to extinguish any internal sense of defensiveness; reacting from a defensive place creates a biased or skewed interaction. It can interfere with decision and choice making, and concretize a negative picture of yourself that you carry around with you in all your relationships. Defensiveness and bias negatively skew how information is interpreted and set the stage for reaction rather than mindful, response.

Bias is sometimes a result of a belief that may have represented a previous experience but is not necessarily truth. Defensiveness can be a result of habit, history or misinterpretation of the other person's intention, tone, or action. In this way defensiveness is like bias. Being clear in a neutral, non-defensive tone, with unbiased and uncharged language allows for fuller communication and an opportunity to rework old issues toward a peaceful, active resolution.

To help you move into neutrality when interacting you need to get a handle on what unhelpful, defensive, or a habit reaction pattern from earlier in the relationship (or earlier in your life) you may be bringing to the situation. You can use the *stop look and listen* method. As soon as something feels off stop and listen to what you and your partner sound like as you are talking. Look for consistencies or disconnection to determine if your feeling of defensiveness is warranted. As you incorporate your sensory guidance system, notice when and to what you are reacting defensively. When you can pinpoint the moment you felt differently, you can identify whether there is a present-moment problem or something from your history that is creating the disconnection. Whether there is something left over, an old unresolved issue or belief, or there is a misinterpretation in the present you still have to let go of the defensiveness and move into a forgiving posture.

Communicate out loud with your partner about what you have discovered. *Determine* how you both want to proceed. *Invite* your partner to discuss these issues with you and to look into what disconnects he or she is experiencing. These steps can be applied to any personal relationship or situation. When applied to your parents you get insight into the complicated meaning about your own power and sense of self, derived from your interpretations of that relationship.

Once you have more insight you can choose to align your beliefs and actions to be more congruent with your authentic truth. For example, if you feel defensive when your partner is flippant with you, you may follow that belief back to a childhood injury with one of your parents wherein you felt like your worries or concerns were unimportant. Feeling dismissed by your partner may bring up that injury and cause defensiveness in you; recognizing this correlation you can communicate with your partner about his word choice and demeanor and ask whether your reactive interpretation is accurate. If you discover that it is not an accurate belief then you have to shift your internal energy and *unlink* your self-perception of being unimportant from flippant comments from your partner, forgive, and accept. Forgiving your parent, your partner and your self, and accepting the truth of who you are and acting from that internal strength.

Defensiveness comes from a need, or interpreted need, to protect yourself from attack. If, you have had miscommunications or mistakes in how you related with your parents then, this defensiveness can be intense, charged, difficult, and multi-layered over time. Following these steps will increase your positive interactions and assist you in working through how you have linked words and actions into a misconstrued belief system that erupts into defensiveness.

If you feel *defensive*

- Wait,
- stop talking,
- breathe,
- open your mind to what the other person is trying to say,
- be ready to receive rather than send communication,
- clarify what you really want from the situation,
- Finally, focus on that, and only that; don't get distracted and moved onto a more negative path, or other tributary issues.

Think about, and feel into, what is behind the defensiveness. Follow it like a thread through your history. This understanding gives you a place to tether the defensiveness. Then you can determine if that original event or set of events is relevant or if you would like to shift the defensive energy. It is through this process that you can identify where you want to focus your interaction with the other person.

If you feel *angry*,

- Wait,
- stop talking,
- breathe,
- open your mind,
- receive what the other person is trying to say,
- discover what is triggering an angry response in you,
- consider whether it is something you need to resolve (if it is an historical issue that is not part of the present interaction – share that
- or let go
- stay focused on the current issue.

If you have a *block or just can't understand* what the other person is saying,

- stop,
- try to look at the issue from a different perspective,
- invert your persepctive
- see if you can identify what perception or interpretation you have that may be blocking your understanding of the other person's point of view.

Get the other person to re-describe their feeling or experience in different words, or give an example so that you can better understand what she is saying.

You may not find agreement immediately.

Strive to understand the other's viewpoint and from that understanding you will discover a new path for interaction.

Shared understanding comes from seeing both perspectives. Remember the figure-ground concept, and the duck/bunny image. Both perspectives are right from the specific perspective and wrong from the other one. Paradigm shift.

FIGURE 15, DUCK...BUNNY....FIGURE/GROUND ILLUSION

Increasing your awareness and applying your mindfulness to the situation allows for increased understanding and connection. This may result in a different course of action. It may not result in a change, but in this case you will be able to support the situation through a more mindful, neutral approach. It may allow for a negotiation that incorporates both paradigms, not a compromise, but a collaboration or blending that meets the needs or perspectives of both parties.

This creates space to see, hear, understand, and interact more fully and gives you the opportunity to look for connections and agreement. It's shifting your perspective without losing your center. Focused on your personal relationships taking into account the history you each bring to the situation from other relationships and earlier experiences together; you're shifting from an *off* position of obstruction *No* to an interested focused *Yes* position of *On* ready to connect and relate fully without reservation. You are stretching the communication, so that you can see the place where you can connect and bring the issue at hand into the present time. The actions identified above shift the focus, dissolve the defensiveness, and increase the opportunity for agreement and collaboration.

Be truthful and honest in the content of your communication, kind and caring in the tone of your communication, and warm and real in your presentation. This is the We-style of relating; it will go the furthest to create a space for a powerful and positive interaction that can increase the depth and breadth of your family, friend and partner relationships.

SEEING FROM FOUR DIMENSIONS AT ONCE: THE 4D WE-STYLE RELATIONSHIP

"...a priori intuitions and concepts provide us with some a priori knowledge which also provides the framework for our a posteriori knowledge..." Immanuel Kant, Critique of Pure Reason (1787)

Working with the idea of the fourth dimension, space and time, is a way of thinking about what happens when you are shifting paradigms. Immanuel Kant in his *Critique of Pure Reason (1787, 1929, 2003)* developed a concept of transcendental philosophy. In Kant's view *a priori* is reasoning or knowledge that proceeds from theoretical deduction rather than from observation or experience; it is a proposition that is not grounded in experience but can be validated by experience. And *a posteriori* is grounded in experience and observation; it is a proposition that is validated by and grounded in experience and observation. When using these concepts *a priori* is intuitive and *a posteriori* is observable so more grounded. Kant's theory about space-time is fascinating as to how it relates to the fourth dimension. Space and time together for Kant are a form of perceiving, and causality is a form of knowing. From his perspective both space and time and our conceptual principles and processes pre-structure our experience.

This develops the idea that paradigms, and paradigm shifting, are a product of perceiving and then introspectively knowing.

For Kant things *as they are* in themselves are unknowable. In his view for something to become an object of knowledge, it must be experienced, and experience is structured by our minds, with both space and time being the forms of our intuition, or perception, and the unifying, structuring activity of our concepts. These aspects of mind turn *things in themselves* into the world of experience so that they can be known.

Seeing in 4D is related to how Kant describes this knowing. Seeing in four dimensions means 1) viewing with your five senses plus intuition, and the concept of time as represented by the now, past (history), and future; 2) recognizing how interpretations in time affect the future; and 3) noting how changing those interpretations actually *changes* your interpretation of reality.

Mindfulness increases your capacity to see in 4D. Mindfulness is a concept that includes spirit, mind, and body responses integrated with information to guide your actions and cognitions, in the space-time continuum of the *now*.

Your integrated spirit, mind, body sensory guidance system is an combined focus on perception, attention, perspective, intention, and time. These are the foci that allow you to see in 4D, giving space for figure/ground perspective and paradigm shifting. Intuition provides a *blink response*, as described by Malcolm Gladwell (2005). This is a cue that there is something wrong or right. It allows you to integrate your observations of your sensing system with your knowledge in the space-time continuum to guide you. The blink quality allows for this integration to come to you as a whole (what Fritz Perls coined as a *Gestalt, Gestalt Therapy Verbatim*, 1969, 1992) in an instant.

Emotions are not distinct knowings: they are triggers, or responses. Your emotions, like an internal alarm system, might alert you that there is someone crossing your boundaries, or they may be emotional triggers to survivor scenarios, or responses as *a posteriori* knowledge. Viewing emotions as experiences but not knowings assists you in determining how to respond to an emotion. A good example is feeling sorry for yourself, *a sense of poor me*. It can erode at your being in an insidious way but is not always rooted in a reality. Recognizing that perceptions and experiences can be temporal but not necessarily real or factual can assist you in seeing in 4D and remaining centered in your life.

If you find yourself feeling defensive, angry, or sorry for yourself, assess whether the feeling is part of a habit reaction pattern or a trigger *or* an accurate assessment of something happening in the present moment. Sometimes these feelings are cues that what is happening now is akin to something historical that needs to be addressed. When the feeling is nagging and bothersome rather than intense and loud, it may be indicative of a problem. If it feels reactive and loud, then it may be more of a habit reaction pattern or trigger. This is counterintuitive but follows the previous concept that the loud, *pushing through to the fore* feeling is fear or a trigger and the quiet, nagging, bothersome feeling is a message from your internal guidance system.

You can make a comparison of the historical event and the now event, to discern which one is in play. You compare the historical event and the now event by comparing your feelings about the experience then and now, evaluating whether your assessment of what the other was doing in the past is truly similar to what your partner is doing now. You compare the whole of how the historical person treated you and the current partner is acting. If, it is a habit reaction pattern then, you will recognize that your fear from the history is driving your reaction to the person in the now. With this knowledge you can shift your perceptions and actions.

Mindfulness is a concept of utilizing your emotional sensory guidance system, and physical sensing system and the *whole* capacity of your cognitive and problem solving skills to evaluate situations and experiences in order to create and guide your way. This is seeing in 4D and allows for a unifying and flexible style of relating in the world. This is the We-style of relating in partnership. Seeing in 4D increases your capacity for centeredness, groundedness, flexibility, and strength.

SHIFTING THE ENERGY OF DISAPPOINTMENT TO THE POWER OF COURAGE: ME TO WE

How you choose to deal with disappointment is an intersection point in life. Whether you apply mindfulness or get lost in a maze of discouragement determines which path you take. The natural pull is toward sadness and despair. Unfortunately, that force can get you caught in a loop of insecurity that pulls you down and diminishes your sense of self, power, and courage.

Life is full of disappointment.

In order to promote joy and inclusion and a sense of individual strength without getting lost in the competitive nature of me against you, you have to focus on your own strengths and limitations and choose goals in alignment with these.

The best, most encouraging response to disappointment is mindfulness. Mindfulness will create the space to shift the energy of disappointment into the strength of courage. Often in retrospect you are able to view the disappointment from a balanced, centered, holistic perspective and see the way in which that disappointment served to strengthen and encourage you. Looking at the disappointment in the present-moment from this centered perspective through mindful, introspection, can give you the insight or knowing that you can use now that comes with retrospection.

Mindful introspection moves you further along your path. It defines and clarifies the path and your inner self within the context of who you are.

Despair in response to disappointment creates a tear in you center and moves you into a loop of depressive thinking that results in circling in a maze without forward movement. It's like an involution onto yourself, a turning inward negatively, that results in depressive thinking and incorrect attachment of meaning and experiences. Despair creates stagnation and linking of cognition and meaning that is self-destructive.

Shifting the energy of disappointment to the strength of courage is a mindful act that results in positive, self-affirming growth and behavior. Use mindful, meditation to move out of despair and into encouragement. This shift happens as a response to your neutrality in viewing the situation. This action is transforming the energy of the disappointment into the energy of change and growth forward. Inverting or shifting your perspective to see the good effect within the disappointment is the key.

Viewing each situation with a neutral, compassionate perspective allows the facts and information most important to you to rise to the fore of your vision so that your perspective shifts and clarity results.

Your goal in life is to be fulfilled, successful, and joyous. This comes from a strengthened courageous perspective within you. The characteristics and qualities that define that path for you are unique. If you have chosen an unattainable goal you will be disappointed. If, you apply a mindful eye to the goal and situation then, you can be encouraged and renewed.

The energy of disappointment leads to insecurity, fear, and despair; it serves to solidify a core insecurity style that interferes with We-style relating and gets you stuck in either a Me or I-style of relating. To address the core insecurity look to shift the energy of disappointment to courage through mindfulness.

Shifting the energy of disappointment to the strength of courage allows for you and your partner to get exactly what you want. This attitude is one that allows for all beings to succeed. This is the way to move through competition and find yourself collaborating. This enhances all parties and allows for expansion because it is wholly individual and group minded, at once. Your focus is on being your best and true self and allowing others to do the same. This intentional energy moves everyone toward their successful selves.

Applying mindfulness accepts the differences between you and another without judgment, so that you both can enhance your strengths and diminish your limitations by following your true inner nature and guidance. Applying mindfulness enhances your strengths, so that you are in the exact place you need to be to succeed in your goals.

Mindfulness with neutrality, perspective, acceptance, understanding, and compassion allows for each individual to choose best for himself. And when the choice is not the best one, it allows for the fine-tuning and adjustment needed to shift disappointment to strength of courage.

The next time you are faced with disappointment, apply mindfulness to your circumstance and see if you can shift your disappointment into courage. This will strengthen you and it will focus your energies and goals on those attributes and experiences that best support your path and your core self.

The secret is the attitude of gratitude, remembering all that is positive in your life along with the disappointment. This allows for a centering of you within the whole of your life, connected to those you love and solid within yourself. This results in an inner resilience, peace, and confidence. Courage is the inner strength found in disappointment. This energy moves you from a Me or I-style of relationship into a We-style of mutual caring, sincere communication, compassionate understanding, and interdependence.

FOCUS YOUR ENERGY AND BREATHE: RESPOND FROM AN INNER BALANCED STATE

Therapeutic listening is an active listening that requires rapid responses, redirection, and guidance offering a sense of calm. The listening is active but not strained. You are present in the foreground in a neutral open way, while in the background your mind, heart, intuition, and senses are evaluating the information on some kind of inner grid; the person's tonal quality, choice of words, and speech as well as the content of what was said and not said. This grid is used to develop a multilevel understanding of the person and the problem at hand, in context.

An attitude of outer calm and stillness with an inner readiness and activity, keeps you in a mindful, state so you can assess risk and transmit calm to neutralize danger. When dealing with a person who is angry or out of control use a quiet, soothing vocal quality. This can drop your and the other person's blood pressure and pulse, even allow others to experience a light trance state. You are telegraphing a sense of calm composure. In the same way an animal can smell fear you can transmit a sense of security and peace to assist the person to return to a sense of calm balanced harmony.

This is something that I developed instinctively over a period of time when working in stressful, dangerous environments. The calmer my demeanor the more likely the danger could be averted. This tactic is directly related to the concept of energy and breath.

It is the sense of safety, visibility without vulnerability that allows the person to move forward to receive the necessary information and support. This sense of visibility in a safe way is soothing and strengthening. Practicing this skill creates an environment for harmony. It is what allows for you to assist others in shifting or shifting yourself. So it's about paying attention and responding to the situation with a sense of calm, neutral interest, through a serious and gentle way of guiding and supporting. These are precisely the terms used to describe mindful, mediation or mindfulness. These actions reduce anxiety, anxious behavior, and feelings of obsessive compulsions. This is the soothing and strengthening experience in therapy you can recreate through therapeutic, active listening, and focusing your breath and energy to outer calm and inner readiness.

Use active listening in your response to yourself. Smile, sit quietly, listen to yourself, your words, your tone, your word choice, what you say and what you hold back. Listen and pay attention with a sense of calm, neutral interest. Appreciating the situation with a gentle seriousness. Focus your energy inward in a gentle, calm, and interested way. Gently question yourself:

what is going on here?,
what do I feel?,
when did it begin?,
what relationships are present?

Listening to each answer that presents itself with a neutral interest, without the need to prove the rightness or wrongness of what is noticed.

Then breathe. Breathe again deeply and fully with a smile in between your exhalation and inhalation, allowing for your heart to open and listen too. A feeling of love and a connection to your spiritual source helps. Feeling a warm caring, sense of spiritual connection allows you to move into your heart even when you have lost your way. Breathe deeply into your belly watching it rise, this decreases anxiety and fear immediately. You can feel an immediate sense of calm. You are providing a space to actively support yourself by simply breathing, focusing your energy, smiling and being open to the perfect answer to the situation presenting itself.

Allowing things to flow can be challenging.

If you have created success through your mind's ability to discover the answer and prove it, you will find this allowing part difficult. Remember that pushing the river takes more energy and doesn't get you very far; go with the flow.

In general, the best answers come to you; they appear or present themselves. This may happen as a result of study and work on the problem, but it is usually after the problem is set to the back burner that the whole picture is revealed along with the solution. Focusing your energy on the problem, setting a desire or intention, and then releasing through a long exhalation. Breathing through the need to make it happen especially when it's out of your control, that is the place of real strength and power.

Focus your energy and breathe. You will feel that inner sense of calm, inner balance and harmony.

From this place you will see solutions present themselves. The more you are centered, actively listening to the whole if the interaction the more you will receive clarified guidance. If you are paying attention to the information you receive from your internal sensory guidance system and from your partner's communications you can integrate this information to see positive, powerful solutions that are mutually satisfying. This process allows you to negotiate in the We-style of relationship, creating interdependence in your partnerships.

YOUR HEART CENTER LINKS MEDITATION AND MEDIATION

Mediation is an art. It requires an ability to listen and see with discernment. It is part intellectual and part intuitive. It is a funny equation of knowing, feeling, and being present with another to hear the subtle messages of tone, shifts in energy, and word choice. Mediation requires you to keep your right/wrong brain out of the equation. It is centered in that mindful, open, compassionate place that seems often unavailable in contract negotiation, couples counseling, and problem solving. The more willing you are to see everything, accept everything as truth to the speaker, and understand that in most situations all participants just want to be heard, cared for, treated with love, and be understood, the more you find a path to healing, clarification, and solutions.

This place of being within requires you stand in your heart center. From that space you can hear and see with mindful, compassionate, lovingkindness.

I find it an interesting spelling oddity that mediation and meditation have a single letter that shifts their meaning. The letter *t*. It's like a clue about how to get where you need to go, because the letter *t* is a wonderful picture of the yoga standing mountain pose, *tadasana* – standing feet together, eyes lightly gazing, with your arms and hands held in a prayer position at your heart.

Mediation done from this heart centered, focused, humbling place creates an opportunity for meditation. Meditation applied to relationship struggles results in acceptance and clarification of what each party wants from heart center, what each person means from heart center, and a centered present-moment place from which to move forward.

The profound benefit of *Tadasana*, the mountain pose in yoga is the inner focus and connection to the present-moment through attention from your heart center. This pose offers a perfect picture of light focus in the now from the heart.

Love, compassion, acceptance, allowing, and forgiveness are heart center emotions. Centering your attention in the present moment, receiving information through the filter of your heart increases harmony, understanding, and *soul*-utions focused resolutions in mediation.

Mediation does not only occur in law or business. It is present in couples collaborative interaction, parent-child relationships, friendships, and work partnerships. It is present in all interactive relating between humans, even between species. Our willingness to come from this centered heart-space increases our capacity to understand and act in ways that uplevel consciousness, increase our interconnectedness, and overall harmony in living.

Since this is a daily part of living, you can begin to practice at any time.

Become aware of the tone, quality, and word choice of others. Pay attention to your own tone and word choice. Don't just think but feel into these various qualities and practice a light attention; practice hearing the intention of another, and yourself, not just content. Shift yourself into a t, into *Tadasana, standing mountain pose*. Stand tall, balanced with a light focus to hear, see, and understand through the filter of your heart. You will find the most amazing gifts awaiting you, powerful threads of understanding, depths of connection, inner peace, and clarity that you have been missing out on in your interactions and relationships. This is the practice of a We-style of relationship. Use these techniques to move your perspective from a Me or I-style of relationship to a We-style relationship. The more you can be present in the now, with neutral interest through open eyes and ears, and centered in your heart, the more your life will evolve into fullness. One letter difference, **t**, connects worlds exponentially. Connecting through your heart center, applying the qualities of meditation to mediation allows for the uplevel of consciousness in relationship from dependence through independence to interdependence.

FIGURE 16, KATE PREPARING FOCUS, PHOTO CREDIT: LISA ALDON

EMBRACING YOUR FLAWS,
SHIFTING YOUR ATTITUDE,
CREATES A WE-STYLE OUTCOME

Energy (read: creation) follows vibration and intention. This theory implies that if you think about something efficiently and powerfully you can create that thing. When living by this theory, it's important to remember fears, worries, and habits are efficiently and powerfully energetic. So that if you *desire* to be A and you worry, fret, or fear that many things may interfere with you creating A, then you are actually working against your own desire via these energetic worries and fears.

In psychological terms, this is anxiety. Anxiety interferes with the process of creating A, it creates what you are anxious about rather than what you desire, A, whereas self-confidence enhances the process of creating A. Self-confidence enhances the process through vibration and intention. When you are self-confident, your vibration and intention are stronger and clearer and you quickly and easily direct energy to the creation desired. Anxiety neutralizes your movement toward the creation of the thing. Fear creates a current away from the desired thing. When you put energy in self confidence and fear you are energizing two currents, one toward your creation and one away from your creation. The result is either to move toward, and away from, in an alternating fashion or to remain stuck in place.

Recognition of problems is an important part of being responsible. You don't want that identification to block creating what you desire. Use response – ability as an effective way to respond to these problems. Awareness through non-attached observation that there may be conflicts or bumps in the road in creating A, isn't problematic as long as you feel that you can respond to these effectively and persevere toward your desired creation.

This behavior and thinking is faith and joy based. It supports the current toward self-confidence and the desired creation and a diminishment of the current of fear or worry. This helps you to focus away from your core-insecurity and toward a neutral joy-based style of relating. You can use these strategies to help you move away from a Me or I-style of relating into a We-style of relating.

You can observe how this works by observing the process of learning yoga. Correct movement into the position (*asana*) requires working with your body, not making your body do something but rather *allowing* the movement into the correct position through breath and faith. Your focus is in creating an *asana* that is correct and to get there you must have non-attached concentration, attention, and breathwork. *The non-attached component* is the part that observes and corrects posture and placement without an evaluation of good or bad (non-attached). Focused breathing while attending to your posture and tension release *is the intention the energy follows*, for the practice; you breathe and allow yourself to find the correct position in a flowing manner. Being in the present moment with your breathing and body, with non-attached attention and concentration creates alignment. As you trust and breathe, focus and align, you easily move into the correct posture.

The process of learning yoga is an accepting and allowing process of breath, attention, and flow. Fear blocks movement and binds the energy from flowing. Deep, intentional breathing shifts the energy and releases blocks, both physical and emotional.

This same process is what underlies the practice of mindful, meditation.

Breath, flow, and non-attached observation in the present-moment creates expansion of your understanding and capacity for mindfulness. It deepens and broadens your perspective. Applying this to communication, rather than proving your point and digging in, you clarify your understanding and deepen your compassion. From this place you may focus your energy and intention toward your desire.

Since energy follows vibration and intention, creation of desires happens most easily and quickly when the desire is unopposed, which is to say clarifying your intention and vibrating in a space through breath of present-moment awareness and clarity of intention assists the process most efficiently. Actions taken from this space will give rise to information about how you are interfering with your intended creation through fear, worry, anxiety, or insecurity.

Standing in your center mindfully through unattached observation and acceptance of truth, *spiritually* through your faith and clarity in your capacity, and *physically* through breath and confident action *allows for energy to flow directly toward your intended creation and result in delivering what you seek*. This allows for enlightenment through the acceptance, reframing, and release of perceived flaws.

Energy follows vibration and intention so when you find you are stuck, look to reset your intention and your vibration through spirit, mind, and body alignment and centering. Visualize yourself in the intended creation. Feel it, see it, accept it and stand in gratitude of it. This amplifies your vibration by removing the worry, anxiety, fear, and insecurity. Once you allow the removal of the current that pulls you away from your intended creation, you will immediately observe an elevation in your progress toward your intended creation.

Being grateful for where you are and for the intended creation as if it has already taken place will serve to strengthen your vibration, intention, and self-confidence. It is as *if by practicing being the you, you want to be, your are practicing change within your consciousness first; and then through creation of that new habit of thinking, being, seeing, and knowing you are shifting who you are, and how you are, from the inside out. Additionally as you see it internally, you see it all around you (in the same way you see a new word you just learned when it was as if it had not existed before).

You can *be* the change you wish to see in the world. You can begin this process at any time. And the more you trust yourself, embrace yourself, and move away from defensiveness toward forgiveness, internal strength, self-confidence, and gratitude, the more you will experience the change in your own consciousness and a reflection of others in your environment like you.

This is how the group consciousness changes and this is how you can effect change in not just your own self-relationship, or couple relationship, but also in your small-group and large-group connections.

It is very powerful and yet very simple.

Accept/embrace, see/shift, believe/allow/create.

With these tools and through these actions you are free and empowered to create the We-style of relationship and choose to relate in your partnerships to increase harmony, mutual satisfaction, and uplevel of consciousness.

FIGURE 17, THE WE-STYLE OF RELATIONSHIP, PHOTO CREDIT: LAURA WOLF

REFERENCE

Asch Experiment, 1950, Solomon Asch, Asch Conformity Experiments, or Asch Paradigm. The Asch conformity experiments are often interpreted as evidence for the power of conformity and normative social influence, desire to be like the identified group and to not go against the grain, to avoid punishment by the group.

Milgram Experiment, 1961, Stanley Milgram, *Obedience to Authority an Experimental View (1974)* "The Milgram experiment on obedience to authority figures was a series of notable social psychology experiments conducted by Yale University psychologist Stanley Milgram, which measured the willingness of study participants to obey an authority figure who instructed them to perform acts that conflicted with their personal conscience."

Abraham Maslow, Hierarchy of Needs Pyramid: *(Maslow, 1954, 1970, 1999)*: Original version had five stages (1954) and then two more were divined from his writings in (1970) and a final *transcendence* in (1999) to clarify movement from deficit needs to Being needs. These were stages placed on a pyramid going from the bottom to the top – each stage must be met to move upward to the next stage: 1) *Biological and Physiological needs* (basic life survival needs: air, food, drink, shelter, warmth, sex, sleep) to 2) *Safety needs* (protection, security, order, law, limits, stability) to 3) *Belongingness and Love needs* (family, affection, connection, relationships, work groups) to 4) *Esteem needs* (achievement, status, responsibility, reputation) to *Self-Actualization needs* (realizing personal potential, personal growth, self-fulfillment, peak experiences).

In 1970, this was model amended to include two stages between the esteem needs and the self-actualization needs; Maslow referenced these elements in his writings as motivational factors for human beings (see his 1943 paper *A theory or Human Motivation, Psychological Review*, 50, 370-396) however he did not incorporate them into his five stage model: so that 5) became *Cognitive needs* (knowledge and meaning) and 6) *Aesthetic needs* (appreciation and search for beauty, balance, and form), moving 7) *self-actualization* at the pinnacle. This model was again amended in 1990 to include above self-actualization, 8) *Transcendence needs* (helping others to achieve self-actualization, altruism, focus on one-ness). The first four are deficit needs. The middle three are being needs of self-actualization. For the purposes of this document, Me to We, the first four are aspects of the Me and I-style insecurities. The attainment of the self-actualized stage allows for interaction in the We-style of relating. The middle stages may indicate a focus of security or meaning in relationship. Work by Stephen Covey, *The 8th Habit* incorporates this issue and *Transpersonal Psychology* is an offshoot of this idea.

Keirsey, David, *Temperament typing*;(1978, 1998) Keirsey perceives the *Sensing and Intuitive* aspects of temperament as the primary dividers: *Observant (S) concrete* and *Introspective (N) abstract* from here he divides the S and N categories into 2 main styles of *Cooperative (SJ, NF) vs. Utilitarian (SP, NT)*

Guardian: (SJ) Logistical – breaks into Informative vs. Directive: *Conservator (SFJ) Supporting or Administrator (STJ) Regulating*, and *Artisan: (SP) Tactical* – breaks into Informative vs. Directive: *Entertainer (SFP) Improvising or Operator (STP) Expediting*, and *Idealist: (NF) Diplomatic* – breaks into Informative vs. Directive: *Advocate (NFP) Developing or Mentor (NFJ) Developing*, and finally *Rational (NT) Strategic* – breaks into Informative vs. Directive: *Engineer (NTP) Constructing or Coordinating (NTJ) Arranging*.

These each break into two more categories each as Introversion and extraversion are added. These final temperaments result in identifying the best job styles. Keirsey uses these to assist in determining how *Brains and Careers* (2008) are related and to describe the four differing intersections roles played in relationship and interaction. He breaks these into *Proactive Enterprising Roles (initiators, contenders)* and two *Reactive Inquiring Roles (coworkers [collaborators 2010]), responders [accommodators 2010])*.

As part of Keirsey's work, he has traced the history of Temperament Typing from Myers/ Briggs MBTI to the ancient Greeks, aligning his temperament styles with the four styles identified throughout this history. For more information and a complete chart, please review his book: Keirsey, David (May 1, 1998) [1978]. *Please Understand Me II: Temperament, Character, Intelligence (1st Ed. ed.). Prometheus Nemesis Book Co. ISBN 1-885705-02-6.*

Meditation Map for focused breathwork in meditation, Turning No to ON: The Art of Parenting with Mindfulness (Gineris, 2011)
Follow breath--Attention, awareness, calm, flow----->----------> distraction --attention, rumination, worry, spin-out------>-important awareness, observation ---->Redirection, Re-orient attention -----with attitude of kindness, compassion, curiosity,----->Follow breath--Attention, awareness, calm, flow----->------------------------->distraction------- attention, rumination, worry, spin-out------>-important awareness, observation-------->Redirection, Re-orient attention -----with attitude of kindness, compassion, curiosity,---------->Follow Breath...

- **Here is a simple meditation technique you can do sitting or laying down:**
  - *Sitting straight, or laying flat with your shoulders against the mat, Breathe in for a count of 5, and breath out for a count of 7. Take in deep breaths from your tummy, each time.*
  - *After several times, allow your breathing to continue, without trying to control the breath at all, just allow yourself to breathe normally and naturally through your nose, in and out, in and out rhythmically.*
  - *Gently be aware of your breathing; Gently paying attention to the breath, watching the breath - breathing in and breathing out. Following the breath in and following the breath out.*
  - *Continue this meditation technique for 60 seconds at first; then you can increase it to 3, and then 10 minutes, as you get more practice.*
  - *When you've finished, end the meditation by taking a deep breath.*

Meditation on Lovingkindness to increase empathy and compassion, mindfulness and detachment, reprint from Turning No to ON: The Art of Parenting with Mindfulness (Gineris, 2011)

- *Sit in your chair or on the floor comfortably if you want to use the sitting pose please do so*
- *Breath in for a count of 5 and out for a count of 7*
- *Notice your body against the chair or floor allowing your breath to continue in and out*
- *Breath in from the top of your head and down through your body, you can imagine a sense of warmth entering your body and allow negative energy or tension to leave through your torso, hands and feet.*
- *Continue breathing and focus inward noticing and allowing your breath*
- *Focus your mind onto a being that you love and feel loved by. Choose a being that is not one of conflict like a pet, cat or dog that you love*
- *See the face of that being shining love toward you*
- *Now shift the picture, as you are holding and feeling that love to your face shining toward you so that you can experience self-love - if this is difficult and you feel the energy fade bring back the being from whom you felt that love and Begin again, once this is fruitful then you may want o put in the face of the being or problem with which you are struggling*
- *Allow for the love you are feeling to smile upon the problem*
- *Again if this is difficult go back to the last loving being and feel that energy and begin again.*

- *Now sit with this loving feeling and with your breath*
- *Now bring in all three, your loving being, your loving self and your loving other/problem*
- *Hold these together as you feel the loving energy flow between these three images into and through you.*

Once you feel you have completed this you may bring your attention to your breath, and to your body in the chair, and slowly open your eyes.

Reprint of Every Twelve Years from, Turning No to ON: The Art of Parenting with Mindfulness (Gineris, 2011) and the Erik Erikson stages of Development:

Every Twelve Years

I like to think about adolescence as a second childhood. It seems like what didn't get resolved in the first twelve years gets a second chance in the second set of twelve years. So thirteen is about year one and fourteen is about year two and so on. It's an efficient neutralizing way of reframing the issues of adolescence. I am using Erik Erikson's psycho-social stages of development, first defined by him in his book *Childhood and Society* (1950, 1963), to refer to the developmental tasks of years one to twelve that I observe as getting reworked in ages thirteen to twenty-four.

I have developed this thesis of Every Twelve Years as a result of my therapeutic work with adolescents and children in my counseling private practice over the last twenty-five years. These stages have a tenacity and solidity to them in how they effect or create personality. However, the resolution to each task has some malleability in that individuals can go back and rework their conclusion thereby effecting a change throughout the entire structure, in both directions. This is how therapy and mindfulness can be used to effect a change in a person's frame of reference, shift paradigmatic perception, release habit reaction patterns, and heal old wounds.

Erikson's stages are divided in the following way, and they build on each other, such that successful resolution of a task sets the stage for success in the next stage-task, and problems in previous stage-task resolutions can create a skew in the child's ability to resolve subsequent developmental tasks. Trauma or loss, are the most detrimental and problematic effectors of this set of stages.

Stage 1, Infancy, Birth to a year and a half—Trust versus mistrust: Task is around nutrition, feeding, nourishment on all levels; important outcome if accomplished successfully, children develop a sense of trust when caregivers provide reliability, care, attention, and affection; a lack of these experiences or qualities will result in mistrust. This is a sense of trust/mistrust at a fundamental level.

Stage 2, Early childhood, two to three years old—Autonomy versus shame and doubt: Task is around toilet training, power-over versus empowerment at an internal level due to forced or internal initiative for training; important outcome if accomplished children develop a sense of personal control over physical skills and a sense of independence, guiding one's life, autonomy; a disconnect in this stage results in an internal sense of shame and/or doubt. These feelings are core issues and interfere with or promote an internal picture of self that is either strong and courageous or fearful and tentative.

Stage 3, Preschool, three to five years old—Initiative versus Guilt: Task is around exploration, a sense of control and power over their environment, this is the external-action-result of the previous stage, how feeling forced or empowered will play out in your child's interface with his environment; important outcome if this is accomplished is a sense of purpose; a disconnect in this stage can result in a sense of guilt either due to a lack of skills from the previous stage or from exerting too much power over the environment and receiving disapproval. These feelings of a sense of purpose or guilt are core issues that then color the child's inner picture of self. Note that because these stages affect the subsequent stages, once an individual begins to have difficulty completing a developmental task this deficiency will negatively affect future developmental stage outcomes. Alternatively, a positive resolution of a subsequent stage may be able to shift the previous stage outcome in the child's inner picture of self.

Stage 4, School age, six to eleven years old—Industry (competence) versus Inferiority: Task is around coping with the new social and academic demands, a sense of competence at meeting the demands and integrating structures; competence is not just the outcome of this stage alone but also requires a sense of trust, autonomy, independence and a sense of purpose, the positive results of the earlier developmental tasks; a disconnect in this stage leads to a sense of inferiority.

Stage 5, Adolescence, twelve to eighteen years old—Identity versus Role Confusion: Task is through social, academic, athletic, and spiritual individual and group relationships around development of a sense of self and personal identity; the outcome of a positive resolution results in being able to stay true to one's authentic self, while a failure or disconnect leads to role confusion and a vulnerable, insecure, weak sense of self; as with preceding stages, this outcome is not just a relationship of the task of this stage but also its integration with the skills developed from previous stages.

Stage 6, Young adulthood, nineteen to forty (for our purposes twenty-four) years—Intimacy versus Isolation: Task is through relation- ships to develop intimate, loving relationships with other people; the outcome is the capacity to form loving relationships that are fulfilling and enduring; a disconnect in this stage leads to isolation, loneliness, and a lack of enduring, intimate relationships. This is the culmination of the previous stages and loss, trauma, or disconnect in an earlier stage will have a negative effect on a person's capacity to create longstanding, close relationships. A person needs to be able to trust, have a sense of autonomy and competence, as well as the capacity for initiative and identity to be able to negotiate and create intimate relationships.

What is great is that the developing psycho-social aspects of adolescents are still open to shifting and mindfulness so that an increased self awareness and a reframe of difficulties in the earlier stages can right the inner sense of self such that the adolescent can develop the earlier skills at these later stages.

By investigating through various techniques of attention, perception, paradigm shifting, self-awareness, and mindfulness, a child, through assistance with loving caregivers and support persons (e.g., parents, counselors, spiritual leaders, and teachers) can discover when a task may have gone awry and set it right. I have observed this in my practice. I have seen many children and adolescents heal their inner wounds to go on to have happy, successful, growth promoting, and fulfilling lives. This is the truly amazing and powerful healing component of mindfulness and paradigm shifting with compassion and lovingkindness and why it is such an important asset in parenting.

I will often ask kids and parents what was going on in those early years when I am working with adolescents, and I find the insights are fascinating. A twelve-year-old who is led into a dangerous relationship in school remembers the loss of her devoted grandmother; a thirteen-year-old dealing with intense power struggles in school reports he had a horrible time with toilet training, he describes memories of a loss in personal control over his own physical body. These are examples of how the disconnect in the earlier stage creates an interference in the current stage and how the tenor of the interference can give you a cue, clue, or hint to when the disconnect occurred so as to deal with those issues directly through reframe and reworking that stage. These stages cannot be directly re-done. The girl's grandmother cannot be returned to life, or the boy's toilet training experience physically re-done. The work is in reframing the experience and offering a healing, mindful, compassionate acceptance and view of the loss, trauma, or disconnect and outcome.

When dealing with adolescents, remember that they act out what is going on. In fact, another part of the work of this period is to get them to talk about rather than act out their issues and psychological injuries. They don't have the self-control to not act on their impulses. They feel deeply, as deeply as adults, but they have a truncated impulse control mechanism. Of course for many par- ents this is the one area in which they have trouble, talking with their teenagers. That's why creating and maintaining the communication pathway early in the relationship is so important.

The best time to build your relationship with your children is when they are children. How you treat them in their early lives sets up the relationship you have with them in their adolescence and adulthood. Children are real people right at the beginning. They have feelings, needs, desires, likes, and dislikes that are all personal to them. They have a temperament about how they take in and process information and how they relate to their environment. It is important to get to know your children and treat them like they are real in this way. That doesn't mean don't discipline them - definitely DO. Do it in a way that is mindful and allows for development of a deep and secure relationship, this requires acting in a congruent way. That is the foundation for creating trust and strength. Trust, strength, self-confidence, and a sense of self are what children need to steady themselves through the storm of adolescence. The closest thing to impulse control for an adolescent is to know himself and feel strong even in the face of adversity. Feeling connected to a parent may be the only thing that helps an adolescent though their existential angst.

~Tools~ This kind of closeness is created, and built, in early childhood. Although you can build on it later and you can rework the foundation, it gets more difficult to create that foundation, as they get older. There's a lot you can heal in the first years of adolescence if you are willing to put in the effort to connect, be present, and be congruent with your child. Focus on creating an atmosphere where your child's feelings and experiences are validated. Set limits and explain why, not as an avenue to change your mind, rather as an avenue to encourage your child to change his and to give him a way to align with what you are setting as structure. This teaches them that you have a plan or reason for what they may feel is arbitrary. It can create a confidence in you that is very positive later.

If your children are very young and you don't think they can understand your plan, think of your explanation as a way of setting theructure for your- self so that you will remember to keep those communication lines open. You'll need those lines later. Children get the unspoken energy of things more than the spoken, so if you are honestly trying to connect and create a structure for them, they will get that and feel that you are creating trust and relationship. If your child is an adolescent, this is harder. First you need to set the stage. Explain you are going to be doing things differently. Talk about the importance of communication and connection and being mindful. Show them that you are available and be congruent; do what you say you are going to do and what you expect them to do. You will find they are not immediately responsive to these actions, but don't stop. Adolescents are always watching for incongruence. If you can hang in there with them, continuing to honestly try to connect, they will note that internally, even if they do not appear to change externally. That is your way in. You will have to be consistent, trustworthy, and real, or they will not trust you. It can take awhile for the shift to happen. Think about how long the habit reaction has been in place. You have to be patient, confident, persevering, and congruent. Apply the *stop, look, and listen* strategy and the attention, intention, perspective, perception strategy to keep yourself in the moment and mindful. Don't bring in the past unless it's directly relevant to the now, or you will lose them. They will feel like you are lecturing rather than connecting. Practice, be patient, be real, and have faith. In order to be there when they need you, you have to create the relationship even when it seems it isn't needed.

I have a very loving and close relationship with my stepson, Max. We refer to each other as mom and son because that is the emotional, spiritual, and social relationship we have created with one another. This is how we instinctively felt toward each other when we first met, when he was twelve years old. When he was sixteen years old, we had difficulty akin to what one observes in many homes between parent and child, but this was not consistent with what we had experienced previously. It was about an injury in his earlier life of loss at age four. My challenge and presence was to offer the opportunity for him to rework this earlier loss by standing by him and being real. Loving him, and being congruent in my words and actions in an unconditional and compassionate response to his behavior resulted in an internal shift within him such that we could return to our earlier positive experience. He felt a deeper sense of trust, autonomy, and a stronger sense of inner control and purpose in his life.

He went away to college and functioned beautifully, with ambition and success. In the middle of his college experience, at age twenty years old, he decided to move home to experience the warm, secure, stabilizing experience of a cohesive family. He identified this as an intentional, purposeful decision to resolve the loss he experienced in his earlier school-age developmental stage at the divorce of his parents. We responded with a welcoming, embracing, and accepting attitude. It was actually a fun experience for all of us and we were able to develop a stronger cohesive family connection.

Through this mindful and intuitive action, he was able to shift his internal paradigm of inferiority to competence. He has gone on to create successful, fulfilling, enduring, and loving relationships in his life.

Posted in *Yogitimes.com*, under the title *Spirit, Mind, and Body: How Yoga can intensify the Connections,* by dr beth gineris on May 3, 2012
Staying centered is remaining balanced. Balanced within your own sphere as well as balanced in your interactions and community. Centeredness and balance infer a collaborative and open response to internal sensations and external expectations.

When you are pulled in one direction or the other this can have the effect of destabilizing you internally and within your environment. It can skew your energy and shift your focus onto a path that is not in your best interest. The best way to stay centered is to maintain an internal awareness of your senses. Paying attention to how you feel through your internal sensory guidance system will assist you in staying centered. This is your five plus one (intuition) senses, integrated. The use of mindfulness and paradigm shifting are of great benefit in developing your relationship to your internal guidance system especially through paying attention and neutral observation of your sensory guidance system responses. One way to develop this relationship to your sensory guidance system is through the practice of Yoga. This is because you will have the opportunity to connect breath, with the integration of physical body positions and energetic spiritual centers it increases your awareness of your spirit, mind and body integration.

In the Yogic tradition there are *bandhas,* Sanskrit for locks, that need to remain closed or locked as you do various positions to assist in building physical strength, as well as increasing the spiritual power of the pose. These *bandhas* correspond with certain energy centers in your body called *chakras.* What is useful for the musculature is related to the emotional component of the center – one is at the root *chakra* and is referred to a *kegel* closure – the root *chakra* relates to survival and may connect to issues of fear. The next important *bandha* that is discussed is the belly button area – holding this *bandha* closed is described as pressing the belly button to the spine – this is related to the second *chakra,* which deals with creativity of all types including sexuality and procreation. The third *bandha* that is discussed is described as holding the chin to the chest – this has a dual effect of closing off the throat *chakra* while opening further the *chakra* at the third-eye or the brow *chakra*, which relates to inner vision and intuition.

By closing off these centers while holding the Yoga positions the practitioner is strengthening the flow of energy within his centers so that the energy doesn't dissipate. This results in strengthening the muscles and the physical core of the practitioner as well as the energetic flow of internal connection between these centers. This is how an intentional Yoga practice can assist you in the strengthening of your sense of wellbeing, and remaining centered. Through the use of breath you can increase your connection to your internal sensory guidance system. Any focused attention with breath to your inner sensory guidance system will produce an increase in your awareness about what and how you are feeling, and responding, in any given situation and can provide guidance about what action is in your best interest which includes a choice to not act from an intentional place. Centering your self is simply paying attention to, observation of, gathering information from, your internal sensory guidance system and responding from a place of compassion, love, and neutrality to that internally connected information, in present time. Remember that centered sensory guidance is in general a calm, and charge-free instinct and results in a sense that something is the best response, rather than a loud, pushing forward, anxiety-filled, reactive response. Simple focused breathing for 30 seconds to 3 minutes can increase your capacity for mindfulness and can re-center you. Longer focused, breathing meditation for 15 - 30 minutes can further increase your centering practice and allow space to reconnect to your inner center; this has a lovely additional effect of reducing your blood pressure and reducing your sense of anxiety by bringing your fully into the present-moment.

SUGGESTED READINGS

Covey, Stephen R. *The 8th Habit.* New York: Free Press, 2004.

Covey, Stephen R. *The 7 Habits of Highly Effective People: Restoring the Character Ethic.* New York: Fireside, 1990.

Damon, William. *The Moral Child: Nurturing Children's Natural Moral Growth.* New York: The Free Press, 1988.

Das, Lama Surya. *Buddha Is as Buddha Does: The Ten Original Practices for Enlightened Living.* New York: HarperCollins, 2007.

Dunn, Philip. *The Art of Peace: Balance over Conflict in Sun-Tzu's Art of War.* New York: Jeremy P. Tarcher/Putnam, 2003.

Epstein, Mark. *Thoughts Without a Thinker: Psychotherapy from a Buddhist Perspective.* New York: BasicBooks/HarperCollins, 1995.

Erikson, Erik H. *Childhood and Society.* New York: W.W. Norton & Co, 1950, 1963.

Erikson, Erik H. *Toys and Reasons: Stages in the Ritualization of Experience.* New York: W.W. Norton & Co, 1977.

Fenske, Mark, Brown, Jeff with Neporent, Liz. *8 Strategies Great Minds Use to Achieve Success, The Winner's Brain.* Harvard University (2010) Philadelphia: De Capo Press, 2011.

Fromm, Erich. *The Art of Loving.* New York: Harper & Row Publishers, 1956.

Gineris, Beth. *Turning NO to ON: The Art of Parenting with Mindfulness.* Charleston, SC: Createspace, 2011.

Gladwell, Malcolm. *Blink: The Power of Thinking Without Thinking.* New York: Bay Back Books, 2005.

Gladwell, Malcolm. *Outliers: The Story of Success*. New York: Little, Brown and Company, 2008.

Hanh, Thich Nhat. *Peace Is Every Step*. New York: Bantam Books, 1991.

Hegel, Georg. *The Phenomenology of Spirit*. New York: Oxford University Press, 1977.

Heidegger, Martin. *The Question of Being*. William Kluback and Jean Wilde, trans. New Haven: College and University Press, 1956.

Heidegger, Martin. *On the Way to Language*. Peter Hertz, trans. New York: Harper & Row, 1971, 1982.

Hesse, Hermann. *Magister Ludi (The Glass Bead Game)*. New York: Bantam Books, 1968, 1980.

Hesse, Hermann. *Siddhartha*. New York: Bantam Books, 1951.

Hicks, Esther and Hicks, Jerry. *Ask and It Is Given: Learning to Manifest Your Desires*. Carlsbad: Hay House, 2004.

Jung, Carl. *Synchronicity*. R.F.C Hull, trans. Princeton: Princeton University Press, 1960, 1969, 1973.

Kant, Immanuel. *Critique of Pure Reason*. Norman Kemp Smith, trans. London: Palgrave Macmillan, 1787,1929, 2003.

Kant, Immanuel. *Fundamental Principles of the Metaphysic of Morals*. T.K. Abbott, trans. Buffalo: Prometheus books, 1987.

Keirsey, Bates. *Please Understand Me: II*. Del Mar: Prometheus Nemesis Book Company, 1998.

Kopp, Sheldon. *If You Meet the Buddha on the Road, Kill Him*. New York: Bantam Books, 1976.

Kuhn, Thomas. *The Structure of Scientific Revolutions*. Chicago: The University of Chicago Press, 1962, 1970.

Levy, Carlo. *Christ Stopped at Eboli*. London: Penguin Books, 1956.

Lockhart, Russell. *Words as Eggs: Psyche in Language and Clinic.* Dallas: Spring Publications, Inc., 1983.

Maslow, A. H. *Motivation and Personality* (2nd ed.). New York: Harper and Row, 1970.

Maslow, Abraham. *Toward a Psychology of Being.* New York: John Wiley & Sons, 1999.

Myers, Isabelle Briggs with Myers, Peter B. *Gifts Differing, Understanding Personality Type.* Mountain View, CA: CPP, Inc., 1980, 1995.

Perls, Fritz. *Gestalt Therapy Verbatim.* Gouldsboro: Gestalt Journal Press, Inc., (1969) 1992.

Piaget, Jean. *Play, Dreams, and Imitation in Childhood.* C. Gattegno and F.M. Hodgson, trans. New York: W.W. Norton & Co., 1962.

Pipher, Mary. *Reviving Ophelia: Saving the Selves of Adolescent Girls.* New York: Ballantine Books, 1994.

Requena, Yves. *Terrains and Pathology Acupuncture, Volume One, Correlations with Diathetic Medicine.* Brookline, MA: Paradigm Publications, 1986.

Saint Exupery, Antoine de. *Le Petit Prince.* New York: Harcourt Brace Jovanovich, 1943, 1971.

Sartre, Jean-Paul. *Being and Nothingness.* New York: Washington Square Press, 1956.

Siegel, Daniel and Hartzell, Mary. *Parenting from the Inside Out.* New York: J.P. Tarcher/Putnam, 2003.

Simmons, Rachel. *Odd Girl Out: The Hidden Culture of Aggression in Girls.* Orlando, FL: Harvest Book/Harcourt, Inc., 2002.

Vygotsky, L.S. *Thought and Language.* Eugenia Hanfmann and Gertrude Vakar, eds. and trans. Cambridge: The M.I.T. Press, 1962.

Wilber, Ken. *No Boundary: Eastern and Western Approaches to Personal Growth*. Boston: Shabhala, 2001.

Wilber, Ken. *Integral Spirituality*. Boston: Integral Books, 2006.

Williamson, Marianne. *Illuminata, A Return to Prayer*. New York: Riverhead Books, 1994.

Follow Beth Gineris's website for additional resources, including seminars, links to other websites, and blogs: www.bethgineris.com; www.InstinctiveHealthMedicine.com

Made in the USA
San Bernardino, CA
14 December 2015